Confronting Colonialism

Resistance and
Modernization
under

Haidar Ali
& Tipu Sultan

Confronting Colonialism

Resistance and
Modernization
under

Haidar Ali
& Tipu Sultan

Edited by Irfan Habib

Anthem Press
London

Anthem Press is an imprint of
Wimbledon Publishing Company
PO Box 9779
London
SW19 7QA

This edition first published by Wimbledon Publishing Company 2002

British Library Cataloguing in Publication Data
Data available

Library of Congress in Publication Data
A catalogue record has been applied for

ISBN 1 84331 060 0 (hbk)
      1 84331 024 4 (pbk)

1 3 5 7 9 10 8 6 4 2

Our grateful thanks are due to
INFOSYS TECHNOLOGIES
for the generous assistance that,
among other things,
made this volume possible

Contents

DIPLOMATIC HISTORY

INTERCOMMUNAL RELATIONS

Contents

Acknowledgements

1 The Ideological and Social Background of Haidar Ali and Tipu Sultan *Barun De*
First published as 'Some Socio-political Implications of the Cognomen "Tipu Sultan"' in *Proceedings of Indian History Congress,* 52, Delhi, pp. 701–07.

2 The Death of Haidar Ali *Irshad Husain Baqai*
First published in *Islamic Culture*, XXI (1949), pp. 167–71.

3 Haidar Ali's Invasion of the Eastern Carnatic, 1780
Jadunath Sarkar
First published in *Islamic Culture*, XV (1941), pp. 214–28.

4 The French in the Second Anglo–Mysore War *Mohibbul Hasan*
First published in *Bengal Past and Present*, LXV, pp. 55–65.

5 Did Haidar Ali Turn a Defeatist in 1782? *D.S. Achuta Rau*
First published in *Proceedings of Indian History Congress*, 15, Gwalior, pp. 313–16.

6 A Conference between Tipu Sultan and Brigadier-General Macleod *Irshad Husain Baqai*
First published in *Islamic Culture*, XVII (1943), pp. 88–93.

7 Cornwallis and the Mysore–Maratha War (1786–87)
B. Sheik Ali
First published in *Proceedings of Indian History Congress*, 26, Ranchi, pp. 148–52.

8 Tipu Sultan's Embassy to Constantinople, 1787

Ishtiaq Husain Qureshi

First published as 'The Purpose of Tipu Sultan's Embassy to Constantinople' in *Journal of Indian History*, XXIV (1945), pp. 77–84.

9 Relations between Travancore and Mysore in the Eighteenth Century *A.P. Ibrahim Kunju*

First published in *Proceedings of Indian History Congress*, 23, Aligarh, pp. 56–61.

10 Tipu Sultan's Projected Confederacy against the British, 1790

N. Kasturi

First published as 'Tipu Sultan's Confederacy against the British, 1790', in *Journal of Indian History*, XIV (1935), pp. 266–71.

11 The French and the Third Mysore War: Testimony of the Mauritius Records *B. Sheik Ali*

First published as 'Mauritius Records on the French and the Third Mysore War' in *Proceedings of Indian History Congress*, 18, Calcutta, pp. 265–67.

12 Tipu Sultan and Sir John Shore *B. Sheik Ali*

First published in *Proceedings of Indian History Congress*, 20, Vallabh Vidyanagar, pp. 243–46.

13 The Seringapatam Correspondence and the Carnatic Nawabi

C.S. Srinivasachari

First published in *Indian Culture*, XII (1946), pp. 207–11.

14 Tipu's Endowments to Hindus and Hindu Institutions

A. Subbaraya Chetty

First published in *Proceedings of Indian History Congress*, 7, Madras, pp. 416–19.

15 Tipu Sultan as Defender of the Hindu *Dharma* *B.A. Saletore*

First published in *Medieval India Quarterly*, I(1), pp. 43–55.

16 Muslim Rulers of Mysore and their Christian Subjects

George M. Moraes

First published in *Proceedings of Indian History Congress*, 7, Madras, pp. 442–48.

Contents

Preface

The fourth of May 1799 was looked at with particular satisfaction by the British rulers as the day on which an indomitable opponent of theirs was at last destroyed. For the same reason the day was looked at with sadness by all who had a care for the memory of fighters against colonialism. It was, therefore, doubly saddening that the fourth of May 1999, the bicentenary year, passed without a national commemoration. The people and government of the state of Karnataka alone remembered their native son and those who had fallen in the fight along with him.

The Indian History Congress, meeting at Patiala in December 1998, decided to commemorate the event on its own. As part of this programme, we are publishing the present volume, which has as its core a collection of papers published in the annual *Proceedings* of the Indian History Congress. In order to locate the papers we have gone through the contents of all the *Proceedings* volumes, except those of the Third and Fourth sessions, which we have unluckily not been able to trace despite much effort.

When these papers were put together, it was felt that there were also valuable papers on Haidar Ali and Tipu Sultan in old issues of journals, which are not easily available to scholars and readers. We are, therefore, printing a number of papers drawn from various sources other than our own *Proceedings*. The Indian History Congress wishes to extend its grateful acknowledgement to the journals from which the papers have been drawn, full references to which are given in the Acknowledgements. While we hold the rights to reprint papers published in our *Proceedings*, we have tried to take permission from all the authors (or their heirs) of other journals whom we could reach.

Professor S.P. Verma has contributed a paper to explain the paintings by the Daniells of the forts of Tipu Sultan, whose reproductions appear in this volume.

I am happy that Professor Irfan Habib agreed to edit the volume. He has also contributed a comprehensive introductory essay on Haidar Ali and Tipu Sultan. The texts and notes of the papers have been retained as originally published, and editing has been confined to removing misprints and to minimal stylistic changes for standardization. The titles of the papers have in some cases been modified to suit their actual contents. The original titles, where changed, are indicated in the Acknowledgements.

The papers in the *Proceedings* were located by Miss Shadab Bano, Mr Sk. Ehtishamuddin Ahmad, Miss Aditi Govil, Miss Amita Paliwal and Mr Aziz Faisal, young and active members of the Aligarh Historians Society, who also checked the processed script at the intial stage. Mr Yusuf Siddiqi, Professional Assistant Librarian at the Centre of Advanced Study in History, AMU, scanned the past volumes of various journals for papers on Haidar Ali and Tipu Sultan.

Thanks are due to the Aligarh Historians Society for computer and photocopying facilities. Word-processing was carried out by Mr Muniruddin Khan, Mr Khushtar Khalique and Miss Yusra Aziz. The staff of the Library of the Centre of Advanced Study in History, have been uniformly courteous and cooperative.

Professor S.P. Verma, Treasurer of the Indian History Congress, has been of inestimable help in this venture. He has advised us on the selection of illustrations. Mujtaba, photographer of the Centre of Advanced Study in History, has prepared the photographic prints.

I am especially grateful to Mr Rajendra Prasad and Ms Indira Chandrasekhar for publishing this volume under the aegis of Tulika, to Mr Ram Rahman for designing the book, and to Ms Salima Tyabji for copyediting the volume and compiling the bibliography.

Throughout our effort we have been greatly encouraged and actively supported by Mr Girish Karnad and Mr Mohammad Moienuddin, both warm admirers of Tipu Sultan. I cannot fully express the extent of my own gratitude to them.

November 1999   SHIREEN MOOSVI
                                         Secretary, Indian History Congress

Introduction: An Essay on Haidar Ali and Tipu Sultan

Irfan Habib

Haider Ali and Tipu Sultan were formidable adversaries who inflicted a severe defeat on the British and came near to breaking the power of the East India Company.... Haider Ali was a remarkable man and one of the notable figures in Indian history. He had some kind of a national ideal and possessed the qualities of a leader with vision.... He realized, long before others did so, the importance of sea power and the growing menace of the British based on naval strength. He tried to organize a joint effort to drive them out.... His son Tipu continued to strengthen his navy. Tipu also sent messages to Napoleon and to the Sultan in Constantinople.

> — Jawaharlal Nehru, *The Discovery of India*,
> 6th edn., London, 1956, pp. 272–73

The Sultans of Mysore, Hyder Ali and Tipu proved much harder nuts to crack. They defied the British and their allies. They fought four valiant wars.... In the fourth war British gold effected what British guns had so far failed to accomplish. The ministers betrayed the master. Tipu refused to surrender and died bravely fighting in defence of his fort.

> — Tara Chand, *History of the Freedom Movement of India*,
> revised edn., Delhi, 1965, I, pp. 226–27

The gloom of final defeat is only relieved by the gleam of personal heroism, and the disaster that eventually befell him [Tipu] was not blackened by disgrace.

> — N.K. Sinha, on Tipu's last stand at Srirangapatnam, in
> *Haidar Ali*, 3rd edn., Calcutta, 1959, p. 274

These quotations help to remind us that in the conception of our past, as held in our nationalist historiography, Haidar Ali and Tipu Sultan have occupied an honoured place. Now, however, at some official levels, at least, there is a strong contrary current. In 1990 a national television serial on Haidar Ali and Tipu Sultan was compelled to carry the admission that the episodes of the serial were not necessarily historical, a disclaimer never attached to any of the other 'historical' or mythological fantasies that abound in our TV world. More recently, when 4 May 1999 came, marking the second centenary of Tipu's last stand against the British at Srirangapatnam, it was stonily ignored by the Government of India and all its agencies. Hostile demonstrations were even organized to oppose the commemorations held in Tipu's own native state, Karnataka. How amused Lt. Col. Mark Wilks, the major British writer on the Mysore wars, would surely feel to find his bitter invectives against the two indomitable opponents of the colonial regime so widely shared in free India!

It is, therefore, particularly important that the Indian History Congress should have decided to observe the second centenary of Srirangapatnam. The Congress has, as part of the commemoration, undertaken the publication of this volume containing papers devoted to Mysore under Haidar Ali and Tipu Sultan. It is a matter to reflect on that from the pre-independence days, the papers presented at the Indian History Congress consistently project a view opposite to that of Wilks and his present Indian fellow-thinkers. Whether what these historians say is right or wrong can be judged on the basis of the evidence they present in their papers. But the writers' attitude is also evidence of an anxiety to defend the memory of the two rulers, which in turn tells us much about the sentiments that had swayed a bygone generation.

While gathering the papers it came to be realized that because of the intrinsically random nature of such an assemblage, a volume confined only to the Indian History Congress *Proceedings* could leave out some important aspects of the history of Mysore under Haidar Ali and Tipu Sultan. A practically equal number of papers from other journals and periodicals, as would not be easily available to the general reader, have therefore also been included. We thus have here, among others, papers by Jadunath Sarkar and C.S. Srinivasachari, great *savants* of their day.

The individual papers naturally assume some basic knowledge

on the part of the reader some basic knowledge about the regime of Haidar Ali and Tipu Sultan and about their careers. It is the aim of this Introduction to provide such information, along with a discussion of some broader historical issues.

Haidar Ali

Of Haidar Ali's antecedents not much is known; what one can say for certain is that his father, Fat'h Muhammad, was in the employ of Dargah Quli Khan, the Mughal *faujdar* (commandant) of Sira (in Tumkur district, Karnataka), in the early years of the Mughal emperor Muhammad Shah's reign (1719–48).[1] The kingdom of Mysore technically belonged to the large *sarkar* of Sira (also called Karnatak-i Bijapuri). The Mysore ruler Chikka Deva Wodeyar (d.1704) had rendered allegiance to the Mughal emperor Aurangzeb (1659–1707) when Mughal armies overran southern India. Part of what happened as Haidar Ali's career developed can, perhaps, be explained by this subordination of Mysore to Mughal authority.

Haidar Ali, born about 1721–22, lost his father in 1728, when he was still a child. A member of the family, Haidar Sahib, had already taken service with the Mysore state; and now Haidar Ali, preceded by his elder brother Shahbaz, also became a cavalry officer in the Mysore army, *c.*1749.

Haidar Ali's recruitment to the military ranks of the Mysore state stemmed from its rulers' general desire to obtain recruits from the Mughal military classes, especially those connected with cavalry. Owing to the technical limitations of Indian muskets (which were still usually matchlocks, not flintlocks), and owing to the advantage, on the other hand, of the great mobility possessed by cavalry, skilled archers mounted on good breeds of horses were regarded at this time as the most effective arm of Indian troops in wars against each other.[2] It was, therefore, natural that unemployed Mughal cavalrymen should seek employment with the new emerging local powers. As Haidar Ali's career was to show, once the Mughal infusion in the army became strong, the next step could be not only a shift in political power in favour of the new military element, but also an infusion of Mughal political and administrative institutions in the state system of Mysore.

But before this could happen, Mysore came face to face with another military truth: the superiority of well-drilled flintlock-using infantry over all kinds of Indian armies. At the battle of Mylapore (Madras) in 1747, a small French force overthrew the Mughal cavalry of Anwaruddin Khan, the *faujdar* of Arcot ('Nawab of the Carnatic'). This was at the beginning of the three Carnatic Wars (lasting till 1763) in which England and France struggled for mastery over southern India. By supporting particular claimants to the office of the Mughal viceroyalty of the Deccan (left vacant by Nizamul Mulk Asaf Jah's death in 1748), to which Mysore was nominally subordinate, Mysore became involved in the Second and Third Carnatic Wars on the same side as the French. For Haidar Ali, appointed *faujdar* or commandant of Dindigul in 1753, and actively participating in the wars, this was the occasion to learn much about European methods of fighting: he was deeply impressed. As early as 1755–56 he is said to have obtained the services of Frenchmen to organize his artillery, arsenal and workshop.

The military basis for Haidar Ali's rapid ascent hereafter was based not only on his personal diplomatic skills, but mainly on the armed power he acquired. This lay in a brilliant combination of the mobile cavalry organized on the Mughal pattern with his increasingly disciplined musket-using infantry. Despite some temporary reverses, this combination proved invincible. Undoubtedly, he was the first important Indian commander to realize the value of European methods for drilling infantry, whom he tried to provide with flintlocks, a rare sight so far in Indian armies. This alone makes him a remarkable man.

Haidar Ali's seizure of power in Mysore was fairly swift. Intervening in the struggle between the raja and his powerful minister Nanjaraj, Haidar Ali's own patron, Haidar took the side of the raja, who had been chafing at being reduced to a nominal status by Nanjaraj. Replacing the latter, Haidar Ali acquired full power over the state in 1760–61, but he did not seek to substitute himself for the raja. When the current incumbent (Chik Krishna Raja) died in 1766, he duly installed a successor. The ceremonial of the raja's court and palace continued to be maintained. Haidar Ali, in fact, looked for the legitimacy of his own power to a different source altogether, one that lay within the framework of the Mughal political system. From Basalat Jang, claimant to the office of the Viceroy of the Deccan, Haidar Ali obtained in 1761 the title of Haidar Ali Khan and the office of *faujdar* of Sira.[3] In this capacity, he could claim to be superior to the Raja of Mysore, whose territory in the better days of the Mughal empire had belonged to the jurisdiction of that officer. The nominal right to supremacy so gained was strengthened when Sira itself fell into Haidar Ali's hands later in 1761, followed by the great town of Nagar (Bednur) in 1763. By his conquests in the north and acquisitions in Malabar, Haidar could well claim that he had added territory far larger in size than the original dominions of Mysore that the raja had reigned over.

Internally too, Haidar Ali's regime represented a combination of the existing institutions of the Mysore *raj* with an influx of Mughal elements. The latter were invoked to increase the state's share in agrarian revenue and to centralize the administration. Before his time, the local hereditary potentates, like *deshmukhs* and *palegars* ('*palaiyak-karars*'), and subordinate holders (*goudas, patels*, etc.) held varied rights, and the state's share in the produce taken in revenue was accordingly much constricted.[4] Haidar Ali took the standard Mughal view that the local potentates were *zamindars* and as such their entitlements were not sacrosanct. He aimed to dispense with their intermediation and imposed the land tax (which was a tax on the produce, equivalent to surplus or rent) directly on the peasants, realizing it through salaried officers.[5] This system, where tax was directly assessed on peasants, came to be the basis of Munro's Ryotwari system. Munro, indeed, heavily drew upon his experience of revenue collection in the district of Baramahal, seized from Tipu Sultan in 1792.

The fiscal resources so heavily augmented needed to be centralized. Haidar Ali did not entirely dispense with the Mughal institution of *jagir*, the temporary or transferable assignment of tax collection in a territory in lieu of obligation to maintain a certain number of troops. An order of Tipu is preserved in which a *jagirdar's* obligation to maintain cavalry, with the branding (*dagh*) of horses, to check their actual maintenance, is referred to in terms that one would have expected from a document of the Mughal imperial administration.[6] But the system of having troops maintained through *jagirdars* was now getting obsolete. The new methods of warfare called for a large standing army. For such an army that had to be directly paid, Haidar Ali had to collect revenues directly and so to limit the extent to which *jagirs* could be assigned. In this he also had well-known Mughal precedents: in 1574–75 Akbar had resumed *jagirs* wholesale in order to obtain better fiscal and administrative control. The Nazims of Bengal in the first half of the eighteenth century, from Murshid Quli Khan onwards, had also largely dispensed with *jagirs*.

By directly collecting revenue in the larger part of his dominions, Haidar Ali was thus enabled to concentrate resources on improving and enlarging his army. Unlike the traditional Indian armies with contingents of varying sizes, each depending upon the size of resources of its individual commander, Haidar Ali established the system of *risalas*, of a standard number of soldiers with fixed allotments of guns and transport, in line with the pattern of troop division in European armies. Each infantry *risala*, for example, was to consist of 1,000 men.[7] Its officers would be appointed by the ruler himself. This modern organization of the army was accompanied by the creation of regular infantry using European or European-style muskets (flint-locks). By 1767 he had 8,000 regular infantry so armed, as against 4,000 old-style matchlockmen, plus 5,000 'grenadier' sepoys and 1,000 'topasses (Indo–Portuguese half-castes) with muskets', all in his regular establishment. He continued to employ rocketeers, or persons adept at throwing gunpowder-powered *ban* rockets, a south Indian speciality (later to lead to the invention of Congreve rockets in England). He introduced a local innovation also by having a large bullock-and-cart establishment to enable him to rapidly transport his infantry and supplies. Haidar Ali, however, remained convinced of the importance of cavalry for its tactical mobility. In 1767 he had 800 'excellent Mughal horses' and 12,000 other cavalry. By this year he had 210 Europeans, mostly Frenchmen, serving him, both in the artillery (he could cast excellent guns) and cavalry.[8] Haidar Ali also tried to develop a navy, which by 1766 comprised 2 ships, 7 smaller vessels and 40 gallivats. He employed a European officer, Stannett, to command the ships when out at sea.[9]

It was thus in his army that Haidar Ali tried to introduce as much modernization as he could, while retaining and developing inherited Indian elements in other spheres of administration. This effort was carried out, however, within a political and ideological framework which was still set by the institutions of the local *raj* and Mughal fiscal and administrative methods. Despotic and centralized, Haidar Ali's regime was untouched by any other effort to develop technology and commerce on modern lines, let alone obtain an opening to science or enlightenment. Without this effort, military modernization itself had necessarily to depend heavily on the presence of Europeans, especially the French, and could therefore be expected to be successful only in the short term.[10]

In the short term, though, the success was considerable. The first war against the English, 1767–69, ended when Haidar Ali 'appeared under the walls of Madras and dictated a treaty'.[11] The next war (1780–84), emerging out of a grand anti-English alliance of Mysore, the Marathas, the Nizam and the French, was in progress when Haidar Ali died (7 December 1782); but although Mysore was soon alone in the fight, this war too, like the first, ended (March 1784) with a mutual restitution of conquests by the two antagonists.

Part of the reason why Mysore could stand up to the English in this manner surely lay in Haidar Ali himself. In 1800 Buchanan, touring the territory that Haidar had governed, was forced to recognize that 'on account of his justice, wisdom, and moderation, his [Haidar Ali's] memory is greatly respected by the natives of all description'.[12] A man driven merely by 'avarice' or 'animal spirits', as Wilks pictures him to be, could hardly have won such approval from his subjects.

Tipu Sultan: Ideology and Polity

Tipu, Haidar Ali's elder son, succeeded to his father's office on 29 December 1782, at the age of 32 (he was born in November 1750).[13] He was immediately immersed in the struggle against the English, continuing the war that had begun under his father and in which he had already taken a vigorous part. Despite difficult circumstances, he succeeded in obtaining advantageous terms by the Treaty of Mangalore (March 1784). A war with the Marathas and the Nizam soon followed (1785–87) ending with military successes but with rather disadvantageous terms of peace: this was apparently because of Tipu's anxiety that these two powers should not combine with the English, whom he consistently regarded as his principal enemy.

In this matter Tipu's attitude was one which Haidar Ali would perhaps have shared. But Haidar Ali acted as if his own power was his main consideration; he was content to base his title to supreme power on a dubious grant of a mediocre office in the vanished Mughal government; and he could also see himself as a guardian of the Wodeyar *raj* and claim the subjects' loyalty on that count. In practice, his administration drew heavily on Mughal institutions and traditions, and he saw no need to proceed beyond their limits. The only area where, as we have just noted, he attempted modernization was the army, which he bequeathed to Tipu in fine condition.

This alone, however, was not enough for Tipu Sultan. Whether it was his personal ambition that demanded loyalty to himself on much firmer ground, or his belief that in order to confront the English he needed to have a cause to which his subjects, or a section of them, could especially feel deeply attached, cannot now be determined. Probably both played a part in shaping his conduct in the political sphere. His own education in Persian (unlike Haidar Ali, who, if not really illiterate, had not received much formal education) made him fairly well-versed in Islamic history and theology, and this too helped to direct him to the course he now took.[14]

From his accession Tipu treated himself as an independent sovereign, not needing any diploma of inferior office from the Mughal court at Delhi. He thus dropped the name and title of the Mughal emperor from his coins, and, according to Wilks, began using the title *Padshah* for himself from January 1786.[15] Tipu could now claim parity with full-fledged sovereigns, like the Sultan of Turkey and the King of France, both of whom personally received his ambassadors (1787 and 1788). While these embassies might not have resulted in any substantial material support for him, in respect of either military resources or commercial advantage, the diplomatic stature gained by him certainly reinforced his prestige at home.[16]

Tipu's separation from the Mughal court was on another plane as well. He does not exhibit himself as a sovereign in the same political fashion as the Mughal emperor. True, the titles of *Padshah* or *Zill-i Ilahi* (Shadow of God) were those in use by the Mughal emperors as well. But Tipu gave to his sovereignty a colour of religious militancy, which was not at all present in the Mughal imperial polity of the eighteenth century. Tipu would not put his own name on the coins he minted; rather the coin legends invoke God as the all-powerful Sovereign, and bring in the name of Muhammad the Prophet, and of Haidar, i.e. Ali, the Prophet's cousin and the model for heroes in Islam.[17] His double-rupee was called *Haidari*, after Ali, and the single rupee *Imami*, recalling the twelve *Imams* whose line begins with Ali. There is little doubt that the motif of tiger, so much emphasized in Tipu's ceremonial symbolism,[18] was designed to link him with the same hero of Islam whose title 'Haidar' also meant a lion or tiger.[19] His formal name for his government, *sarkar-i Khudadad* ('God-given government'), also recalled his assertion that his was no ordinary government, but one with a divine-ordained mission. The religious orientation of government was underlined by the orders to appoint a *qazi*, especially for imparting instruction in elementary principles of Islam to Muslim children.[20]

Islam, then, suddenly becomes with Tipu, which it never was for Haidar Ali, one great ideological prop for his power. It may be argued that he turned to it in order to retrieve the loyalty of his Muslim officials and troops who were up till now accustomed to honour titles to power certified by the Mughal emperor, and therefore, to allegiance at least nominally rendered to that figurehead. But what is more likely is the fact that, by invoking Islam, Tipu was trying to appeal to the 'holy-war' (*ghazwa*) spirit of his followers. When in 1783 he directed the compilation, through Zainul Abidin Shustari, of a manual of military organization and tactics, he significantly titled it *Fat'hul Mujahidin*, the Victory of Holy Warriors.

> This Holy War was to be directed against the English. In the instructions that he penned for his envoys to Constantinople he drew a picture of how the English had become a grave danger by their conquests and acquisitions. The Ottoman sultan was to be told that the English have acquired the country of Bengal, with revenues of twenty crores of rupees, the country of the Carnatic, with revenues of three crores, and the country of Surat, Gujarat, etc., with revenues of three crores, in total twenty-six crores of rupees. This territory was in possession of the King of Hindustan, which they have seized either through collusion with, or treachery against, the potentates of the said territories. They have converted many Muslims to their own faith by inviting them to Infidelity (*kufr*); they have enslaved many Muslim women and children; they have destroyed Muslim mosques and tombs to build their idol-houses [churches] thereon. When the assault of Infidelity (*kufr*) [i.e. of the English] became unbearable, and the ardour for Islam was enflamed, our (then) Master [Haidar Ali] made war on these faithless Christians.

Tipu goes on to explain that the assistance given by Haidar Ali and himself to the French (who were, of course, Christians) was owing to the enmity between the English and the French; and he was currently (1785) fighting the Marathas only because 'the Marathas, owing to their own position as Infidels (*kuffargi*) had joined the English, and so made a [separate] peace with the English [in 1782].'[21]

It is the English who, despite the dictates of Muslim theology to the contrary, were held to be infidels, the major enemy of Islam. All other enmities were secondary; all friendships were to be defined on this primary basis.

One can understand in the case of Tipu, as in that of the Rebels of 1857, why religion should be appealed to for strength and ardour against an alien foe.[22] But religious fervour can also run away with one. Tipu's actions of punishing rebels in Coorg and Malabar by forced conversions cannot be covered by any apologia: they became the basis for interested allegations against him of persecuting and destroying or closing Hindu temples. Buchanan accuses him of having 'wantonly destroyed their [the Hindus'] temples',[23] and Wilks alleges that Tipu 'oppressed and insulted his Hindu subjects'.[24]

Yet the evidence to the contrary is almost definitive. Tipu, like Haidar, continued Hindus in government employment. One of his major ministers to the end was Purnaiya; but there were a number of other high and trusted officers.[25] In 1800, Buchanan, in his critique of Tipu included in this volume, says that brahmans remained in control of Tipu Sultan's revenue department.[26] Tipu in his letters and orders notes the appointments of Marathi and Kannada ('Kanhari') clerks (all Hindus wherever named) in the treasury and of 'Hindawi' clerks in other offices.[27] One of Tipu's orders relates to the assembling of his brahman officers at Srirangapatnam in 1792–93 where Tipu announced he would forgive all faults of his servants; and the brahmans, having duly taken a bath, took an oath of loyalty to him, whereafter they were all feted at the cost of the government.[28] Another order of the Sultan, issued around this time, decrees that all land grants to brahmans conferred by the old authorities (apparently of the Wodeyar *raj*) were to be deemed confirmed; and if any astrologers and *shastris* held grants revenue-free, without any documentary support, their cases should be submitted to the court so that their grants too may be approved.[29] Tipu maintained in dignity the family of the raja, who was never deposed; and, if the tiger was his symbol, so was the elephant (put on the coins), involving the age-old Indian esteem for that animal.

Tipu, like Haidar, went beyond mere tolerance. Wilks makes fun of the fact that before he made his last stand at Srirangapatnam, 'the moolla and the bramin were equally bribed (!) to interpose their prayers for his deliverance'.[30] What Wilks cannot see is that for Tipu there was no contradiction in his belief in the efficacy of both Muslim and Hindu prayers, just as there was no logical conflict for him in his making a divinely-conferred government (*sarkar-i Khudadad*) support brahmans and *shastris.*

The discovery in 1916 of Tipu's letters to the Sringeri *math* shed fresh light on how far Tipu was willing to go. These were analysed by Surendranath Sen in 1930; but the present volume reprints a very long and fuller survey by B.A. Saletore.[31] In 1793, Tipu tells the Swami of this famous *math*: 'You are the *Jagadguru*, Preceptor of the World.... In whatever country holy personages like you may reside, that country will prosper with good showers and crops.'[32] In a paper at the Indian History Congress session at Madras, 1944, A. Subbaraya Chetty gave an impressive list of Tipu's grants and other favours to temples, derived from a number of sources.[33] Both the Sringeri *math* letters and the other grants show that Tipu's own fiery faith in a militant Islam had a context other than any supposed confrontation with Hinduism. Directed in the main to his struggle with the English, his emphasis on Islam involved no conflict in his mind either with his Hindu subjects or with their faith and temples. In the record of his dreams, which he confidentially put to paper, he tells of one (16 November 1798) in which he saw a big damaged temple. Inside it were many idols whose eyes moved. One of the two female idols told him they had all been praying to God. Tipu commended the deities, and ordered his men to repair the building.[34] It was not only policy, then, but an unconscious sharing of beliefs too, that was at work behind his attitude of benevolent tolerance.[35]

In 1792, as the English army moved into the heartland of Tipu's dominions, the chronicler of the campaign noted the prosperity of the territory, and made the following comment:

> Whether from the operation of the system established by Hyder; from the principles which Tippoo had adopted for his own conduct; or from his dominions having suffered little by invasion for many years; or from the effect of these several causes united; his country was found everywhere full of inhabitants, and apparently cultivated to the utmost extent of which the soil was capable; while the discipline and fidelity of his troops in the field, until their last overthrow, were testimonies equally strong, of the excellent regulations, which existed in his army. His government, though

strict and arbitrary, was the despotism of a politic and able sovereign, who nourishes, not oppresses, the subjects who are to be the means of his future aggrandizement: and his cruelties were, in general, inflicted only on those whom he considered as his enemies.[36]

Clearly, then, whatever Tipu wanted to do, he did not want to make war on the bulk of his own subjects. On the contrary, despite undoubted constraints, he was driven by a desire to improve the conditions of his people and thereby add to his own resources.

Tipu Sultan: Economic Improvement and Modernization

Since agriculture was the main sector of the pre-modern economy of Mysore, Tipu's major concern was naturally with agricultural improvement. An order issued by Tipu shows concern that if revenue was collected at the wrong time, this would pauperize peasants by compelling them to sell their cattle. Such untimely collections were to be avoided, and 'the resource-less' (*nadar*) peasants were to be given *taccavi* loans 'in the form of cattle and grain' in order to enable them to undertake cultivation. Old canals and embankments were to be repaired, and new ones built. Similarly, old dams thrown across rivers were to be repaired, and new ones constructed. Headmen ('*patels, shanbhogs*, etc.') who oppressed peasants were to be punished.[37] These regulations were largely in conformity with the traditional principles of earlier regimes including the Mughal administration. Buchanan's gibe that Tipu merely interfered with and spoilt earlier irrigation works from a desire to set up his own,[38] is not borne out by the concern shown in these injunctions for keeping the old works in good order.

Nine miles from Srirangapatnam is the famous modern dam on the Kaveri, built to create the great lake of Krishna Raj Sagara. When excavation work for it began in 1911, an inscribed slab was unearthed: dated 12 June 1798, this announced that Tipu Sultan had laid the foundations of the dam on this very site to provide water for irrigation; and a quarter of the revenue was to be exempted for those who thereby brought new area under cultivation.[39] Since Tipu fell within a year of the foundation of the dam, it is no discredit to him that the work was left incomplete and neglected by the British-controlled regime that followed. But it speaks much for his acumen and interest that he should have chosen the exact site for the dam that modern engineers were to select more than a hundred years later.

Tipu was also interested in furthering agricultural manufactures. This is shown by a very interesting order he issued for raw-sugar manufacturers to be summoned and trained in the making of candied sugar and white sugar so that they might manufacture and sell these finer varieties in their own localities.[40]

Another indication of Tipu's farsighted innovation was the introduction of sericulture in Mysore, which was to grow later into such a successful industry. The raising of mulberry trees was assigned to particular land-farmers (*talluqdars*). Twenty-one centres (*karkhanas*) for the culture of silkworms were established; the worms were to be produced on a monthly basis; and the (sale?) proceeds paid into the treasury: Tipu looked forward to an increase in silk production year after year.[41]

Such interest in agricultural improvement could be creditable enough. But it was in the sphere of manufactures that his endeavours especially distinguished him from all contemporary Indian potentates. We have already seen that Haidar Ali had concentrated on modernizing his army and the manufacture of muskets. In 1787, Tipu instructed his prospective ambassadors to France to tell the French king that he had in Mysore 'ten workshops (*karkhanas*) where countless muskets (*banadiq*) were being manufactured'.[42] These muskets were modelled after those of Europe. Cossigny, governor of Pondicherry, examining one 'produced by Tipu Sultan's workers' in 1786, thought it equal to any produced in Europe. This was also the judgement in Paris pronounced on two pistols presented by Tipu's ambassadors to Louis XVI in 1788.[43] Tipu's ambassadors to the Ottoman court (1785–86) were asked to exhibit proudly to the Turks the muskets carried by the men in their train, that had been made in Mysore.[44] But Tipu wanted further improvement, and he asked his ambassadors to Paris to request the French monarch to send him 'other craftsmen who could make muskets of novel designs, *manjaris*(?), cannon-pieces, and iron guns (*baitaroi*)', to all of whom he would pay suitable wages.[45] A founder, with four master craftsmen, was actually brought from France in consequence.[46] Buchanan refers to a machine installed at Srirangapatnam by 'a French artist' to bore cannon: it was to be driven by water power, but was actually worked by bullocks.[47]

Where Tipu went significantly beyond his father was in his anxiety to introduce modern technology outside the area of weaponry. He asked his ambassadors to France to get, on their own, 'a printer of books, on suitable wages'. And the French king was to be requested to obtain for him the services of 'a clock-maker, a maker of Chinaware and a maker of glass and mirrors'.[48] By 1797, he was demanding from France 'ten cannon founders, ten ship-builders, ten manufacturers of Chinaware, ten glass and mirror makers, ten makers of ship clocks (literally wheels), and wheels (or engines) for raising water and other kinds of wheel work, and workmen versed in gold plating'.[49]

Tipu could not establish a printing press, but he did succeed in making paper by modern methods ('formed on wires like the European kind').[50] He also succeeded in manufacturing 'watches and cutlery'.[51] There was certainly a French watchmaker working at Srirangapatnam in Tipu's late days;[52] and his services might have been utilized in setting up clock and watch manufacture. As for cutlery, Tipu refers in his orders to his own workshop for the manufacture of knives, scissors and needles. Its superintendents were to gather ironsmiths from different localities and train them in the technique of manufacture, so that they might manufacture and sell these goods on their own in their own localities.[53] In view of this exhortation, Buchanan's allegation that Tipu wished to keep the new techniques a secret from his subjects,[54] seems especially ill-founded.

And can one say after all this that Tipu Sultan was 'an innovating monarch, [who] made no improvements';[55] or that his aim was simply to impress his subjects rather than 'to improve his country'?[56]

It is obvious from these endeavours of his that Tipu was well aware that technology lay behind much of the Europeans' success. He also simultaneously held the view that European powers had acquired their dominance by developing certain financial and commercial institutions and practices (companies and monopolies), and building and operating navies and fleets. Here too they could be emulated, but, as with the technological devices, this could be done only under the aegis of the state. Tipu, therefore, tried to build in Mysore an immense state-run trading enterprise, a veritable primitive public sector.

There is no doubt that pre-colonial Indian regimes often undertook commercial activities to augment their income. Seventeenth-century potentates on the western coast, like Malik Ambar and Shivaji, had ships trading across the Arabian Sea;[57] and many rulers on the Karnataka and Kerala coasts controlled or monopolized the pepper trade.[58] Haidar Ali had realized, as we have seen, that to protect his ships against the English, a navy was also essential. With Tipu not only did these ideas assume a far more vigorous form, but he developed them into a full-scale project to imitate the European East India Companies and make Mysore a sea power based on naval strength and maritime trade.

Accordingly, Tipu Sultan proceeded actively to rebuild the navy that Haidar had established and then lost in the Second Mysore War (1780–84). When, in 1792, the English seized Honavar ('Onore'), they found on a fortified island nearby naval stores that contained 'almost the whole iron work for a ship of sixty guns', the ship having had to be scuttled by Tipu's men when 'nearly completed', in order to escape capture by the English.[59] Despite this fresh setback, Tipu set about planning to build a navy afresh after 1792: this was designed to consist of 7 warships (*jahazat-i jangi*), each to be mounted with 30 to 50 guns (*darakhsh*).[60]

Tipu's major interest was, however, in building ships which could be used for trade, though, being armed for defence, as was usual with merchant ships of the time, these could also be used in naval action. The initial area for their use in commerce and future naval ambitions was naturally the Arabian Sea. His ships already used to sail to Musqat (Oman), where a factory (trading house, *kothi*) of his government (*sarkar*) had been established before 1785.[61] That year his larger plans led him to send an embassy to Constantinople.

This embassy, really consisting of a board of four officers, had both diplomatic and commercial objectives. In the official diary of the mission, which is unfortunately incomplete, commercial transactions dominate.[62] The embassy and its large retinue and cargo was put aboard three ships, *Fakhrul Marakib*, *Fath-i Shahi Mu'izzi*, and *Nabi Bakhsh*, and a galliot (*ghurab*) *Surati*, which sailed from the port of Tadri to Musqat (Oman) on 20 March 1786. The cargo carried by the ships consisted mainly of black (round) pepper, sandalwood, cinnamon and textiles, which was to be sold off at Musqat, the Iranian ports and Basra (Iraq).[63] Tipu was, however, not spending so much money merely to sell goods: he hoped to make Basra a permanent depot for the trade, with the port under his own control. He asked his ambassadors to try to secure for him a farm (*ijara*) of the port from the Ottoman monarch; this would give a safe haven to his vessels during the monsoons, and Constantinople would gain by what he would pay it for the farm.[64] Clearly, he wished to act like the European Companies by establishing an overseas settlement of his own!

Tipu was also looking beyond the Indian Ocean, and wished to open his own direct shipping line to Europe. In 1787, he proposed to send to France a ship with four hundred Indians aboard along with his embassy—this would have been 'the first Indian ship to appear in European waters'.[65]

In the event both the schemes collapsed: the Ottoman court was not willing to go beyond a diplomatic recognition of Tipu's royal position; moreover, three of Tipu's four vessels that had carried his envoys across the Arabian Sea were destroyed while anchored near Basra—one by fire, two others in a storm.[66] And the royal government of France was not willing to annoy England by too strident support for Tipu, and so would only let the Mysore envoys come on a small French ship.

The defeat in the Third Mysore War (1790–92) set harsh limits to Tipu Sultan's overseas ambitions, but even so he gave to his schemes of developing commerce, both maritime and inland, even more concentrated attention.

What was in effect a state commercial corporation was now (1793) created. This corporation was headed by nine members of a board (the names of four only being recorded in his order) with the designation of *Malikut Tujar*, entrusted with

> the management of the affairs of trade carried on through ships and factories (*kothis*), and [in camps of] the victorious army of the country of this government (*sarkar-i Khudadad*), and [in] the territory of other [states], trade in coined money and bullion, such as gold, silver, etc., and in fine textiles, sandalwood, round pepper, cardamoms (small and large), betel-nut, coconut and its fruit, rice, camphor and elephants and other merchandise.

They were to employ merchants and establish factories and maintain proper accounts.[67]

Factories were to be established within Tipu's dominions at thirty places, including Srirangapatnam, Bangalore and Mangalore, and at seventeen places outside, including Madras, Pondicherry, Mahe, Pune, Nagore, Kutch, Karachi and Musqat.[68]

Much of the capital for this enterprise had necessarily to come from the treasury with an initial investment of four lakhs of *rahatis* or pagodas, equal to Rs 12 lakh.[69] But in a very interesting order Tipu asks the officials of the corporation to raise capital from the public as well as through inviting deposits. These were to be held on an annual basis, the principal to be returned after a year along with the prescribed interest (*nafa*). The interest rates were to vary with the size of the deposit, the smaller depositors getting higher rates, viz.:

Depositors	Deposit	Interest
Smaller	5–500 *Imamis*	50%
Medium	500–5000 *Imamis*	25%
Higher	>5000 *Imamis*	12%

Note: *Imami* was the name given by Tipu to his rupee.

The distinction was expressly made in order to encourage 'the weak, the helpless and the non-affluent'. Receipts were to be duly given, the amounts invested in trade, and the principal and interest immediately repaid on demand (on maturity?).[70] Tipu's attempt was obviously to attract the small investor; but the interest rates were obviously far too high, and it is not certain how rich persons were to be prevented from making small deposits under fictitious names. Yet, the scheme had an obvious welfare element built into it, and it hardly deserves the calumny poured on it by Wilks and others.[71]

The corporation was to obtain its supplies locally through another agency headed by a board of nine members (six of whom are named), each given the title of *asif-i huzur*, and entrusted with civil administration, maintenance of warships, management of the state workshops producing muskets, cannon pieces, cutlery (knives, scissors and needles) and silk, and maintenance of the bullock department (20,000 heads) and of sheep (50,000 heads). This board was required to meet the demand of the trade corporation (*maliku-t tujars*) for rice, coconut, pepper, sandalwood, cinnamon, cardamom, honey, wax, etc., which it was to buy locally on behalf of that corporation's factories (*kothis*).[72]

These supplies were to be mainly exported; and, as we have seen, Tipu planned to establish for his corporation a number of factories outside Mysore. Four such factories already existed, two at Musqat and two in Kutch.[73] For establishing trade with Karachi and beyond, a mission was sent in 1796 to Zaman Shah, the Afghan ruler, who then held Sind. Trade with these ports was carried on through Tipu's own ships for which he had established yet another department headed by eleven admirals (*mir-yams*).

Tipu's orders show that at this time (1792–93), he planned to have forty three-masted ships of two classes, viz., large, with 72 or 62 guns each, twenty in number; and small, the remaining twenty, each with 46 guns. These were to be based at the ports of Mangalore, Coondapoor and Tadri, placed under the charge of the *mir-yams* and a hierarchy of marine officers with a complement of navigational staff, sailors, smiths, carpenters, etc.[74] The English found, after Tipu's destruction, eight ships of his fleet in good order, with many smaller vessels, when they occupied the three ports in 1799.[75]

Tipu's plans obviously exceeded the resources, both organizational and technical, that he could command; though time too, despite his own feverish vigour, was against him. One weakness, as one can see now, was his failure, as of all other independent Indian rulers of his time and subsequently, to obtain access to modern science and technology directly through the learning of European languages by his subjects. It is possible that when he thought in 1787 of sending a ship with four hundred persons to France, he imagined that they would come back learned in the French language and trained in French crafts. Through his ambassadors in 1788 he also proposed to send one of his sons to France to obtain secondary education there.[76] But neither plan came to fruition.

Tipu himself was certainly interested in scientific instruments, like thermometers and barometers, and mathematical instruments,[77] and in mechanical things, like a toy tiger, that made noises when its mechanism was made to work—it was presumably made for him by some French craftsman.[78] But there is no evidence that he himself went beyond the obvious technological products of Europe to seek acquaintance with its great advances in theoretical science. He gathered with much care a large library of Persian and Arabic books. To judge from what survives of this library, ravaged by the victors in 1799, it contained books on theology and law, as well as secular sciences. But there was apparently little material here that had been translated from the European languages.[79] Tipu's intellectual horizons thus remained restricted to the old inherited learning. Here his innovations ran either on traditional lines—thus his invention of yet another era, a solar one, calculated from the Prophet's birth[80]—or into eccentricities, like writing numbers with the digits arranged from right to left.[81]

Tipu and his Mysore were, therefore, still far away from a real opening to modern civilization, despite his own bold and restless endeavours.

Resistance, To the End

The same year (1784) that the Treaty of Mangalore brought the Second Anglo–Mysore War to a close, the British Parliament passed a comprehensive piece of legislation known as Pitt's India Act, laying down the constitution for the governance of British territories in India through the East India Company. In this Act, the Parliament was pleased to proclaim, as an undisputed truth, that 'to pursue Scheme of Conquest and Extension of Dominion in India, are Measures repugnant to the Wish, the Honour and Policy of the [British] Nation.' The claim, in view of how English dominion had grown in India during the years since Plassey (1757), was laughable in its ingenuousness; and the two Mysore wars that were now to follow (1790–92 and 1799) were in due course to show that, even as a statement of intention, the sanctimonious self-denial amounted to no more than a display of the usual parliamentary hypocrisy of the time.

Mysore, in fact, was singled out for bitter hostile propaganda. Haidar and then Tipu had had the insufferable effrontery to defeat British forces and capture British officers and men; even General Mathews had become a prisoner in 1783. Upon their release, the English prisoners told of their ill-treatment by Tipu's men, and the stories did not lose any colour in the retelling.

Very few asked, then, as few have done later, how the English had treated *their* prisoners of war. But some had, even then, been troubled by this matter, including the publisher of a gruesome tale of Tipu's 'barbarities' by one Captain Henry Oakes. Along with this tale was published in an appendix, a letter of Lieutenant John Charles Shean, who had belonged to Mathews' army. According to him, when General Mathews' troops, after occupying Bednur, attached the fort of Anantapur:

> orders were issued for a storm *and no quarter*, which was immediately put into execution, and *every man put to the sword*, except one horseman, who made his escape, after being wounded in three different places. A most dreadful sight then presented itself:

above four hundred beautiful women either killed or wounded with the bayonet, expiring in one another's arms, while the private soldiers were committing every kind of outrage, and plundering them of their jewels, the officers not being able to restrain them.[82]

When, in October 1791, Tipu's garrison at the fort of Penagra surrendered, one hundred and fifty men of the garrison were 'put to the sword' in cold blood—for having 'violated the rules of war' by not surrendering earlier.[83]

The fault of Tipu, then, was that he gave quarter and took prisoners alive. The English gave no quarter, and so they had few prisoners with them to ill-treat.

The publisher of Oakes' blood-curdling account of Tipu's 'cruelties' was therefore led to admit that: 'His [Tipu's] Conduct was evidently founded upon Principles of Retaliation; and Candor must acknowledge that the Conduct of the [English] Company's Army goes a considerable Way in Justification of that of the Enemy.'[84] But this was a voice in the wilderness. It was immediately challenged. Modern propaganda through the printed word succeeded in portraying Tipu as a brutal villain, whose head British vengeance demanded, and against whom every war could be justified.

Tipu did not need to be aware of this propaganda in order to realize that the English, having conquered so much of India, would want to conquer more; and Mysore being in their way, conflict was inevitable. His measures for improving his army therefore proceeded in earnest. A manual for military organization and tactics, the *Fathu-l Mujahidin,* had been written in 1783 by Zainul Abidin Shustari, at Tipu's direction and partly, perhaps, at his dictation.[85] This tract bears a strong imprint of the new organization of the army into fixed divisions. (The main unit was *qushun,* held by the English to correspond to a brigade.[86]) Tipu viewed it as an important text: not only was it widely distributed through transcribed copies (there are 26 copies in the Asiatic Society Library, Calcutta, and 22 copies in the India Office Library, London), but it continued to be cited by Tipu in his letters and orders throughout the subsequent years.[80] We have also already seen how Tipu was endeavouring all the time to improve his weaponry through the manufacture and import of muskets and cannon.

Apparently confident of the loyalty of his subjects, Tipu was also singular in envisioning a kind of people's war. Early in his reign, he required his revenue collectors 'to themselves carry a musket, and to call upon the peasants too to carry muskets: every day the revenue-collector should come out of the inhabited area with all the peasants, and hold target practice against a wall.'[88] This was, however, a burst of excessive enthusiasm, for there would not have been muskets, even matchlocks, enough for the purpose.

Equally unrealistic proved to be Tipu's hopes, put on paper in 1785, of inducing the Ottoman Sultan to send troops to Mysore, with expenses to be met by Tipu,[89] and the French King to send troops to India, in order to act in alliance with Tipu so as to share with him the British possessions in South India (and then, hopefully, Bengal).[90] Turkey did not have either the wish or the capacity to send troops; and France, after its costly war with Britain (ending in 1783), was in a financial crisis and heading towards the Revolution of 1789. So Tipu had to face British power alone in what was to become the Third Mysore War (1790–92).

That war was already planned by Cornwallis when, on 1 July 1789, he offered to give to the Nizam a military contingent, provided it was not used against adjoining Indian powers, from which Mysore was deliberately excluded. An offer was also made to share with the Nizam in future territories that then belonged to Mysore. At the same time full protection was offered to the ruler of Travancore, though he himself provoked a war with Tipu by acquiring two forts from the Dutch in disputed territory. When Tipu answered by attacking the 'Travancore Lines', a long fortified wall, in December 1789, Cornwallis obtained the opportunity he was waiting for.

The Third Mysore War (1790–92) was fought in a situation totally unfavourable to Tipu. The French maintained complete neutrality; and, in fact, with the revolutionary regime deeply suspicious of the royalist army, there was little that France could actually do to help Tipu. On the other hand, the Nizam and the Marathas joined the British to despoil Mysore, and Tipu had to face enemies on all sides of his dominions. Despite this, he and his troops fought well. Tipu first began a war of manoeuvre, and breaking into the Carnatic, he was able to approach Pondicherry in January 1791; in May that year he forced Governor-General Lord Cornwallis to retreat from the approaches of Srirangapatnam back to Bangalore. But the Marathas forces' union with Cornwallis changed the situation, and Tipu was ultimately compelled to accept British terms in the Treaty of Srirangapatnam, in February 1792.

This treaty divested Tipu of half his dominions, and imposed on him an indemnity of 3.30 crores of rupees, an immense sum for those days. This was to be paid *within a year*, with two sons of Tipu

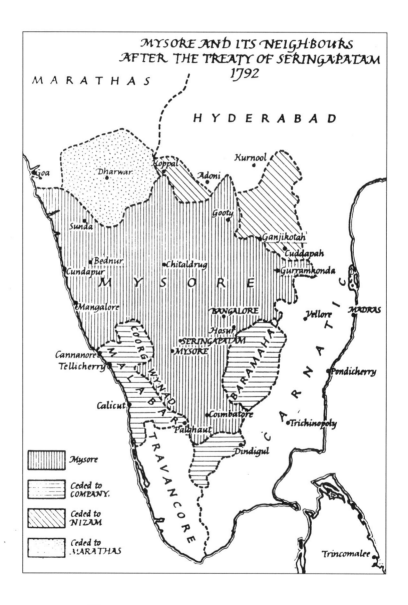

held as hostages.[91] According to a British estimate of the time, the revenues of Tipu's dominions before the war amounted to £2.5 million or Rs 2.20 crore.[92] Since he was now deprived of half his kingdom, he was in effect being required to pay a sum amounting to three times the annual gross revenues of the territory left with him!

Cornwallis probably expected that the amount would not be paid, and still harsher terms could then be imposed on Tipu. But Tipu succeeded in making the payment, though the process devastated the country within the reduced limits frrom which it had to be exacted. He had perforce to impose a levy of Rs 1.60 crore on his subjects, the remainder coming from the treasury (Rs 1.10 crore) and forced 'gifts' from the army (Rs 0.60 crore). The oppression that naturally resulted became another excuse for the demonizing of Tipu by the very same British who had forced him to this extremity.[93]

That Tipu's government survived, and that he was in the succeeding years busily at work in schemes for developing agriculture, commerce and industry, and reorganizing his army and rebuilding his fleet, is a tribute not only to the man, but also to the system that could still function after such a heavy setback. Some of his most interesting innovations, as we have seen, belong to the period of this interlude, 1792–99, before the final war.

Tipu must have known that his efforts to rebuild the military and economic power of Mysore were being vigilantly watched by the English, who had reduced him in size but had not been able to impose on him any curtailment of his independence. One last hope for him now was help from France.

During the entire period of the Third Anglo–Mysore War (1790–92) France had been involved in its own internal problems, as both the monarchy and aristocracy conspired with foreign powers to oppose the revolution. As the invading Prussians were repulsed, monarchy was at long last abolished (September 1792). All the other great powers of Europe rallied against France, and war with England began early in 1793. It was now Tipu who was neutral, and France which was at war and anxious to have allies against England. Tipu was willing to respond to these approaches, and in 1796 he sent a draft agreement for future joint military action, provided the French landed 10,000 men in south India—but such an enterprise France was no longer capable of undertaking.[94]

Individual Frenchmen could, however, still be entertained, and with them came the new ideas of revolutionary France. A Jacobin Club was established at Srirangapatnam; and on 15 May 1797, the Republican flag was hoisted, and the Tree of Liberty planted, in the presence of 'Citizen Tipu', with a salute of 2,300 guns. Whatever its immediate lack of relevance, the event is memorable for the first declaration of the principles of Liberty and Equality on Indian soil.

Of any substantial help from France, however, there was little sign. A mission to the French islands of Mauritius in 1797–98 obtained the services of 99 Frenchmen, who volunteered in response to a proclamation by Malartic, governor-general of the Islands, issued on 30 January 1798. This document was practically worn through in providing the justification for the final British invasion of Mysore in 1799.

This invasion took place just as Tipu was expecting to receive the English envoy John Doveton. Troops under General Harris crossed into Mysore on 5 March 1799, under orders issued by the governor-general, Lord Wellesley. The reasons given for this act of aggression could not stand any legal test. There was no bar imposed on Tipu by the Treaty of Srirangapatnam of 1792, on maintaining good relations with foreign powers. Even under international law, as understood in Europe at the time, neutral countries had the right to deal with both belligerent powers. And Tipu was a neutral in respect of the war between England and France. Nor could any fear of French invasion have lain behind Wellesley's action, since with Nelson's victory over Napoleon's fleet in Egypt in the Battle of the Nile (1798), all danger of a French expedition to India from Egypt (a possibility always belonging in any case to the realm of fantasy) disappeared. Wellesley himself triumphantly announced the victory to Tipu in his letter of 4 November 1798.

The reason for the invasion was a simple one—conquest and acquisition, providing thereby a further source for the tribute, the major motive for colonial expansion in India. Within six months of the fall of Srirangapatnam, Wellesley was writing to Henry Dundas, President of the Board of Control (i.e. the British minister in charge of India):

> If you will have a little patience, the death of the Nizam will probably enable me to gratify your voracious appetite for lands and fortresses. Seringapatam ought, I think, to stay your stomach awhile; not to

mention Tanjore and the Poligar countries. Perhaps, I may be able to give you a supper of Oudh and the Carnatic, if you should still be hungry.[95]

There was nothing jocular about this: what Wellesley was proposing here soon came to pass, in respect of both Oudh (Awadh) and the Carnatic.[96]

No reason given at the time, nor a partisan reconstruction of Tipu's 'secret' activities against the English *post-facto*,[97] can hide the real character of Wellesley's action: it was naked, colonial aggression.

Tipu resisted coolly and skilfully, first trying to manoeuvre in the open, and then retreating to Srirangapatnam. His authority over his troops and subjects remained unimpaired; but with his territory already halved, the Nizam joining the English, and the Marathas looking the other way, the odds against him were overwhelming. His last decision too was a cool one: no surrender, but a fight to death. English officers who broke into his palace on 4 May, expecting to find him there with an offer of surrender, misjudged their man. He had died fighting at the so-called Water Gate. English soldiers had after- wards killed all they found there, including women; and his corpse was covered over by bodies 'heaped in mass over each other'.[98]

Srirangapatnam was given over to reckless rapine and slaugh- ter by the victorious army. The only thing done with grace was Tipu's funeral, with military honours. Perhaps this was found necessary in order to assure everyone that the dreaded enemy was dead, so as to prevent any further resistance.

An English observer present on this occasion wrote that the people of Srirangapatnam, even as their houses and property were being plundered by the victors, lined the streets through which the funeral procession passed—'many of whom prostrated themselves before the body, and expressed their grief by loud lamentations.'[99]

That was how his own people felt about Tipu two hundred years ago.

Notes and References

[1] For Haidar Ali my facts are ordinarily drawn from N.K. Sinha's careful bio- graphy, *Haidar Ali*, 3rd edn., Calcutta, 1959. This may be supplemented by B. Sheik Ali, *English Relations with Haidar Ali*, Mysore, 1963.

[2] The matchlock 'up to the middle of the 18th century was looked on with less favour than the bow and arrow, which still held their ground. The

matchlock was left chiefly to the infantry who occupied a much inferior position to that of the cavalry in the opinion of Moghul commanders' (William Irvine, *The Army of the Indian Moghuls*, London, 1903, p. 103).

3 Mark Wilks, *Historical Sketches of South India*, Vol. I, ed. Murray Hammick, Mysore, 1930, pp. 491–92. Wilks' original text of Vol. I was published in 1810; that of Vol. II in 1817. All references to Wilks in these notes are from the Hammick edition.

4 Cf. ibid., I, pp. 172–73.

5 Cf. Francis Buchanan, *A Journey from Madras through the Countries of Mysore, Canara, and Malabar, etc.* [1800–01], I, London, 1807, p. 300. This journey was undertaken at the direction of Lord Wellesley, and Buchanan, therefore, shows a visible bias against the fallen regime.

6 See Geo. P. Taylor, *The Coins of Tipu Sultan*, Calcutta, 1914 (reprint, New Delhi, 1989), pp. 21–29.

7 *Hukmnamaha-i* [*Tipu Sultan*], India Office Library, Persian MS., I.O. 4685, f. 67a.

8 *Risala* is an Arabic word, literally meaning a troop of horse. But Haidar Ali apparently generalized it to mean both cavalry and infantry units of the size of a regiment.

9 The information for 1767 comes from Orme MSS, Vol. 23, cited by N.K. Sinha, *Haidar Ali*, p. 258.

10 Ibid., pp. 144–45. See also Surendranath Sen, 'Haidar Ali's Fleet', in his *Studies in Indian History*, Calcutta, 1930, pp. 146–50.

11 This applies, with similar force, to those who followed in Haidar Ali's footsteps, like Mahadji Sindhia and Ranjit Singh.

12 V.A. Smith's summing up in his *Oxford History of India*, 2nd edn., London, 1922, p. 485.

13 Buchanan, *Journey from Madras*, I, p. 300.

14 For these and many other facts on Tipu's life and reign I have drawn on the standard biography by Mohibbul Hasan, *History of Tipu Sultan*, 2nd edn., Calcutta, 1971. It can be supplemented by a readable and well-documented book by Denys Forrest, *Tiger of Mysore: The Life and Death of Tipu Sultan*, Bombay, 1970. See also B. Sheik Ali, *Tipu Sultan*, New Delhi, 1971.

15 Barun De, 'Some Socio-Political Implications of the Cognomen "Tipu Sultan"', *Proceedings of the Indian History Congress*, 52nd session, Delhi, pp. 700–07 [Art. No. 1 in this volume], seeks *sufic* origins for Tipu Sultan's militancy. This could be an additional factor. Shiite influences on Tipu are, however, more perceptible, though Tipu showed respect to all the four Pious Caliphs.

16 Wilks' letter, cited by Kate Brittlebank, *Tipu Sultan's Search for Legitimacy: Islam and Kingship in a Hindu Domain*, Delhi, 1997, pp. 71–72 & n. On the entire matter of Tipu's assertion of full sovereign titles, there is much factual material in Brittlebank, pp. 57–81.

17 Cf. I.H. Qureshi, 'The Purpose of Tipu Sultan's Embassy to Constantinople', *Journal of Indian History*, Vol. 24 (1945), pp. 77–84 [Art. No. 8 in this volume], where the embassy is related to Tipu's decision to abandon

any legal dependence on the Mughal court.

[18] On this motif see Brittlebank, pp. 140–46.

[19] The designation *Asadullahi* was used for Tipu's Muslim soldiers. See *Hukmnamas* of Tipu Sultan, Asiatic Society of Bengal, Calcutta, Persian MS No. 1677, ff. 7a, 57a–b. The term *Asadullahi*, 'Of the Tiger of God', again invokes the war-image of Ali.

[20] *Hukmnamaha-i* [*Tipu Sultan*], I.O. 4685, ff. 85a, 120a-b.

[21] Asiatic Society of Bengal, Persian MS No. 1677, pp. 14b–15b. This letter is dated 14 Muharram 12[00], 17 November 1785; and so are all the other letters in this volume. Tipu, of course, heavily overstates the revenue resources of the territories conquered by the English; and his accusation that the English were intent on converting Muslims had little basis.

[22] Cf. Surendranath Sen, 'The Shringeri Letters of Tipu Sultan' in his *Studies in Indian History*, pp. 155–57. Mohibbul Hasan, *Tipu Sultan*, pp. 362–63, disputes the large figures of converts claimed by Zainul Abidin Shustari in *Sultanu-t Tawarikh*.

[23] Buchanan, *Journey from Madras*, I, pp. 70–73 [Art. No. 21 in this volume].

[24] Wilks, Vol. II, p. 766.

[25] Mohibbul Hasan, pp. 357–58.

[26] Buchanan, *Journey from Madras*, I.

[27] *Hukmnamaha-i* [*Tipu Sultan*], I.O. 4685, ff. 130a, 152a, 159a–b, etc.

[28] Ibid., f. 3b–4a. This is dated Jafari, 1221 Mauludi. I follow the concordance reconstructed in Geo. P. Taylor, *The Coins of Tipu Sultan*, p. 19.

[29] Ibid., f. 112a–b.

[30] Wilks, Vol. II, p. 735.

[31] Surendranath Sen, *Studies in Indian History*, pp. 155–69; B.A. Saletore, 'Tipu Sultan as a Defender of the Hindu *Dharma*', *Medieval India Quarterly*, 1, (1950), pp. 13–55 [Art. No. 15 in this volume].

[32] Saletore, p. 54.

[33] See Art. No. 14 in this volume. This paper has been strangely neglected by writers on Tipu.

[34] *The Dreams of Tipu Sultan*, translated from Persian [India Office MS] by Mahmud Husain, Karachi, n.d., Dream XXII (pp. 78–79).

[35] I find Brittlebank's treatment (pp. 125–30) of Tipu's attitude to Hindu beliefs and temples fairly well balanced; and one would have no quarrel with her view that Tipu belonged to a milieu where Hindu–Muslim coexistence in the religious sphere was an accepted part of culture and polity. Her interpretation of Tipu's religious views tends to become one-sided, however, owing to her contextualizing his Islamic symbolism in terms of its presence in a 'Hindu domain' only, rather than setting it in its real context—resistance to English power.

[36] Major Dirom, *A Narrative of the Campaign in India, which Terminated the War with Tippoo Sultan in 1792*, 2nd edn., London, 1794, pp. 249–50.

[37] I.O. 4685, f. 110a–111a. For a much longer collection of agrarian regulations of Tipu Sultan, see 'Original documents of Tipu Sultan and his officials, 1783–89', Persian MS, I.O. 4683, ff. 10b–23b (incomplete copy, ff.

2b–8a), issued in 1784, and ordered to be read daily by officials. Further regulations to be read 'morning and evening' were issued in 1786, and are given on ff. 51a–73b of the same volume. Tipu's agrarian regulations, as translated by Burrish Crisp in 1795, are reproduced in Nikhiles Guha, *Pre-British System of South India*, Calcutta, 1985, pp. 175–219, and are discussed by Guha on pp. 20–29.

38 *Journey from Madras*, I, pp. 70–71; II, pp. 82–3, 164, 235.

39 Photograph of inscription in Mahmud Khan 'Mahmud' Banglori, *Tarikh-i Saltanat-i Khudadad* (Urdu), Bangalore, 1939, opposite p. 456; see also text, pp. 454–58. Since the slab is displayed at the site, and the dam is a tourist spot, the inscription is naturally very well known.

40 I.O. 4685, f. 95a.

41 Tipu's order in I.O. 4685, f. 98a–b. All the places where the silkworms were cultured are listed in the order. Buchanan, *Journey from Madras*, I, p. 222, makes his usual derogatory remarks about Tipu's 'arbitrary measures' to introduce sericulture, but acknowledges that the mulberry trees in the dead Sultan's gardens had grown well.

42 *Hukmnamas*, Asiatic Soc. MS, f. 61a. After Tipu's loss of territory to the English in 1792, the number of the musket-manufactories was reduced to seven; these are listed in *Hukmnamaha-i* [*Tipu Sultan*], I.O. 4685, ff. 94a–95b, in an order where concern is shown for recruitment of the workshops' staff from amongst local 'ironsmiths, carpenters, traders (*kumati*), etc.'

43 M.P. Sridharan, citing documents in Archivee Nationale Paris, in 'Tipu's Letters to French Officials', *Proceedings of the Indian History Congress*, 45th (Annamalainagar) session (1984), pp. 506 [Art. No. 18 in this volume].

44 *Hukmnamas*, Asiatic Soc. MS., f. 16b.

445 Ibid., f. 61a.

46 Mouriset, employed in French royal foundries, agreed to go to India with Tipu's ambassadors, along with two foremen, a carpenter and a turner (Suman Venkatesh, tr., *The Correspondence of the French during the Reign of Haidar Ali and Tipu Sultan*, III, Bangalore, 1998, pp. 280–81).

47 Buchanan, *Journey from Madras*, I, p. 70. There is no reason to accept Buchanan's sneer that Tipu was 'little sensible' of the value of the use of water power; probably the waterwheel installed did not work efficiently enough. The use of bullocks should have needed an additional gearing mechanism if the original apparatus had vertical waterwheels (as usual in Europe) and not horizontal (as in Asia: but these would not have given sufficient power). To construct such gearing, which would have to be of iron to transmit so much power, must surely have required a creditable level of craftsmanship.

48 *Hukmnamas* of Tipu Sultan, Asiatic Society MS., f. 61a. Cf. also Sridharan, p. 505, for Tipu's interest in acquiring a printing press and clocks from France in 1788, as indicated by documentary material in the French archives.

49 *Asiatic Annual Register*, for 1799, London, 1801, p. 97, quoted in Ashok

Sen, 'A Pre-British Economic Formation in India of the late Eighteenth Century: Tipu Sultan's Mysore', in *Perspectives in Social Sciences-1*, ed. Barun De, Calcutta, 1977, p. 96.

[50] Buchanan, *Journey from Madras*, I, p. 70. In 1783, 'Burrah Mire', a high officer of Tipu, surprised English prisoners of war by enquiring whether any of them 'understood the method of making musket-flints, paper or black lead-pencils, offering great rewards to any person who would instruct him in these arts' (Captain Henry Oakes, *An Authentic Narrative of the Treatment of the English … by Tippoo Saib*, London, 1785, p. 32).

[51] *Journey from Madras*, I, p. 70.

[52] Mentioned in Joseph Michaud, *History of Mysore under Haidar Ali and Tipu Sultan*, [original French ed., Paris, 1801], English tr., 1926 (reprint, New Delhi, 1985), p. 107.

[53] *Hukmnama-ha-i* [*Tipu Sultan*], I.O. 4685, ff. 94Ab–95a.

[54] *Journey from Madras*, I, p. 70.

[55] Wilks, Vol. II, p. 763.

[56] Buchanan, *Journey from Madras*, I, p. 70.

[57] For references to Malik Ambar's ships, see W. Foster (ed.), *English Factories in India, 1624–29*, Oxford, 1909, pp. 33–71; for Shivaji's ships trading with the Gulf and the Red Sea, see W. Foster (ed.), *English Factories in India, 1665–67*, Oxford, 1925, p. 10.

[58] For an agreement of the ruler of Cochin in the 1660s to deliver all pepper and cinnamon grown in his country to the Dutch alone, see K.N. Chaudhuri, *The Trading World of Asia and the English East India Company, 1660–1760*, Cambridge, 1978, p. 315.

[59] Major Dirom, *A Narrative of the Campaign in India*, p. 107.

[60] I.O. 4685, f. 93a-b. Are these the two-decker *ghurabs* (galliots), built for naval (*jangi*) purposes, each carrying 25 to 30 guns (ibid., f. 138a–b)?

[61] *Waqai Manazil-i Rum* (for which see the following note), Persian text, p. 11.

[62] This has been printed: *Waqai Manazil-i Rum*, ed. Mohibbul Hasan, Bombay, 1968. This diary needs to be read with the letters of instructions issued to the embassy by Tipu that are contained in the Asiatic Society MS, Persian No. 1677, already cited, running from f. 1a to f. 59a.

[63] *Waqai Manazil-i Rum*, Persian text, p. 47 & passim.

[64] *Hukmnamas*, Asiatic Soc. MS, ff. 11a, 15b–16a.

[65] Sridharan, p. 504 [Art. No. 18 in this volume].

[66] *Waqai Manazil-i Rum*, pp. 59–60. Only the largest vessel *Fakhru-l Marakib*, which had not sailed beyond Musqat, survived this fateful voyage.

[67] I.O. 4685, ff. 6b–7b. The connected documents are dated in Tipu's *mauludi* calendar, giving years 1221 and 1222, so that the corporation was probably created in 1793. The documents relating to this enterprise were partly translated by W. Kirkpatrick in *Select Letters of Tipu Sultan*, London, 1811, and these have been conveniently reproduced in Nikhiles Guha, *Pre-British State System in South India*, pp. 160–74. Since I have used the Persian

documents, I have not checked the accuracy of Kirkpatrick's translation.

[68] The two lists of factories inside and outside his dominions are carefully set out (I.O. 4685, ff. 17a–19a).

[69] I.O. 4685, f. 12a. I take a *rahati* (equated with a pagoda by Kirkpatrick) to be equal to Rs 3. But if Taylor, *Coins of Tipu Sultan*, p. 13, is right in identifying *rahati* with a *fanam*, the total amount loaned from the treasury would have been Rs 1.20 lakh only.

[70] Ibid., ff. 20a–21a.

[71] Cf. Wilks, Vol. II, pp. 570–71 ('a swindling loan').

[72] I.O. 4685, f. 84a–85a, 108a.

[73] Ibid., ff. 141b–142a, 184b–185a.

[74] Ibid., ff. 171b–187b. In another order (f. 138a–b) Tipu plans to build at the three ports twenty three-masted ships with 80–85 guns each, and twenty two-masted ships (*ghurabs*), with 25–30 guns each. The larger ones built were to be handed over to the *mir yams*, and the *ghurabs* to the officers (*asifs*) entrusted with commerce.

[75] Mohibbul Hasan, *Tipu Sultan*, pp. 355–56.

[76] Sridharan, p. 504 [Art. No. 18]. See for French comments on this proposal, Suman Venkatesh, tr., *The Correspondence of the French*, III, pp. 200–05.

[77] Wilks, Vol. II, p. 584, and Sridharan, p. 505 [Art. No. 18], for thermometers and barometers; for 'mathematical instruments of London make' see Major Dirom, *A Narrative of the Campaign in India*, p. 153n.

[78] D. Forrest, *Tiger of Mysore*, pp. 214–15, basing his description on Mildred Archer, *Tippoo's Tiger*, Victoria and Albert Museum, London, 1959.

[79] A portion of the library is now to be found in the India Office, London; some MSS from it are in Asiatic Society Library, Calcutta. For the latter collection, see Hidayat Hosain, 'The Library of Tipu Sultan', *Islamic Culture*, XIV (1940), pp. 139–67.

[80] See Geo. P. Taylor, *The Coins of Tipu Sultan*, pp. 15–21, especially the concordance of his solar and Christian era years on p. 19, which suggests its epoch is to be placed in AD 571. The era was set to begin from the Prophet's birth (traditionally placed around AD 570), conforming to its own name *maulud-i Muhammad*. The supposition in Hidayat Hosain, *Islamic Culture*, XIV, p. 162, followed by Mohibbul Hasan, *Tipu Sultan*, p. 400, that the era was held to begin from AD 609, when Muhammad received the Revelation of his Prophethood, is, therefore, ill-founded.

[81] Mahmud Husain, *Dreams*, p. 29. As Mahmud Husain, p. 10, notes, Tipu's spelling was atrocious. Probably, he was accustomed to hearing books read out to him, and to dictating his own orders or regulations. The recollections of his dreams were written out by him in a confidential notebook apparently for his own eyes alone.

[82] Captain Henry Oakes, *An Authentic Narrative of the Treatment of the English who were taken Prisoners ... by Tippoo Saib*, with an Appendix containing an account by Lieut. John Charles Shean, pub. by G. Kearsley, London, 1785, pp. 77–78. Italics ours.

[83] Dirom, *A Narrative of the Campaign in India*, p. 56.

84 Publisher's Advertisement in Oakes, *Authentic Narrative*, p. vii.

85 There is an MS copy in Maulana Azad library, Aligarh, Habibganj collection, 56/2.

86 Cf. Dirom, *A Narrative of the Campaign in India*, p. 174.

87 E.g., I.O. 4685, ff. 62a–63a.

88 Persian MS, I.O. 4683, f. 19a.

89 Tipu's letters, Asiatic Society MS, f. 11a-b (letter dated 17 November 1785).

90 Ibid., f. 29b–30a: also dated 17 November 1785. For French response (or responses) to Tipu during this period and subsequently, see Aniruddha Ray, 'French Attitude to Tipu Sultan: a General Review' in B. Sheik Ali, ed., *Tipu Sultan: a Great Martyr*, Bangalore, 1993, pp. 51–76.

91 For the text of the five articles of the preliminary treaty, see Dirom, *A Narrative of the Campaign in India*, pp. 226–27. This was followed by a detailed treaty dated 18 March 1792 (full text in ibid., pp. 275–82).

92 Ibid., p. 249. On p. 300, a rupee is rated at 2s., 3d.

93 See, e.g., Wilks, Vol. II, p. 562–63.

94 This draft agreement is cited by D. Forrest, *Tiger of Mysore*, pp. 242–43, from A.K. Antonova's translation of its Persian text in *Central Asian Review*, I: 2, 1963.

95 Quoted in Forrest, p. 310. Tanjore (Thanjavur) had been taken over in October 1799.

96 Half of Oudh was seized in January 1801, and the Carnatic was annexed by a proclamation in July 1801, the latter on the specious ground of its nawabs having maintained secret correspondence with Tipu (on which see C.S. Srinavasachari, 'The Seringapatam Correspondence and the Carnatic Nawabi', *Indian Culture*, XII, 1946, pp. 207–11 [Art. 19 in this volume]).

97 After the publication of the *Official Documents relating to the Negotiations Carried on by Tippoo Sultan with the French Nation*, issued by Order of the Governor-General-in-Council, Calcutta, 1799. Then came W. Kirkpatrick's *Select Letters of Tippoo Sultan*, London, 1811, and Wilks' two volumes, London, 1810 and 1817—all being part of the campaign to justify the destruction of Tipu.

98 Wilks, Vol. II, 751. See Constance E. Parsons, *Seringapatam*, London, 1931, p. 86, for the women killed there.

99 Alexander Beatson, *A View of the Origin and Conduct of the War with Tippoo Sultan*, London, 1800, p. 148.

Tipu Sultan by a Mysore artist, 1796–99
Courtesy: Victoria and Albert Museum, London

Tipu's uniformed infantryman

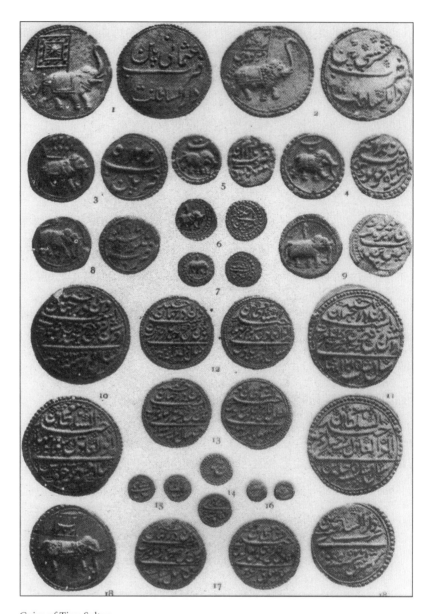

Coins of Tipu Sultan

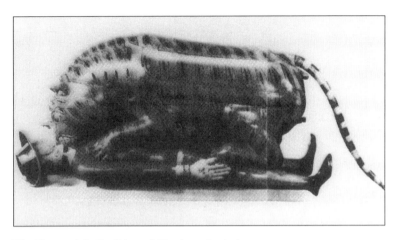

'The Tiger and the Englishman', Tipu's mechanical toy
Model now in Victoria and Albert Museum, London

VIEW OF THE HOALLY GATEWAY IN WHICH TIPPOO SULTAUN WAS KILLED.

The Water Gate where Tipu was killed

The Two Rulers

1

The Ideological and Social Background of Haidar Ali and Tipu Sultan

Barun De

ipu Sultan, Mysore's last independent ruler, was distinctly an alternative element in late eighteenth-century South Asian political culture.[1] Unlike the nominally independent Nizam Ali Khans, Asafuddaulahs, Nana Fadnavis or other princes and statesmen of an age when colonialism was destroying the Indian ancient *regime* brick by brick, Tipu, like his father Haidar Ali and his northern contemporary Mahadaji Sindhia, refused to be pliant and complaisant about British diplomatic blandishments allied with military threats during the age from Warren Hastings to Wellesley. Plebeian in his social origins, more of a *ghazi* than the average feudal carpet-knight, he was a throwback to the pre-Mughal Deccan Sultan, seeking acceptance of his imperial aspirations from West Asian and continental European peers, so as to effectively challenge British Indian competition for dominion in South India.[2] More than any other indigenous ruler in eighteenth-century India, Tipu was interested in state power and its commercial capacity. But more than any of them, except his father and Mahadaji, he recognized the need to fight for it. He did this in a pragmatic way, using French absolutist alliance, Jacobian ideology, as well as the neo-Madari principles of a *shaheed*, without any scruples of artificial consistency, or ideological purity.

Tipu's contacts with France in its pre-Revolutionary and Revolutionary generation are fairly well known. What is practically unexplored are the implications of the dialectics of Sufi plebeian militancy in Tipu Sultan's family traditions and cognomen. This note seeks to initiate discussion on the data, which may be carried out by people more qualified to do so, i.e. by those who, unlike the present

3

writer, can read the Persian sources themselves, a field now sadly neglected by scholars of South Indian history, except perhaps by some in the U.S.A. like J.F. Richards and R.M. Eaton. It also seeks to arouse debate on the variety of indigenous reactions to political conditions in eighteenth-century India.

Plebeian Oeifyina of the Lineage

Mohibbul Hasan, still Tipu's best biographer, noted many years ago that the veracity of tales about Haidar Ali's ancestry 'is for the most part obscure' and that the only detailed pedigree—by the anonymous author of the *Karnama-i Haidari* about his distant forefathers moving as Quraish from Mecca, to Sana'a in Yemen to Baghdad, to Ajmer in the seventeenth century and its *dargah,* to Shahjahanabad (Delhi) was 'possibly ... manufactured to bolster up the domestic prestige of Haidar and Tipu'. But it is certain that his more proximate forefathers were *dargah* servitors, then land managers, then petty warriors. Their description in Mohibbul Hasan's evocative narrative bears rereading.[3] Tipu Sultan's grandfather's grandfather, Shaikh Wali Muhammad 'came to Gulbarga from Delhi with his son Muhammad Ali during the reign of Muhammad Adil Shah (1626–56) of Bijapur, i.e. at the time of the break-up of the latter Vijayanagar domains ruled from its refuge at Chandragiri, an age of Deccani expansion into Karnataka.' A religious man 'he' attached himself to the shrine of Sadr-ud Din Husaini, commonly known as Gisu Daraz on a monthly subsistence allowance. His son was married to a servitor's daughter. On his death, Muhammad Ali trekked further south to Kolar on the edge of the plateau to look after and rent fields and gardens. His four sons forswore the 'life of devotees'. They took to warfare—in an age when Aurangzeb Alamgir's troops were pressing into Tamilnadu from Golconda. After his death in 1697, his third son Fath Muhammad went further south in the service of the new Mughal ruler of Arcot, Nawab Sadatullah Khan, who made him a *jamadar* and gave him the command of 200 foot and 50 horse in the lowest rung, perhaps below the *mansabdari* system.

Fath Muhammad Khan thus moved from a *dervish*-cum-land management background to being a soldier of fortune. He briefly served the Nayak of Sira, an official of the later Mughals, where Haidar Ali was born in 1721. Haidar stayed in his father's profession, but

4

retained the pious connections. His first wife, who was paralysed for life after childbirth, was the daughter of a *pirzada* Sayyid of Sira. His second, Fakhr-un-Nissa, however was of higher and military rank. Daughter of a quondam *qiladar* (castellan) of Cuddapah, when she 'became pregnant ... with her husband [she] paid a visit to the tomb of Tipu Mastan Aulia in Arcot ... built by Nawab Saadatulla Khan in about 1729 ... and [they] prayed for her safe and easy delivery and for the birth of a son... [who], born to her at Devanhalli [in 1750] ... was named Tipu Sultan after the name of the saint.' Also he was called Fath Ali after his grandfather, Fath Muhammad Khan.[4]

The juxtaposition of cognomens signifies the duality of the two parts in the lineage, part Sufi servitor, part petty military adventurer.[5] This was a social position far below the elite compradores of colonialism in the eighteenth-century Indian ruling class in Hyderabad, the Maratha Confederacy, Awadh or Bengal. Indeed this ancestry was not even that of 'service gentry', a term coined in the early 1980s by C.A. Bayly of Cambridge to categorize the relatively stable socio-economic base of the later Mughal, U.P. petty rural, *madad-i maash* grantees, prebendaries, or the now semi-permanent *taluqdars* or *jagirdars*.[6]

The Muslim *naiks* of late eighteenth-century Mysore were certainly below the status of small-town *ulema*. Their immediate background was the lowest rung of military adventurers whose status was gained by their arms, cunning, self-assertion, i.e. popular heroic, in Gramscian terms with common sense rather than elitist intellect. With myths of Arab origin and tenuous claims to broken Quraish, i.e. the Prophet's kin lineage, they were not even legitimate princes, since the Wodeyars were still immured in Seringapatam palace itself. They lacked the foreign ethnic specificity and racial elitism of the Turani, Irani, Kashmiri or Rohilla adventurers of the North. Neither foreigner nor *Navyat* (direct newcomer to South India) the Quraish rulers in Mysore were fully plebeian.

The Dervish Streak

In Tipu's struggle against encirclement there is however a deeper strand. What British romantic imperialists like John Buchan or P.C. Wren in the late nineteenth or early twentieth century, fantasizing about 'the thin red line' fighting the Mahdi's dervishes in the Sudan, or even later the Saudi *Ikhwan-al Muslimeen* in the southern Iraqi or Najd deserts, or the Pathan followers of the Faqir of Ipi in Waziristan in the 1930s, called the *ghazi* streak. A recent popularizer of the Mysore resistance has sought to score a cheap point over historians better than himself, in correcting 'Lord Macaulay who [in his *Historical Essays*] goes to the ... extreme of imputing that Haidar's extraction was humble. His father had been a petty officer of revenue, his grandfather a wandering dervish. One must forgive the English historian the liberties he took with historical facts for the drama and thunder of his prose.' Praxy Fernandes then notes that the dervish was Haidar's great-grandfather who had actually wandered from Delhi to Gulbarga: he then proceeds to make a slip of fact as trivial as that for which he forgives Macaulay.[7] However, the hare coursed by Macaulay in his mid-nineteenth-century elitism about social origins will be well worth tracking.

The original in Tipu's cognomen, the Mastan Auliya, was a Muslim ascetic presumably to the point of ecstatic fantasy (*mastani*). A Persian manuscript, the *Rauzat-ul Auliya* mentions his death in 1725 (the tomb-shrine as we know was constructed in 1729). The Auliya's residence in the late seventeenth century was at Shahpur Hillock outside Bijapur city, where many Sufis congregated from Bahmani times; he then lived as a migrant in Arcot, where Nawab Saadatulla Khan set up the Eastern Carnatic principality of the early eighteenth century. The parallelism with Muhammad Ali and Fath Muhammad's time and shifts may be noted. The *Tarjama-yi Rauzatul-Auliya-i Bijapur* further noted him as 'one of Amin-al-Din Ala's murshids Tipu Auliya ... who is said to have ignored the distinguished Shaikhs of his time' and was a naked fakir like Shah Nangi *Majzub* (d. 1713) whose name was the give-away.[8]

Such *majzubs* as the 'Mastan', mad or intoxicated with the spirit, 'dead to the world', with the aid of narcotics such as *bhang* or *charas*, have been socially described by Eaton in his *Sufis of Bijapur*. He particularly emphasizes that 'miniature paintings of seventeenth-century dervishes of Bijapur reflect these features and some also reflect that entranced expressions on their faces... None of them is known to have written anything himself, and the hagiographic biographies provide only the briefest sketches of their lives. Their doctrinal positions ... were to varying degrees unorthodox ... their accentric behaviour attracted attention to them in the seventeenth century, just as the unique dance ceremony of the *Mevlevi Sufis* of nineteenth-century Ottoman Turkey attracted the attention of contemporary European observers who on this account forever associated the adjective "whirling" with "dervish".[9] Eaton proceeds to quote Muhsin Fani's description in the *Dabistan-i Mazahib* comparing the 'Madarian' with 'Sanyasi Avadhuts'. Both sported common signs—matted locks smeared with *bhasma* (ashes), iron chains around their heads and necks, flaunting black turbans and flags, smoking *bhang* seated round fires. Tipu *Mastan* is mentioned as a new initiator, and by no means a follower in late pre-colonial *Madari* practice. It is not surprising that Haidar Naik and Fakhrunissa in their religious faith, should also in a pragmatically secular way, invest the attribute of 'Mastan' to the more sovereign value system connoted by 'Sultan', from other-worldly ecstasy to this-worldy authority, from the extremely spiritual to the highly temporal. There is a large element of social aspirations in the cognomen, Tipu Sultan: the factually subaltern *naik* wanted to become *Padshah-i Ghazi*, as Tipu actually did become in 1787, when he declared that the infirm Delhi Padshah, blinded by a swaggering Rohilla captain, had become unfit to rule.

Many Sufi devotees were deeply imbricated in state power as part of the social dialectics of religious free thinking. Eaton's analysis of 'The State and the Family of Bandanawaz Gesudaraz', i.e. of Saiyid Muhammad Husain's family, constructed from a series of over twenty-five *farman* from the Bijapur court over the period 1659–76, documents the Gulbarga locale. A large lower class following an economy of seasonal fairs displaying and selling, according to the Abbé Carré, a French traveller, 'streamers, bells, whirligigs, pots, plates, cradles', which implied a market economy, was linked with a gentry class. *Sajjada-nashins* and *pirzadas* were increasingly involved in Hindu–Muslim social violence in seventeenth and early eighteenth century Deccan and Karnataka, which escalated as Hindu *naiks* and *palegars* began to resist the Bijapur–Golconda thrusts south into Mysore and upper and western Tamilnadu, and Mughal imperialists pressed hard on the thrusters from further north. The reflection of this was to be found in the *chakkinamas* or foodgrain grinding-wheel accompaniments dirges sung by the lower classes, as much as in local accounts of *pirzada* gentry violence against Hindus.[10]

'The political and social disruptions accompanying the dealing of the kingdom [of Bijapur] were followed by further disruptions after the Mughal conquest,'.[11] Cholera in 1689–90, the Bhima river floods in 1696, a terrible famine in 1717, and growing tensions amongst the Deccan ruling classes which the later Mughals sought to standardize: there was also the subordination of the dialect of Dakhni Urdu by northern forms of speech of the imperial camp, patronized by the imperialists and their *ghair-mulki* (extralocal) followers. A *chakkinama* of the year Aurangzeb conquered Golconda, which is kept in the Hyderabad Salar Jung Museum, is redolent of a mood of embittered snobbery:

> The twelfth century [Hijri, i.e. 1689] has arrived and Aurengzeb is king. Pawns have leaped to become queens.
>
> Those who used to be nobles now have to serve these mean people. Kayastha, Khatris and Brahmans of the army [who] have gained much, and have become an estranged retinue.
>
> North Indian leather-workers, tanners, and untouchables, washermen, oil-dealers and gardeners, all have become rulers.[12]

There one gets the same refrain as one gets in the *Shahr-i Ashobs* of the eighteenth century North, about the Indian social structure and its mental world turning upside down.[13]

In this disruptive world of social disharmony, the choice of a *Madari* cognomen may appear trivial nomenclature. But in its deep structure may be found the popular faith in a *Madari* holy man, one who was no ordinary fanatical *Madari*, but had donned—in a sort of extra-communalist, apocalyptic, religious authority.[14] In the mid-eighteenth century, coexistence of social symbiosis and communal (in the sense of social class and rank ordering, and not just religious distinction, as we find reflected in the *chakkinama* quoted above) did continue. Such a composite culture did represent a secularizing force, since dervish-veneration with its implied alternative to landed-gentry authoritarianism may have given a greater plebeian, 'common-sense' hegemony to a rising mercenary ruling class in South Eastern Carnatic.

That such *majzub* simplicity ideally, if not practically, appealed to Tipu's own imagination may be inferred from illustrated manuscripts depicting vignettes of utterly plebeian Sufis in prayer and ecstasy which were found in his rich library in Seringapatam. Looted by the British army, parts of this ultimately found their way to The Asiatic Society of Bengal and also the India Office Library, London. Some of them, utterly simple in their representational form, were on display in the Exhibition held at the national seminar on Tipu Sultan, in January 1992 at Bangalore. More research on the people actually venerated by Tipu, and the elements of ideology in his 'Dreams' which are purported to have been collected, will be necessary by scholars who can not only study Persian but also take note of the social psychological aspects.

Some Interim Conclusions

Characterizing the Sufi landed gentry, R.M. Eaton correctly ignores the late N.A. Siddiqui's fantasy about Muslim *a'immadars* or land grantees as an integrative social yeast among a predominantly sectarian Hindu population at the *pargana* levels. He opts for Irfan Habib's earlier categorization of such *ulama* as 'bastion[s] of conservatism because they had nothing except orthodoxy to justify their claims to the state's bounty' and 'what the Mughal Emperor Jahangir called his army of prayer'.[15] Tipu's position, as far as his social origins went, was below this sort of gentry estate. But he did not go beyond such bastions of conservatism in his attitude to religion or communal matters, whether syncretist, orthodox or modernizing missionary, in Mysore, Coorg or coastal Kanara, where his arbitrary absolutism of the *cujus regis ejus religio* variety was no different from the seventeenth-century Sultans and Padshahs.

However, we can go further. In their non-elite, plebeian aspect the dervishes were implicit cultural alternatives to the Deccan landed gentry elite, whether Muslim or Hindu. As conditions at the level of polity, i.e. of stable state power, crumbled at the central level, but jutted out in regional outcrops by the 1750s, Indians in different parts of the subcontinent began to share only a sense of helplessness before the increasing 'rapine, plunder and anarchy', the labels with which Irfan Habib branded in 1963 the internal, precolonial conditions of early eighteenth-century indigenous rule in India which colonial rule compounded by overassessment and drain of wealth. The cultural aspect of this sense of general crisis and insecurity of life and property is brought out by Eaton thus:

> Referring to 'the decaying Mughal–Maratha–Rajput Civilization' of eighteenth century North India, Herman Goetz observed that 'the retirement from worldly affairs into a life of pious devotion is not less remarkable in this age. This *dervish* and the *jogini* are likewise a

favourite theme of art and literature, the simple, sober life without many wants and fears, far from the vanities, the lies and the ferociousness of the courts, became an almost sentimental desire'.[15]

Goetz recognized that the phenomenon of withdrawal from society on the part of certain individuals represented a response to certain historical conditions. It was their perception of these historical conditions that seems to have caused them to form what Victor Turner has called 'communities of withdrawal and retreat'. This involved, wrote Turner, 'total or partial withdrawal from participation in the structural relations of the world, which is, in any case, conceived of as a sort of a permanent disaster state'.[16]

As the Marathas punched holes in the Mughal provincial system in the Deccan, Gujarat, Central India, Rajasthan, and Bengal, as the Indian armies of Awadh and Hyderabad were defeated by the Persians at Karnal and the Afghans later began to conquer the Indus Basin *subas*, as the defeats of the Carnatic Nawabs at San Thome on the Adyar and at Ambur by the French showed up the utter fragility of the regional powers (with some few exception as in Kerala where Marthandaverma defeated the Dutch in Colachel in 1741) and as all the major contestants for North India slogged to a stalemate, twenty years later, by the time of the Third Battle of Panipat (1761), the 'disaster-state' premised by Turner had many new reactions. British colonialism which ultimately won out was only one.

Another was inversions in different ways into withdrawal intoxication (*mastani*). The flipside of that coin—the politics of the alternative culture—was Haidar and Tipu's rise as a new 'national-popular' alternative in Karnataka—an alternative power but not anti-structure. It is the clue to the defiance of his berserker[17] resistance to the principal contradiction for Indians, i.e. the newly-emergent British colonialist imperialism. Tipu's attempts to modernize against the grain of Indian socio-economic practice of cultural decay in the late eighteenth century, and his destruction at the hands of British repression, whose first clear manifestation in India was directed against him in an all-out way and only after that against the Marathas or the Sikhs, can be explained in this context of his aspirant absolutism. The British in the end turned to imperial absolutism themselves.[18] But that is another story.

Notes and References

[1] This paper is a brief statement of the thesis informing data presented in my longer paper entitled 'Some Observations about the Social Origins and Naming of Tipu Sultan' which was read in the actual Session meeting (Modern India Section) at Delhi in February 1992.

[2] I am grateful to Dr A.K. Pasha of the School of International Studies, Jawaharlal Nehru University, New Delhi, for new insights on this point, given in his paper presented to the National Seminar on Tipu Sultan at Bangalore University, 18–19 January 1992.

[3] Mohibbul Hasan, *History of Tipu Sultan* (Calcutta 1951, 2nd ed. 1971), pp. 1–2.

[4] Ibid., p. 6.

[5] A recent reference to Tipu by Sanjay Subrahmanayam in 'A Note on Some Early Nineteenth Century *inam* Records in the Karnataka State Archives', *IESHR*, Vol. XXVII, No. 4, Oct.–Dec. 1991, refers to 'The defeat and death of Fateh Ali Khan, better known by the sobriquet of Tipu Sultan'. The name was Fath, not Fateh, Ali. Praxy Fernandes, *The Tigers of Mysore: A Biography of Haidar Ali and Tipu Sultan* (New Delhi, 1969, revamped, 1991) repeats Mohibbul Hasan, in writing 'The additional name Fath Ali ... does not appear to have been used much.'

[6] C.A. Bayly, *Rulers, Townsmen and Bazars: North Indian Society in the Age of Expansion, 1770–1870* (Cambridge, 1983), pp. 43, 49–50. This ascription of social stability in the eighteenth century was first put forward by Noman Ahmad Siddiqui, *Land Revenue Administration under the Mughals, 1700–1750* (Aligarh, 1970) in unspoken contradiction of the dourly secularist critique of the rural and small town *ulama* class, beneficiaries of much of the *a'imma* as 'creatures ... natural apologists and propagandists' of the Mughal state, made in Irfan Habib, *The Agrarian System of Mughal India, 1556–1907* (first ed., Aligarh, 1963) ch. VIII, pp. 310–11.

[7] Fernandes, *The Tigers of Mysore*, pp. 17–18. As usual, in taking his facts from Mohibbul Hasan, they are garbled thus: 'Mohammad Ali migrated south in the service of Nawab Mohammad Shah'. Shah Muhammad is as different from Muhammad Shah as a great-grandfather from a grandfather.

[8] Richard Maxwell Eaton, *Sufis of Bijapur: Social Roles of Sufis in Medieval India* (Princeton, 1978), pp. 266, 269–270.

[9] Ibid., p. 267, quoting from D. Shea and A. Troyer, *Translation of Muhsin Fani's Dabistan*, (Paris, 1843), p. 123.

[10] Ibid., pp. 239–40, 243–44.

[11] Ibid., p. 270.

[12] Quoted in ibid., p. 272.

[13] The earliest and still the best account of this mood will be found in Ralph Russell and Khurshidul Islam, *Three Mughal Poets: Mir, Sauda, Mir Hasan* (Harvard, 1968) chapters 1 and 2, particularly pp. 64–68, for the account by Sauda of the desolation of Delhi.

[14] This aspect of *Madari* expression of extra-communal spiritual authority is

11

dealt with in Ashim Dasgupta, *Fakir and Sanyasi Uprisings* (Calcutta, 1992). A sidelight on an early nineteenth-century Mymansingh fakir called Tipu *Pagal* (The mad) will be found in Gautam Bhadra, *Unish Sataker Bangle Krishak Chaitanyar, ek Adhyay* (Calcutta, 1992).

[15] Eaton, *Sufic of Bijapur,* pp. 219, 242, and quoting from Habib, *Agrarian System,* p. 310.

[16] Ibid., pp. 279–80 quoting H. Goetz, *The Crisis of Indian Civilization in the Eighteenth and Early Nineteenth Centuries* (Calcutta, 1938) p. 18; and Victor W. Turner, *The Ritual Process: Structure and Anti-Structure* (Chicago, 1969), p. 154 fn.

[17] If the meaning of the term 'berserker' has to be explicated, I would go back to Edward Thompson, *The Making of the Indian Princes* (Oxford), p. 4: 'Haidar and Tipu brought the East Indian Company nearer to ruin than any other Indian foes had brought it and nearer than any subsequent foe was to bring it. But they were an episode only lasting less than forty years. They took no root among the country powers.'

[18] The character of Tipu's absolutism and of the British awareness that it represented the real indigenous challenge to their alien colonialism will be found in Ashok Sen, 'A Pre-British Economic Formation in India of the Late Eighteenth Century: Tipu Sultan's Mysore', in Barun De, (ed.), *Perspectives in the Social Sciences, I: Historical Dimensions* (Calcutta, 1977) and Burton Stein, *Thomas Munro, The Origin of the Colonial State* (Delhi, 1989), p. 20.

2
The Death of Haidar Ali

Irshad Husain Baqai

The death of Nawab Haidar Ali Khan was an important event in the history of South India. Nearly all contemporary authorities agree that it occurred on 7 December 1782, at Narsingh Rayanapet, near Chittoor. There is, however, some confusion regarding this date as the news of the Nawab's death was kept secret for military reasons. Tipu was at that time conducting operations against Colonel Humbeston on the Malabar coast; his presence was absolutely necessary before the sad news could be announced.

Throughout 1782 Haidar Ali was in indifferent health. He had for a long time been suffering from a cancer in his back.[1] Two years earlier, too, he was seriously ill while conducting operations on the Coromandel Coast. Haidar tried many remedies, consulted many hakims, vaids and even French physicians,[2] but without success. He had come to Chittoor to spend the Muharram.

It was Purnaiya who suggested that the news of Haidar Ali's death should be kept secret till Tipu's arrival.[3] Kishen Rao, the other minister, agreed, and therefore soon after Haidar Ali's death the body was embalmed and was secretly sent to Kolar[4] among chests carrying valuable things. Meanwhile courtiers were sent to Tipu asking him to return immediately.

In spite of these precautions, rumours broke out. Haidar Ali's serious illness had already aroused the suspicions of the people about his death. In a letter from Fort St George dated 28 January it was stated: 'On the 10th December 1782 a letter from the Commanding Officer at Tripassore, dated the 8th, mentioned that the current report of those parts was that, about five or six days ago, Hyder Ally went with his army to Chittore, there to celebrate a feast, and that he was since dead of the violent discharge of a Boil on his Back.'[5] If Haidar died on 7 December, then the Commanding Officer at Tripassore (or Tiruppathur) came to have the news almost immediately, or probably he relied upon the rumour that must have become current in consequence of Haidar's serious illness. Macartney also wrote to the Governor-General on 6 December that 'Hyder some days since had moved from Maymundulum to Chittoor, where it is said he will pass the feast. By the most authentic account he is in a very declining state of health. It is indeed pretty confidently asserted among the black people that he is actually dead, but I do not give credit to it.'[6] Three days later Macartney wrote again to the Governor-General enclosing a copy of a letter from Nawab Walajah of Carnatic giving additional strength to the rumours of Haidar Ali's death. Nawab Walajah's informant was one Faqir Muhammad, a commandant under Haidar Ali but formerly in the service of the Nawab. He gave 7 December or the first of Muharram as the date. Macartney in his letter commented that this event, if confirmed, should be used to the best advantage of the company and himself promised that 'Every effort shall be made by me to turn so important an event to the best account.'[7]

More information poured in as days passed. One Colonel Malcolm wrote to Lord Macartney on 21 December that his 'dubash'[8], who was taken prisoner by the enemy the last time the army marched to Vellore and made his escape yesterday at two in the morning from Conjeeveram and has just returned from there, says, that Hyder died fifteen days ago and that Hyder before he died had written to Tipu Sahib and one of his principal Sardars not to trust the French but to establish an alliance with the English before he quitted Carnatic.'[9] A more detailed account was sent to Major-General Stuart by one Murad Ali, described as Amaldar of Tripatore[10] and General Stuart was one who least believed the news. Forwarding this letter to Sir Eyre Coote he made no comments on the news contained therein, implying that he regarded it as a mere rumour without foundation. The Amaldar's letter was in Persian, and translated by one B. Clove it read: 'Praise be to God for his benefits. The accused Naik departed from this life on Thursday 28th Zee Hudge (4th December) at 3 p.m. and from the expectation of Tippoo's arrival, matters were kept secret for three days and on the night of 1st Muharram (6th of December) his corpse was forwarded to Colar.'[11] Murad Ali Amaldar of Tiruppattur wrote his letter on the second of Muharram 1197 and while all other authorities agree that Haidar Ali died on the first of Muharram (6–7 December) his letter suggests that 4 December 1782 was the date on which Haidar Ali died and 7 December as the date when his body was removed to Kolar. The source of information of the Commanding Officer of Tripassore and of Lord Macartney is perhaps the same as of this Amaldar of Tiruppattur, for their dates regarding Haidar Ali's death agree and imply that it occurred on 4 December 1782. It may be pointed out here that the *Tarikh* inscribed on Haidar Ali's tomb, i.e. Haidar Ali Khan Bahadur, only gives 1195 Hijri as the year of death, while 7 December 1782 corresponds to the first of Muharram 1197 A.H. and 4 December to 28th Dhil-Hajj 1196 A.H.[12]

Meanwhile Tipu's arrival was being anxiously awaited at the Court. Abu Muhammad Chaubdar had instantly sent word to Tipu informing him that the dead body was being taken to Kolar.[13] Almost all the chiefs who were taken into confidence remained faithful to Tipu excepting one Muhammad Amir. He formed a project with Shams-ud-Din Bakshi to instal Abdul Karim, Haidar's second son, on the throne. A French officer called Boudenot was also stated to have joined in this plot. This conspiracy however came very soon to the knowledge of the authorities and they dealt immediately with the conspirators.[14] Moreover, Tipu's own personal popularity with the chiefs, the officers of the army and the soldiers had made his succession to the throne a certainty. He was undoubtedly a person much superior to his younger brother Abdul Karim, whom some chiefs were reported to be supporting. One Fath Muhammad Sepoy, who had managed to reach the camp of Haidar Ali to get intelligence for the British, wrote that 'from conversation with his relations he could perceive that the army in general had the highest opinion of Tippoo's Humanity, and Abilities to command them and were highly confident that they would succeed while he remained at the head, but that their idea of Curreem Shah was very different as they imagined he had neither experience nor good sense sufficient to guide him successfully in an important situation and that as far as he could judge there does not seem to be any room for the most distant hope that Tippoo will meet with any rival of consequence'.[15] Indeed there was not the ghost of a chance for anyone else against Tipu, whose reputation as a prince was of the highest order.

The news of Haidar Ali's death was kept secret simply for military reasons. It was a great opportunity for the British to strike the

Mysorean army at a time when its leader was dead and his successor was far away. General Stuart, who alone was in a position to take such a step, was reluctant to believe the news received by him two days after Haidar Ali's death. When the Madras Government urged such action he answered his immediate superiors that he did not believe that Haidar was dead, and if he were, the army would be ready for every action in proper time.[16] When pressed further, he pleaded that the army was not in a state to embark on any undertaking against the enemy. This excuse was even more provocative, for on 17 November 1782, the Madras Council had passed a resolution that 'the army on its present establishment ought to be at all times ready to move,' and General Stuart had assured the members that 'upon any real emergency, the army might and must move and would be ready to do so.' Wilks' comments are bitter on this pledge given by Stuart, and he describes it as 'obviously lax and imprudent, under the circumstances of famine which divided the army and its equipment during the monsoon; but which either ought not to have been given, or ought to have been effectually redeemed on the real emergency of the death of Hyder'.[17]

Sir Eyre Coote, who was at this time in Bengal recouping his shattered health, also lamented bitterly that at such an opportunity the Company's army was unprepared for action. In a Minute on the military proceedings of Fort St George he wrote: 'It needs not the assistance of argument to prove, how little my recommendation of keeping the army ready for immediate service has been attended to, its not having moved, at so important and favourable a crisis for obtaining advantages, as the death of Hyder Ali Cawn, is an unfortunate testimony thereof. Even the appearance of an army in the field on that even, would have produced the most salutory and beneficial effects. The dissensions incident to such an occurrence amongst the dependents of an usurped government, and the universal discontent which had been long known to reign amongst Hyder's troops, as well from personal dislike as from an aversion to the service which had now become in its nature one of great danger and fatigue, without the least prospect of either present or future advantage, would by an immediate advance of our army towards them, have been heightened to a part which in all probability would have terminated in the dispersion and final ruin of the dispirited remains of Hyder's Force. The bad consequences arising from the loss of this glorious opportunity are self-evident.'[18] Considering the exaggerated hopes entertained by Sir Eyre Coote, his bitterness is understandable. Because, when told of the news of Haidar Ali's death he had joyfully exclaimed: 'It opens to us the fairest prospect of securing to the Mother Country the permanent and undisturbed possession of these Eastern dominions.'[19]

Before any action could be taken by the British army Tipu reached the camp of his father. He had received his first news on the afternoon of 11 December, and he left the Malabar coast on 12 December. On his way he met Arshad Beg Khan and asked him to remain on the defensive at Palagautcherry. He reached the Pennar river, where his father's army was waiting for him on 31 December and the next day he assumed control of affairs. No ostentatious ceremonies were held on this occasion as a mark of respect for the late Nawab.

At this time some chiefs, who were probably in the pay of the English, advised Tipu to enter into an alliance with the East India Company. Even before he had reached his father's camp some attendants of Haidar Ali came to him and thus counselled him: 'Collect your scattered forces at Colar and despatch a person with a letter of peace to the heads of the English army and if the Nawab Walajah desires anything as a recompense for the destruction of his kingdom, settle matters by agreement and live contented in your kingdom.' A rumour was also spread that Haidar Ali had left instructions for Tipu to seek an alliance with the English. It was stated that Tipu had found, when he was employed in performing the last rites for his father's body, a small scrap of paper in one corner of Haidar's turban which contained the following words: 'I have gained nothing by the war with the English, but am now alas! no longer alive. If you, through fear of disturbances in your kingdom, repair thither without having previously concluded peace with the English, they will certainly follow you and carry the war into your country. On this account it is better first to make peace on whatever terms you can procure, and then go to your own country.'[20] The instructions ended by asking Tipu to make contact with Srinavas Rao, Wakil of Sir Eyre Coote, with a view to negotiating with the English. But Tipu was not to be taken in by such machinations. He did not conclude peace until the English asked for it and at that time (the Treaty of Mangalore) he appeared as a conqueror.[21]

In the political field, the passing away of Haidar Ali was a very important event for India. He was looked upon as a bulwark of strength against the British. Indian princes of that time, though notoriously devoid of patriotism, could count upon him as a sure ally whenever they could combine to form an alliance against the British. In fact such an alliance was being canvassed at the courts of the Peshwa and the Nizam just before Haidar Ali's death. Nana had not yet signed the Treaty of Salbai and delayed it till 20 December, after he had received intelligence of the death of Haidar Ali.[22] Among the Indian rulers, perhaps Nawab Walajah alone found great satisfaction in the passing away of Haidar Ali.

Notes and References

[1] An entry dated 15 December 1782 in *Memoirs of the Late War in Asia* (p. 109) says: 'He [Haidar Ali] died of an ulcer in his back which had afflicted him for seven years'.

[2] Wilks, *Historical Sketches of South India*, p. 167.

[3] Ibid., p. 168.

[4] At Kolar is the mausoleum of Fath Muhammad, father of Haidar Ali, who was born at Budikota, about 10 kilometres from there, the vicinity having been held by Fath Muhammad on a service tenure. Muhammad Ali, grandfather of Haidar Ali, and other members of the family were buried in the same tomb. (Bowring, *Eastern Experiences*). It was originally intended to bury Haidar Ali there also, but Tipu decided differently and the body was removed to Seringapatam where it was interred in Lal Bagh.

[5] Love, *Vestiges of Old Madras*, Vol. III, p. 241.

[6] Secret Consultations, 31 December 1782, No. I-B, (Imperial Record Department).

[7] Ibid., 6 January 1783, No. 1.

[8] Interpreter, one knowing two languages.

[9] Secret Consultations, 10 January 1783, No. 4.

[10] Tiruppattur, subdivision and taluk in Salem district.

[11] Enclosure to General Stuart's letter to Sir Eyre Coote (Secret Consultations, 10 January 1783, No. 3).

[12] See Brown's *Ephemeris* or Dr Wustenfeld's *Vergleichungs-Tabbellen der Muhammedanischen und Christlichen Zeitrechnung.*

[13] Forrest, *Selections from Select Committee Proceedings*, Vol. III, p. 916.

[14] Wilks, *Historical Sketches.*

[15] Secret Consultations, 10 January 1783.

[16] Wilks, *Historical Sketches*, p. 174.

[17] Ibid., p. 175.

[18] Secret Consultations, 3 February 1783, No. 5.

[19] Ibid., 10 January 1783.

[20] Forrest, *Select Committee Proceedings*, Vol. III, p. 916.

[21] *Cambridge History of India*, V, p. 333.

[22] Forrest, *Selections from State Papers* (Maratha Series), Vol. I, Introduction, p. xxiii.

Episodes of
Resistance

3

Haidar Ali's Invasion of the Eastern Carnatic, 1780

Jadunath Sarkar

A French military adventurer in India, named Maistre de la Tour, calling himself 'a General in the Army of the Mogul Empire,' published a life of this great ruler, entitled *Histoire d'Ayder-Aly Cawn, ou Nouveaux Memories sur l'Inde* (Paris, 1783, 2 Vols., 12 mo.), which was afterwards translated into English. Though the author claimed to be 'an eye-witness of his conquests', yet he naïvely confesses: 'We can give no details of the operations of Haidar in the present war, having no other materials than the relations of the English; and on these we can place no dependence, because they are fabricated in India to deceive the English government....'

It may gratify the shade of this Frenchman in Hades to learn that there is still preserved in manuscript an account of this campaign from its beginning to the fall of Arcot (28 May to 4 November 1780) written by a French officer of Lalée's corps who was personally involved in it. Though composed in French, the narrative is preserved among the Portuguese records in Goa (*Livro das Moncoens*, No. I6rB, ff.469 et seqq.). From a rather defective transcript of it, I have made the following English translation. Here we see in great detail the French side of this famous campaign, of which a shorter account is also preserved in a letter from M. de Lalée to his brother (not yet published in English).*

Translation

May 28th.—Today all the tents of the army have been erected one half league from Seringapatam; the vanguard has been sent

* French original published in *La Revue de l'histoire des Colonies Françaises*, May 1934.

21

towards Bangalore; and the rearguard occupies Graille. As the Brahman astrologers have assured him that the day is auspicious, the Nawab,* who rather believes in their superstitions, has given orders for sending to the camp all the troops who are cantoned in the Island. They have crossed the river in the afternoon, except the party of M. de Lalée and that of M. Pimorin. Our politicians are forming diverse projects, but these will come to light only after some months. Nearly all of them agree in saying that the Nawab will not pass the ghats, and that if he approaches them [with] his army, it will be only for cantoning during the winter [i.e., the rainy season] and sparing the forage of his country. Mons. de Lalée alone holds that he will depart immediately, and that he is going to attack the English with superior forces.

May 29th.—The Nawab issued from the city at ten o'clock in the morning, after making sacrifices [of buffaloes] at all the gates, and he has arrived in the camp with the greatest pomp; and from today entrance into Seringapatam, following the usage, has been closed to all Europeans.

May 30th.—The party of M. de Lalée crossed the river two hours after noon; he has encamped in the vanguard of the army to the left of Muhammad Ali; it is the post that has been assigned to him during the entire campaign.

June 1st.—The artillery has been distributed to the *risalas*; there are in each [*risala*] two pieces of 4–6 calibre, and the same number of 8, two munition wagons and one cart.

The heavy artillery has been sent forth. It consists of 13 pieces of large calibre, four *colubrinces de douze* [culverins or long narrow guns], two howitzers (*obuses*) six swivel-guns (*pierriers*) and a large number of munition wagons (*caissons*) and carts.

June 3rd.—M. de Pimorin has come to the camp. He has occupied a position one muscat-shot behind M. de Lalée. The departure for Bangalore is fixed for next Friday.

June 7th.—In the morning a body of 3,000 cavalry started and the heavy artillery has been set going.

June 9th.—This morning half an hour before daybreak, the Nawab set out on his march with the greater part of the cavalry. The infantry defiled in two columns. The contingent of M. de Lalée

---

* Throughout the following text, Haidar Ali is referred to as 'the Nawab' or 'the Prince'— Editor.

marched at its head on the left. The artillery formed a third column, and the carriages (*equipages*) a fourth. The remainder of the cavalry has become the rearguard.

June 14th.—The Nawab arrived at Bangalore at noon, and has lodged in the fort. The army has encamped to the west of the place. The vanguard has been placed towards Hosur. The Prince [Haidar Ali] has made a halt of 22 days here. During this interval, the troops of the distant psovinces have joined us. From the depot have been issued some siege-guns besides, and quantities of munition. It is said (*on pretende*) that there have been *pourparlers* with the English, which have produced no effect.

July 6th.—The army has received orders to hold itself in readiness for marching. It is composed of 20,000 sepoys, 20,000 cavalry, 10,000 Bidars, 15,000 Peons, 6,000 Carnatis, 2,500 Pathans, and a number of [oxen] sufficient for conveying 40 field-guns very liberally supplied with munitions.

The corps of M. de Lalée and that of de Pimorin can number a total of 450 Europeans of whom 230 are mounted on horses. Besides these, there may be in the camp 300 Europeans of diverse nationalities, who are under the discipline of the *Kachary* (Haidar). But as they do not form any corps and as besides they are all prisoners, or to put it better, slaves, they cannot be placed among the number of the forces of the prince. He has assigned the greater portion of these people to serving his pieces [of cannon], and the rest have been distributed among the *risalas*. He formed, not long ago, a company of infantry which he has placed under the orders of a mestich (Eurasian) of Pondicherry.

Our politicians begin to be a little embarrassed. They are, however, always of the opinion that the army will not go further from Bangalore: But M. de Lalée always asserts against them, that before eight days there will be a great irruption into the Carnatic.

Today the Nawab, in order to end his halt at Bangalore, and to leave there without doubt the memory of a despotic and cruel authority, has caused a *jamadar* of cavalry to be dragged at the feet of an elephant throughout the camp. It is said in public that he (the *jamadar*) had retained something out of the pay of his troops.

July 7th.—The infantry has taken up its march in one column and the artillery on the right, and has encamped four *kos* from Hosur.

July 8th.—The infantry has taken up its encampment to the east of Hosur. Two hours afterwards, the Nawab arrived with all his cavalry. He has come from Bangalore in one march.

July 11th.—All the army has been set on the march in the usual order. They have come to encamp at the entrance to the first ghat (mountain pass).

July 12th.—The infantry has made a halt. The Prince has passed to the front with his cavalry in order to avoid the embarrassment of the crowd in a bad and narrow path.

July 13th.—The infantry has marched in column, and we have crossed the ghat in good order. The worst place is passed for about half a league, bordered on the left by a very spacious wood which clings to the mountains. There is on the right a fort on a rock which appears to be considerable; it would be very difficult to force this passage, which forms the first barrier of the country of Bader (=Baramahal).

July 17th.—The Nawab has detached 15,000 cavalry most lightly armed. This corps on issuing from the ghat will form four divisions, each one of which has a special destination given in secret.

He has placed at the head of the larger [force] Karim Sahib, his second son. It is the first command that he has conferred on the latter. The instructions which he has given him and the zeal of which the young prince is full, make one hope for the greatest success. It is said that he has been charged with the pillage of Porto Novo, which he is to enter on Thursday next during the night. He has with him 200 camels each of which carries two sepoys. This news has made a great noise in the camp. All the people are convinced that we are going to attack the English.

July 21st.—The army has passed the second ghat, and has at last entered the province of Arcot. The road in it is bad and is capable of being guarded by a few troops. We have come to encamp before Changama, which has surrendered without our having to open fire. This place, although on the frontier of Muhammad Ali Khan, is a bad mud fort built on the bank of a river, one league from the mountain chain. The approach to it cannot be very easy. We have found here four pieces of cannon; its garrison was 100 sepoys and ten horsemen. The Nawab has sent forces to invest Kolaspak and Polur.

July 23rd.—March to Kolaspak which was taken immediately on the arrival of the Nawab. This fort appears to have some bastions built of brick, each furnished with one piece of cannon. A dependency of this place is a village (=*petta*), immense in size, very rich and full of labourers and artisans. It is enclosed by a poor earthen wall only.

July 25th.—The army has entered Polur which had made a considerable fire upon the troops who invested it. [But] it surrendered in the end. This fort stands at the mouth of the gorge in a charming situation. It has 12 bastions of stone armed with some pieces of cannon. There was within it a garrison of 100 sepoys and some black horsemen. This place is a dependency of another and very much larger place named Carnatgarh. The latter is situated on a mountain almost inaccessible, one league from the former.

The Nawab has sought, by the mediation of the *qiladar* of Polur, to induce the *qiladar* of Carnatgarh (who is a relation of his) to admit his garrison into the place; but all his efforts and promises have been fruitless. In consequence, the Nawab sent two days afterwards four *risalas* for plundering and burning the country at the foot [of the fort]. The troops returned in the evening after having set fire to it. Today M. de Lalée has been detached with Muhammad Ali to go and encamp on the road to Vellore and Arcot.

July 30th.—The camp has marched upon Trinomali. The journey has been very hard. This Pagoda, around which the Europeans have joined together four bastions on which there are in all five pieces of cannon, could not make a long resistance. The place is commanded and is of easy approach. It surrendered on the 31st in the evening after firing some cannon balls on the camp. The garrison consisted of three companies of sepoys and about 80 peons. They have made a [move] outside to a place which is in the mountains. Our troops on their arrival found it evacuated. It is, however, much larger than a Dharamsala. Karim Sahib has returned with his detachment. It is said that he has taken immense booty.

August 5th.—We marched on Chitpet; the infantry has made only five *kos*, and the Nawab has arrived today before the place with his cavalry.

August 6th.—The infantry arrived before Chitpet at noon. M. de Lalée has encamped with Muhammad Ali on the road to Arcot. This place cost the French very much blood and labour; it is advantageously situated, has 12 good bastions built of stone, besides three strong *cavaliers*, one excellent *fausse braye* and a ditch, and is armed with at least 16 pieces of cannon and munitioned in a superior manner. Ah well! this place opened its gates to the conqueror the very evening of our arrival, without waiting for us to make the least movement to attack it.

It merely made during the day great fire from all parts. The city and its environs have little support from the vicinity of Arni. The Nawab immediately afterwards set up the 'tent of mercy' and all the inhabitants have returned to their homes. The garrison of Chitpet was 200 sepoys and 100 peons.

August 10th.—The army arrived before Arni. The infantry was subjected to the fire of some volleys of cannon and defiled in order to take up its camp. The fort continued the firing on the 11th and all the daytime of the 12th. M. de Lalée has encamped on the road to Arcot with the division of Asdar Ali Beg.

August 12th.—This night the Nawab caused two batteries to be made behind the bases of a village which is almost contiguous to the fort. The pieces had not yet been placed when they offered to capitulate. This place is situated on the bank of a small river, surrounded by blocks of houses and very large. It has many bastions all built of lime and brick. There are at the gate European works which have a very beautiful appearance. The ditch looks large and well kept. Our old soldiers say that such a place ought to have held out at least eight days, although it had the defect of all the other forts in the country. It has an easy approach because of the small villages that they have built around it.

It is said that the Nawab has found in Arni a large amount of treasure. Muhammad Ali made it one of his principal depots, and it is asserted that all the objects which he took out of Tanjore are still in the magazines here. Many jewellers and a number of rich people retired to this place since the invasion of Haidar Ali. Its garrison consisted of 200 sepoys, 100 black cavalry and many peons.

August 15th.—Today we have received the first news of the movements which the English have made for assembling an army. They have sent out a battalion of sepoys from Trichinapalli, which has crossed the wood and joined the detachment of Pundicheri. They may amount to a corps of 200 Europeans, 3,000 sepoys and 8 pieces of cannon. On the 12th instant they took the route of Permacoil, and on the 17th they encamped on a high hill, where they found a body of 800 Europeans, 400 sepoys and 10 pieces of cannon. M. Munro will be the commander of the army.

Here the policy is confusing. The English, who have

astonished all the princes of Asia by their vigilance, their activity, and above all by the promptitude with which they have begun their military operations, have not yet presented one man to oppose the progress of an enemy who has come from a hundred leagues' distance to attack them. Those who led two years ago 40,000 combatants before Pondicherry,—who during all the time of their last war with [Haidar Ali] Bahadur placed on foot two large armies,—who in one word maintain on this side 30 battalions of sepoys,—undoubtedly greatly dazzled by the reputation they have made, have either given to their *fonds* (?forces) some secret destinations, or disposed of their troops for certain operations which I do not know. In the brilliant situation in which they find themselves they have thought that there is not in Asia any Power in a condition to attack them. The mistake that they made in not assembling their army during their first contests with Haidar Ali, is proved. This mistake is irreparable. In a country in revolution like this, and above all since there are powerful and ambitious neighbours, they ought to have a corps always ready to march at the first need and sufficiently large for covering the frontiers. The different posts which the Nawab has occupied by means of his cavalry, have now taken away from the English all the means of assembling a large force. It has brought an end to their prosperity. The events that follow will make known whether our enemies themselves have arrived at that end.

The continual rains, which have lasted for eight days, have greatly retarded the operations of the Nawab. He has, however, sent out two detachments to invest Chambargarh and Dobigarh; they have yielded after five or six days of resistance. These two posts, as well as some others that he has occupied, entirely assure to him communication with his own country.

August 20th.—The camp has marched to Arcot. Timery, which is two leagues distant from it, capitulated to the Nawab when he was passing by. It had fired only some discharges of cannon on the pillagers. All the army has encamped in the region south of Arcot.

The 21st, 22nd, 23rd and 24th passed without our doing anything except making grand preparations for the siege. M. de Lalée has been charged with reconnoitring the place, sometimes with the Bakhshis, sometimes with the Prince himself.

The Nawab has changed his camp; its situation was bad. He has gone to encamp on the road to Madras, at the same distance from the place.

In the afternoon, he set a trap for the posts which guard the approaches to the city. He concealed in a ravine 300 peons, and caused 200 Carnatics to pass at a small distance from them, loaded with fascines and escorted by some sepoys only. When the men in the fort perceived them, they sent out a company of sepoys to chase them. The Nawab, who was advantageously placed for observing the movements on the part of the other side, judging that these unfortunate ones were very near, caused a rocket to be fired: at once the peons sallied forth from their trenches and fell upon the sepoys, sword in hand. They cut off the heads of 13 of them, wounded many others, and put the rest to flight. During this affair the fort fired many cannon balls, which had no effect. The Prince has lost only 3 men. He has given Rs 5 to each of his soldiers who brought a head to him.

August 28th.—M. de Lalée departs with the Bakhshis and some other chiefs to observe the English army which left Punamali five or six days ago. It is to go to Conjevaram and there wait for a detachment which is coming from the northern districts under Colonel Baillie. It is announced outside that the corps is considerable, but M. de Lalée, who has observed it from very near during a march of nearly two leagues, asserts that it contains above 1,200 Europeans, 7,000 sepoys, 30 white cavalry, 150 black cavalry and 15 or 18 pieces of cannon. This army is obliged to carry with itself not only victuals but also forage and [cooking] fuel which are necessary for it. The Bidars who harass them as soon as they go out, crowd them together to such a degree that this morning out of five Europeans who had the misfortune to fall out of the ranks, three have been taken prisoner and two others have been sabred 30 paces from the column.

The Nawab has sent off to Arni his large artillery and all the munitions which he had caused to be brought for the siege.

August 30th.—All the army has departed and gone to Mousseripa.[1] They have left there absolutely all the baggage, even the tents were kept standing when the Nawab passed the river with all his cavalry. M. de Lalée followed him with his company of whites, and left the command of his infantry to M. Renard, the major of his party. Two hours later the infantry crossed the river with the field artillery. It was placed in battle order on the other bank, and there made a halt of nearly two hours. The spies having reported that the English who had set out on the march in the morning, instead of taking the road to Arcot, had gone to encamp under Conjevaram, the Nawab ordered his army to skirt the place in going up; it has reached one *kos* from Kaveripak. As it was late, it halted under the trees, barring all the roads to Arcot and there passed the night. There has been a very bad [misfortune in the form of] heavy rain which lasted more than 18 hours and greatly inconvenienced the troops.

August 31st.—The Nawab has raised across the plain six batteries of five and seven pieces of cannon each, at a distance of two musket-shots from one another, and he has placed all his infantry behind the batteries. He has placed under the orders of M. de Lalée one division of five *risalas*, who may amount to a total of 3,000 men. These troops will be exercised in the French manner and commanded by the officers of the [French] contingent at three hours after noon. They are coming to take up their place with us, behind the battery on the left.

September 2nd.—M. de Lalée departed with the Nawab to reconnoitre the English camp; its position, however advantageous to them, appeared to be a little commanded by the embankment of a tank which is on the left. The vanguard is towards Arcot, and the rear-guard adjoins the Pagoda of Greater Conjevaram.

September 3rd.—The army has marched. The infantry defiled in four columns, each carrying its artillery at its head. All the cavalry has gone in advance. We have encamped one *kos* and a half from Conjevaram. We found the batteries immediately and worked there without relaxation.

September 5th.—The Nawab detached his eldest son Tipu Sultan Sahib with the division of Asdar Ali Beg, and 5,000 horsemen in order to go and encounter Colonel Baillie, according to the report of the spies. It will tomorrow go and encamp 5 *kos* from Conjevaram.

September 6th.—We have broken camp and have come to the presence of the enemy. The infantry marched in three columns, the artillery on the right, and the munitions on the left. All the cavalry passed in front. The intention of the Prince is not to attack, but to observe the movements of General Munro, and to prevent him from joining Colonel Baillie. The English, informed of the march of the Nawab, have broken camp and have entered Conjevaram. Our infantry has been ordered to defile behind the cavalry and to go and place itself on a height which is a good cannon-shot from Conjevaram in the western side. This manoeuvre has made us come close to the path that must be followed by Messrs. Munro and Baillie if they wish to join forces.

29

Three hours after noon the bivouac guards informed us that the English had marched out and taken the road to Chinglepat. Immediately the cavalry galloped ahead in order to cut their road; and the infantry marched behind. When we perceived the enemy, they were in battle order within Great and Little Conjevaram, with their backs to a small fort; the bank of a large tank covered their left, and they had on their right impassable marshes. They fired some volleys of artillery on the cavalry, which pressed their rearguard a little.

The two armies passed the rest of the day in observing each other. The Nawab has only made some discharges of rockets (*fouguettes*), which have not produced the least effect. At the fall of night, the infantry received orders to return and take up their position of the morning, and the cavalry remained in bivouac. Our general [de Lalée] has greatly approved the manner in which the Prince manoeuvred all the day, his chief concern has been always to cover the march of his infantry by his cavalry.

September 7th.—Today we have received details of the affair which took place between Tipu Sahib and Colonel Baillie. The success has not totally corresponded to the hopes which we had formed concerning the talents and bravery of this young warrior. The English did not march that day at all, and they had the good fortune to discover, the day before, a compensation for their situation which was most advantageous. Two tanks and some large marshes covered them at nearly all points. These difficulties did not at all restrain the ardour of Tipu. He made his army advance; his infantry showed itself in two columns in such good order that the English themselves were deceived; they believed for an instant that it was General Munro who was coming to them. But some rockets which were fired by the cavalry on the wings made the English quickly discover their error. They at once replied by a general discharge of all their cannon. Their artillery was better served and made our infantry bend. Next Tipu put himself at the head of the cavalry and fell upon the enemy who formed a square. A crooked stream which it was not possible for him to get over, prevented him from arriving and seizing the left side and forming in battle order on the road to Arcot. Fortune did not serve his desire. A short distance from the enemy was found a terrain suitable for covering the infantry and placing the artillery advantageously. The pieces were mounted in batteries all the night, and they fired on the English square with all possible success. M. de Lalée marched ahead with his two pieces; all his business was to observe even the least movements of the enemy. It being perceived that they had placed their munitions behind a small ravine which was before him, he ordered his artillerymen to aim at it. They had the good fortune to explode a munition cart at the second discharge, another not much later, and then a third. These accidents totally disconcerted the enemy; they made afterwards only a feeble fire; the black troops felt themselves defeated and took to flight. M. de Lalée, whom none of their movements escaped, sent orders to his white cavalry to make a charge. His example emboldened the cavalry of the Nawab, which was on the wings and which was waiting for a signal. The heat was so violent and the crowd so great that [at the onset of] the squadron of M. de Lalée the enemy could neither advance nor retreat. The Europeans, who were nearly the only people that faced us, were all killed, wounded or made prisoners. There is not in India an example of a similar defeat.

However, the corps, after the junction of the detachment of General Munro, numbered at least 700 Europeans, 500 sepoys, with 10 pieces of cannon 6 lbs. and 15 munition wagons. It had marched since eight o'clock at night, and after we had joined it, it was not able to make two *kos*. This affair took place between Catolur[2] and Perambak, three leagues from Conjevaram in the north-western [really N.E.] direction. It lasted from ten o'clock a.m. up to noon.

Two hours after noon we set out on our march and encamped three leagues from Conjevaram in the south-western direction.

If the Nawab, instead of making this manoeuvre, had followed the advice of M. de Lalée, who counselled him to return to the camp from which we had departed in the morning, all would have been said for that campaign about the power of the English, and M. Munro would have been obliged to throw down his arms, and submit himself a prisoner of war with all his army. But the Prince, who knew more than anybody else what he could do with his army, and who is besides accustomed to pushing his prudence to excess, preferred to remove to a little distance in order to avert all surprise on the part of M. Munro. He was content to detach his eldest son with a new corps of cavalry for obstructing the march of his enemy. This failure, which betrays great timidity, ought to be a very valuable test for all the European chiefs. It proves to them that they have always an assured resource against the greatest powers of India. I mean to say, vigour and activity.

After M. Munro was informed of the defeat of Colonel Baillie, and learnt that the Nawab was not far from him, he instantly took the only course which was convenient to him, namely to retreat, whatever it might cost him. Without losing any time, he took the road to Madras, as lightly as was possible for him. This march cost him much hardship and fatigue. Now harassed by the cavalry, and now attacked by the infantry in ambush, he was obliged to make many halts and to clear a passage by force of gun-fire. Happily for him, he gained at the end of the day, the bank of a river; he skirted it up to Chinglepat, where he arrived during the night, and next day he arrived at Madras with 700 Europeans, 3,000 sepoys and his field artillery, his munitions, provisions and his military wagon. He had abandoned at Conjevaram four pieces of 18, one of 3 and 3 mortars and many carts.

September 11th.—We marched and came to encamp at $1^1/_2$ *kos* from Conjevaram, in a place where the second batteries had been constructed. The Nawab sent to Bangalore the Europeans whom he had made prisoner. They were of the number of 55 officers and 430 musketeers. He kept with himself Colonel Baillie and four other officers.

September 15th.—The army arrived at Conjevaram, the presence of the Nawab there being necessary for settling certain matters. He placed his tent[3] in that once famous Pagoda, of which the fortifications however were now destroyed.

September 18th.—The camp made [one] *kos* of the return to Arcot. The infantry marched in only one column, the artillery on the right.

September 20th.—Tipu Sahib was detached with the division of M. de Lalée to attack the place in the western direction. We crossed the river at noon, and encamped between Vellore and Arcot, at about ¾ of a league from the city.

September 25th.—This night trenches were opened in a large mosque (i.e. Pagoda) which is close to the bank of the river.

September 27th.—Today the Swiss contingent mounted the trenches at seven o'clock in the morning. They will be on duty for 48 hours; and up to the end of the siege, out of four nights they will pass two in the trenches and two in the camp.

September 29th.—M. de Lalée came to the darbar to claim the protection of the Nawab in favour of the inhabitants of Pondicherry who were found to have come by one of his Brahmans who collected the customs duties at the gates of the limits [of the camp]. The Prince gave our General the most gracious welcome, and granted all that he asked for from him, and in order to signify his satisfaction with the manner in which he had conducted the affair of 10th September last, he granted him a large increase of pay.

October 10th.—This night we have constructed a breaching battery of seven pieces of cannon. It is 150 fathoms from the place and at an almost equal distance from the Vellore Gate and from the River Bastion. We have opened a *boyau* (narrow covered passage) with communications with the works on the river.

October 13th.—The enemy made a sortie upon the works on the river bank. They have been repulsed with loss, the fire lasted twenty minutes.

October 19th.—We have commenced to batter the breach with five pieces of 18 and two of 24. One bastion of five large pieces which faces [us] and of which we have not taken care to silence the fire, has dismounted five of our pieces. We have had a large number of soldiers slain and wounded.

October 20th.—Tipu Sahib has called up M. de Lalée. He has charged him to remain in the battery and direct its fire at his will, with the two pieces that remain. He has succeeded in silencing the fire of the large bastion as well as that of a small one and also of a piece which stood on the curtain. We have sent to the battery during the night two pieces of 18.

October 27th.—We have battered the breach all the day with the greatest success.

October 28th.—This morning someone issued [from the fort] to parley with our works before the breach and on the bank of the river. Under the fosses we have already thrown a quantity of wood and fascines. However, the breach is not yet practicable. It is said that the breach on the east of the Nawab, who has attacked the place on the eastern side, is very large. There are in his battery six pieces which have fired day and night since the 19th instant.

At five hours and three-quarters of the morning, the Nawab delivered an assault on the city of Arcot. It was taken after a lively resistance at the western breach. The contingent of M. de Lalée suffered much by reason of their not having been properly supported by the troops of the Prince. Undoubtedly his orders have not been executed with all the precision which such an attempt demanded. One portion of the enemy troops had the time to enter the fort, the rest were put an end to, and either killed or made prisoner.

The same day, M. de Penierasse,[4] Captain Commandant, asked for a suspension of arms and offered to capitulate. But the Nawab who knows no other laws than those of the most absolute despotism, has given him no other answer than this: 'I wish that all the world should come to me without reservation and without conditions.'

November 3rd.—M. de Montgomery, 3rd captain, has come out to arrange terms with the Nawab. His insinuating manner, and it may be some political reasons, have at last determined the Prince to agree that only the English troops should issue up to the glacis of the fort with the honours of war, that they should there pile up their arms, and that immediately afterwards, they should take the road to Madras with their effects, all this subject to the express condition that they will not bear arms against him during all [the rest of] this war.

November 4th.—The English troops which were in the fort of Arcot issued at eleven o'clock in the morning in the manner to which they had agreed. There were six officers, 153 musketeers and 300 sepoys. The remainder of the garrison of a place so large as Arcot were the sepoys of Muhammad Ali Khan. No agreement has been made with regard to them.

Notes and References

[1] This word is a copyist's error for Muservakam, a town on the north bank of the Palar river, seven miles west of Great Conjevaram (J.S.).

[2] A mistake for Polilur.

[3] *Il met son tinate dans cette pagode* ... in my MS..., which makes no sense. If we read *tente* for *tinate* we get the above meaning, though the expression is unidiomatic. Can this puzzling word be the Muslim administrative term *tainati*, meaning 'a minor officer deputed to collect revenue'?

  [Professor E.E. Speight says Littré gives an old word '*tinage*', which he defines as 'a man, two oxen and a wagon,' Ed. I.C.]

[4] An error for 'Prendergast'. 'The place was surrendered on the 3rd November. The capitulation was signed by Captain Dupont; Captain (Thomas) Prendergast, the Commandant, having been severely wounded. The garrison, composed of 157 men of the 1st battalion, 1st regiment, about 1½ company of the 5th battalion of sepoys under Lieut. Leighton, and a party of the Nawab's sepoys, suffered to depart in conformity with the terms' (Wilson, *History of the Madras Army*, ii,12).

4

The French in the Second Anglo–Mysore War

Mohibbul Hasan

he bitter disappointments which Haidar experienced at the hands of the English between 1769 and 1776 turned him hostile towards them and compelled him to seek the friend-ship of the French.[1] Immediately after dismissing Muhammad Ali's ambassadors in 1775, Haidar entered into communication with the French at Pondicherry who received his proposals for an alliance with open arms, and readily promised him support against the English.[2] But when Haidar attacked the Carnatic in July 1780 they failed to render him any assistance beyond furnishing him with military stores. The reason was that, although they had themselves been at war with the English since 1778, they had not yet received any reinforcements from France.[3]

It was exactly four years after the rupture of peace between England and France, and over a year and a half after the outbreak of the Anglo–Mysore War, that a small land army consisting of about 2500 men under the command of Duchemin appeared on Indian soil. It was brought by Bailli de Suffren and reached Porto Novo on 25 February 1782.[4] Its object was to reconquer the French possessions in the country, and to assist Haidar who was to act as the mainspring of a coalition of Indian rulers for the expulsion of the British from India.

When Haidar heard of the arrival of this army he felt overjoyed,[5] because with its help he hoped to crush the English. But very soon he became disillusioned, for Duchemin refused to act

* I am obliged to Calcutta University for giving me financial assistance to visit Pondicherry and consult unpublished documents related to this period.

35

according to his advice and displayed a general lack of initiative and enterprise. Haidar proposed to him, and he was seconded in this by de Suffren, to attack immediately Nagapatam which, not being properly defended, was easy to capture, and which was the key to the rich province of Tanjore from where the French could obtain supplies for their troops.[6] But Duchemin not only did not follow this proposal, he even refused to disembark unless and until Haidar agreed to enter into a treaty with him: and he sent Piveron de Morlat and two officers, de Moissac and de Canaple, to the Nawab with his proposals. But Haidar evaded the proposal for a treaty, although he assured the French agents that all the needs of the French troops would be looked after, and immediately ordered his treasure, to send to Porto Novo one lac of rupees.[7]

Partially satisfied with this reply, Duchemin ordered the disembarkation of his troops,[8] and by the end of March, reinforced by the Mysorean army under Tipu, left Porto Novo. Owing to the instructions of Haidar he was well supplied with the means of transport and provisions. In fact, with the exception of bread there was nothing lacking.[9] Still, instead of proceeding towards Nagapatam, as desired by Haidar, Duchemin marched towards Cuddalore, and invested it on 2 April 1782.[10] As the place was poorly defended, it capitulated the next morning without offering any resistance. But in spite of this success, for nearly a month Duchemin remained inactive. He justified his inactivity on the grounds that he lacked funds and was short of troops whose number was daily being thinned due to sickness and disease.[11] He refused to undertake any campaign until the arrival of Bussy for fear it might compromise the honour of France.[12]

But Duchemin did not relax his efforts to conclude a treaty with Haidar, and on the return of Piveron de Morlat sent de Chenneville accompanied by de Canaple to reopen the talks. Haidar felt disgusted with Duchemin 'who occupied himself with negotiations, when it was necessary to fight and take advantage of the consternation in the English army and among the inhabitants of Madras'.[13] Nevertheless, he received the French agents kindly and deputed his three Brahman officers to negotiate with them. Haidar was willing to accede to the territorial demands of the French, but, as he was not prepared to give them more than a lac of rupees per month, the conference adjourned and de Chenneville took his leave.[14] It was again resumed at Cuddalore where Haidar sent his agent Banaji Pundit with his proposals. Haidar demanded that, even if hostilities between England and France were to cease in Europe, the French in India would continue to help him until he had made peace with his enemies. Duchemin agreed to this, but the negotiations, which lasted for fifteen days, broke down on the question of the soldiers' pay. Haidar refused to give to the French more than a lac of rupees per month, as neither his own resources not their achievements justified it.[15]

Although the attempt to enter into a treaty with Haidar failed, Duchemin remained his ally, since there was no other alternative before him. He could not expect any help either from the Marathas or the Nizam, for both of them had made their peace with the English; Haidar was the only Indian ruler who was still continuing the war. Duchemin was, therefore, compelled not to break with him, for without his support the little French army would be easily destroyed by their enemies.

After various evasions and dilatory tactics, at last on 1 May 1782, Duchemin, accompanied by Tipu, left Cuddalore, and advanced to join Haidar who was preparing to besiege Perumukkal, a hill fort situated about 20 miles north-west of Pondicherry. The combined armies of the French and Haidar appeared before the place on 11 May. As soon as Coote heard of this he marched to its relief; but, owing to a violent storm accompanied by heavy rain, his progress was arrested. The result was that when he reached Karanguli he heard that Perumukkal had capitulated on 16 May.[16] From Perumukkal the allied armies marched towards Wandiwash. Coote, anxious to save the place, marched to its relief. Haidar asked Duchemin to give the English battle, but he refused on the grounds that he had been ordered by Bussy and de Souillac not to risk any general action till the arrival of sufficient reinforcements from France, for a defeat would compromise the French prestige.[17] This refusal to fight was a great blunder committed by Duchemin because the combined armies of the French and Haidar, being numerically far superior to the English forces, could have easily defeated Coote.[18] Haidar was, therefore, very annoyed with the French commander and threatened to make a separate peace with the English. He even refused to supply them with any money or provisions.[19] He had nothing but contempt for the French troops who were devoid of discipline, and whose officers spent their time in mutual bickering and jealousies, and in a shameful scramble for power and prestige.[20]

Duchemin died on 12 August 1782, and was provisionally

succeeded by Court d'Hofflize. But this did not improve Haidar's relations with the French; for the new commander, being 'a prisoner of
the situation created by his predecessor, hardly appeared to be better
qualified to take up the initiative.'[21] In fact Haidar felt so disgusted
that he would have made a complete break with them had it not been
for de Launay and de Suffren who continued to humour him and
assure him that a large army under Bussy would soon be arriving from
France.[22] The memory of the exploits of Bussy was still fresh in the
minds of the Indian princes, and so Haidar retained his friendship with
the French, hoping that, on the arrival of Bussy, he would be able to
defeat the English. But Haidar Ali died in December 1782, and Bussy
reached India three months later.

d'Hofflize, who had hitherto remained inactive, woke up on
hearing the news of Haidar's death. He at once decided to march on
Chittoor, where Haidar had died, in order to ensure the succession of
Tipu who was regarded by the French as the most worthy successor of
Haidar and capable of waging a vigorous war against the English.
However, on being assured that there was no cause for anxiety or
alarm, he stayed back at Cuddalore keeping a close watch on events at
Chittoor.[23]

On hearing of the arrival of Tipu in the Carnatic, d'Hofflize
moved out of Cuddalore and joined him at Chuckmaloor in South
Arcot on 2 January 1783. Together they marched against Stuart, and
encamped in the vicinity of Wandiwash. On 13 February 1783, the
armies of Tipu and the English prepared for battle at Neddingul, sepa-
rated only by a tributary of the river Palar. Throughout the day there
was only an exchange of desultory firing between the hostile armies.
But early next morning the English retreated to Wandiwash, closely
pursued by the Mysoreans who wounded and killed nearly 200 of the
enemy.[24] Stuart had decided upon this course probably at the sight of
'the order and discipline of the Sultan's army and the imposing appearance of the French battalions'.[25] Tipu was, however, unable to follow
up his victory, as he was obliged to quit the Carnatic and proceed to
the defence of his Malabar possessions which had been invaded by the
English forces under General Mathews. Tipu wanted d'Hofflize to
accompany him to the Malabar coast, but the latter refused on the
grounds that he was expecting the arrival of Bussy and so could not
leave the Carnatic. However, he allowed Tipu to take with him 600
French troops under the command of de Cossigny.

Bussy left Cadiz on 4 January 1782, and arrived at the Isle of France on 31 May. Here he was detained for a long time because he fell ill and a large number of his troops were affected by scurvy. However, as de Suffren was constantly urging him to hasten to India, he embarked on 18 December with about 2200 men, although both he and the majority of his troops were still convalescent.[26] Bussy wanted to disembark between Karikal and Nagapatam in order to conquer the latter place, for it was a better military base than Cuddalore. But as the English, having suspected the attack, had strengthened Nagapatam,[27] Bussy proceeded to Porto Novo where he disembarked on the night of March 16 and 17.

When Duchemin had been sent to India it was understood that this was a temporary arrangement, and that very shortly he would be replaced by Bussy, who, because of his past exploits in the Deccan and his experience of the country, was regarded as the best person to form a confederacy of the Indian princes in order to crush the power of the English in India.[28] In reality, however, the appointment of Bussy was a mistake, for he was no longer the Bussy of twenty years earlier. He was now an old man of 62 whose vigour of mind and body had been impaired, and who had lost his powers of self-confidence, initiative and enterprise.

From the time Bussy landed in India he estranged Tipu by his tactlessness and by pursuing a policy of unenlightened national interest. He unjustly blamed Tipu for the lack of sufficient supplies for his troops, and wrongly complained of the Sultan's departure from the Carnatic before his arrival in India[29] and of the failure of Sayyid Saheb to wait on him when he disembarked at Porto Novo. It was the failure to have everything his own way that led Bussy to indulge in bitter invectives against Tipu. Even Haidar was not spared for he had refused to be dominated by Duchemin. Bussy, therefore, denounced both father and son as 'brigands and tyrants' on whose words no reliance could be placed, and maintained that the French should not have entered into any alliance with either Haidar Ali or his son Tipu Sultan. They should have established friendly relations with the Marathas and particularly with the Nizam.[30]

However, as the attempt to negotiate a treaty with them had failed, and as there was no prospect of its success in the near future, Bussy maintained friendly relations with Tipu, realizing that, if the Sultan left them or made peace with the English, the position of the

French would become very embarrassing. But he hoped that, with the arrival of fresh troops from France under de Soullanges, he would be able to act effectively, declare his true intentions and 'give the law'.[31]

These vituperations of Bussy against Haidar and Tipu were quite unjustified. In reality it was the French who had not fulfilled their part of the promise. In spite of their repeated declarations they had failed to render any effective help to the Mysoreans: Bussy had come nearly three years after the outbreak of the Second Anglo–Mysore War and with a smaller army than had been originally announced. Haidar had waited for him in vain, and Tipu had delayed his departure for the Malabar coast. The Sultan could not have stayed any longer in the Carnatic because his Malabar possessions were very seriously threatened by the English. However, he left behind a large army under the command of Mir Muin-ud-din, commonly known as Sayyid Saheb, who was required to cooperate with the French and render every assistance to Bussy on his arrival in India.[32] Accordingly, when Bussy landed at Porto Novo he was given whatever assistance, in provisions and means of transport, Sayyid Saheb was capable of rendering.[33] The latter himself could not be present to help in the disembarkation of the French troops as he had to proceed to the relief of the garrison of Karur whose commander had thrice demanded help from him. The place had been attacked by Colonel Lang who, after destroying its fortifications, was preparing to breach the fort.[34]

From Porto Novo Bussy at once marched to Cuddalore. The total army under his command, including the troops under d'Hofflize, consisted of 3500 Europeans, 300–400 Africans (Caffres) and 4000 sepoys.[35] Besides, he had also at his disposal the Mysorean forces left by Tipu in the Carnatic. In spite of this, Bussy remained inactive. Instead of undertaking a campaign, he spent his time in ease and comfort in the company of his admirers and courtiers.[36] Even when he heard of the successes of Tipu on the Malabar coast he did not move. His experienced officers advised him to take the offensive and occupy Perumukkal which, because of its great military importance, General Stuart was proceeding to occupy.[37] But Bussy refused to leave Cuddalore on the ground that he had no cavalry. He even prohibited d'Houdetot, who had been left by d'Hofflize to observe the movements of the English army, from attempting to prevent its advance.[38] As a result, despite his dilatory movements Stuart occupied Perumukkal on 9 May 1783, and, after fortifying it, advanced towards Cuddalore.

40

On realizing that Cuddalore was in danger, Bussy wrote to Sayyid Saheb to hasten to his aid. Sayyid Saheb, in compliance with this request, immediately came, and placed all his forces, amounting to about 10,000, at the disposal of Bussy.[39] But the latter, instead of undertaking an offensive, busied himself only in strengthening the defences of Cuddalore, and again refused permission to d'Houdetot who, reinforced by some Mysorean cavalry, was anxious to march against the English. d'Houdetot was only required to watch the movements of the English army.[40] Owing to these defensive tactics followed by Bussy, Stuart was able to march from Perumukkal unopposed and reach the river Pennar on 4 June.[41] But as the French forces were strongly entrenched on the opposite bank near Cuddalore and as the crossing appeared difficult, Stuart marched to the west along the river. Bussy also made the same movement, but stopped as he did not want to be too distant from Cuddalore. Stuart, on the other hand, moved further west and the next morning succeeded in crossing the river without meeting any opposition. After this he made a successful movement towards the south of Cuddalore and reached the sea on 7 June. The English army encamped two miles to the south of the fort, and employed itself from 7–13 June in making preparation for the siege of Cuddalore with the help of the naval forces under Sir Edward Hughes.[42]

On 13 June, the operations commenced. Early in the morning Colonel Kelly attacked a post situated on a height and commanded by the Mysoreans. The latter, taken by surprise, fled without offering any resistance, and so it was occupied. The second post to the right of this was next attacked, and although Colonel Blynth, who commanded it, put up a stiff resistance, it was also captured. After this, at 8.30 in the morning a general attack on the main French position was made. But, due to the courage and skill of d'Hofflize, it was repulsed with great loss. Two more attacks were led and they also met with the same fate.[43] Emboldened by these successes, the French emerged from the trenches and pursued the English to a considerable distance, inflicting upon them great losses. But they were obliged to withdraw in consternation as one of their positions was dexterously occupied by an English detachment.[44] However, Cuddalore had been saved. The bullocks and other military supplies provided by Sayyid Saheb had proved very helpful in its defence,[45] while the Mysorean light troops had performed useful service outside the town.[46] The French also had fought with great valour, and Bussy, elated with victory, embraced d'Hofflize and Boissieux, and with tears in his eyes cried out: 'My friends it is to you, it is to your brave regiment that I owe the success of this day.'[47] The total English casualties during the day amounted to 1116, while the French lost only 450 men.[48] The number of troops on the French side was a little larger than on the English side.[49]

The French officers advised Bussy to take advantage of the English defeat and attack the enemy during the night, when it was tired, demoralized and short of ammunitions. But in the words of Mill, because 'the spirit of Bussy was chilled with age and infirmities' he 'restrained the impetuosity of his officers who confidently predicted the destruction of the British army'.[50] He even decided to withdraw the same night all his troops from positions outside Cuddalore, and to shut himself up in the town. This caused great consternation in the army. 'The officers were furious and the soldiers swore vehemently. They said that the army had won the battle in spite of the General, but that today he has lost it in spite of the soldiers.'[51] Taking advantage of Bussy's mistakes, the English recovered from their defeat and once again became ready to lay siege to Cuddalore. Bussy, thereupon, immediately wrote to de Suffren for help. The latter at once sailed for Cuddalore where he arrived on 15 June, just when Hughes was going to attack it. By outmanoeuvering the English admiral, de Suffren succeeded in covering Cuddalore and occupying the position held by Hughes. And after he had completed his preparations by embarking 600 European and 600 Indian soldiers furnished by Bussy, he attacked the English squadron on 20 June. The fight lasted the whole day. The British admiral wanted to come to close quarters; the French admiral kept up a distant cannonade which cost the enemy in the course of three hours 532 men. As the English vessels had suffered severely, Hughes sailed away the following morning to Madras in order to refit, leaving Stuart at the mercy of the French.[52] de Suffren was quick to take advantage of the situation. He re-landed the 1200 troops which had been supplied to him, together with 1100 men from the fleet, and planned with Bussy an attack upon the English.[53]

On 25 June, at three in the morning, the Chevalier de Dumas, with 800 Europeans and 500 sepoys led a sortie, but as it was badly conducted he was defeated with great losses and taken prisoner.[54] Stuart, however, failed to take advantage of the French setback because of the deplorable state of his own army which was wasting away due to sickness and casualties and suffering from a great scarcity of provisions, while there was no prospect of aid either from the fleet or from Madras. If the French had made a resolute counter-attack at this time, the English army would certainly have been destroyed. But, as usual, Bussy showed a great lack of boldness and enterprise. Owing to the failure of the sortie he thought that the English were still too strong to be attacked from the front. He, therefore, decided to wait until, after exhausting their strength, they should raise their camp for retreat.[55] But this opportunity never came because within a few days he was obliged to cease hostilities. On 23 June 1783, news reached Madras that Preliminaries of Peace had been signed at Versailles on 9 February 1783, between England and France. This news was immediately communicated to Bussy. Under different conditions, to quote the words of the French General, the Madras government 'would not have hesitated to conceal from us the news which they had received',[56] but now, in order to save the English army before Cuddalore from destruction, it at once sent two Commissioners, named Staunton and Saddlier, with letters to Bussy and de Suffren informing them that since peace had been made between the French and the English in Europe, hostilities should cease between the two nations in India also. The Commissioners reached Cuddalore on 30 June in a frigate bearing a flag of truce, and after a delay of three days, during which the terms of the armistice were adjusted, hostilities ceased on 2 July 1783.

To the Indian powers who had been fed for a long time on promises, and hopes that a large army under Bussy would soon be arriving to wage war against the English, the news of the peace came as a great surprise; for hardly had they been informed of Bussy's arrival than they heard of the cessation of hostilities. In the words of Bussy, 'Little of the advantage which this peace will procure for us, it will be difficult to preserve the reputation and glory of the nation.'[57]

Immediately after the armistice, Bussy sent orders to the French troops, who were engaged with Tipu in prosecuting the siege of Mangalore, to cease fighting.[58] Accordingly, Cossigny refused to fight. Even Lally and Boudenot, who were in the employment of the Sultan, withdrew. This made Tipu very indignant with the French, and he characterized their conduct as treacherous for having backed out just when Mangalore was about to fall, and for having made their peace with the English without informing him and without caring for his interests.[59] He tried to compel them to fight, but they refused, and apprehending an attack from the Sultan, prepared to defend themselves. de Cossigny left the camp after a few days and remained for some time at the Jesuit monastery of Mount Marian.[60] From there he proceeded to the English possession of Tellichery on the Malabar coast, without even waiting for the instructions of Bussy.[61] Lally and Boudenot, however, remained at Mangalore, although they held themselves aloof from military operations.

On the same day that Bussy sent orders to the French troops at Mangalore to stop fighting, he also wrote to Tipu to make peace with the English, promising him, in this connection, every help that was within his power. Two or three days later, he sent a Brahman, named Kishen Rao, to the Sultan to explain to him the aims of the French policy.[62] He also asked Piveron de Morlat, the French agent with Tipu, and other officers at Mangalore, to persuade the Sultan to cease hostilities.

Bussy was anxious to bring about peace between Tipu and the English, in the first place, because, in accordance with the 16th article of the Treaty of Versailles, both the English and the French were required to ask their allies to participate in the general pacification. In the second, because the evacuation of the Carnatic by the Mysoreans being also considered a condition of that treaty, the Madras government wrote to Bussy that 'whilst Tipu will not recall the troops from the Carnatic, it cannot proceed to return the French territories.'[63] Moreover, Bussy realized that if war continued, Tipu was bound to succumb to the coalition of the English, the Nizam and the Marathas which the Bengal government would succeed in organizing. Bussy was anxious to prevent the defeat of Tipu, because he felt it would lead to the strengthening of the British power in India.

At first Tipu refused to listen to the advice of Bussy. In the end, however, better counsels prevailed. Deprived of his French allies, tired of a long war, and threatened by a confederacy of the English and the Marathas, he agreed to an armistice which was signed at Mangalore on 2 August 1783.[64]

After the conclusion of the armistice Bussy tried to bring about a peace treaty and to play the part of an umpire.[65] But he was ignored both by Tipu and the English. The Madras government had sought his assistance to secure a cessation of hostilities with Tipu, but now that fighting was over, it no longer wanted his interference[66] because that would enhance the French prestige in India. Tipu, on the other hand, did not desire the French mediation in the peace talks, partly because he had not yet recovered from the shock of their betrayal, and partly, because he did not trust them and suspected that they would accede to all the English demands. This was the reason why Sayyid Saheb despatched the two Mysorean Vakils, Appaji Ram and Srinivas Rao, to Madras in September without informing Bussy, although the latter had asked him to send them accompanied by the French agents.[67] This was a sufficient indication that Tipu did not want French interference in the peace negotiations. In spite of this, Bussy persisted and sent Paul Martin, accompanied by a Brahman interpreter named Kishen Rao, to participate in the negotiations and keep watch over the French interests. But both Martin and Kishen Rao were ignored by Tipu's deputies who did not even care to meet them.[68] Kishen Rao was obliged to leave after some time; Martin remained till November, but his presence was futile, since he was neither taken into confidence by the agents of Tipu nor by the Madras government.[69] In the subsequent negotiations also, which led to the Treaty of Mangalore, the French were not invited to share in the discussions and had to remain only as passive spectators.

For this treatment Bussy was filled with great resentment and gave expression to bitter tirades against Tipu. It seems he had forgotten that the role of the French in the Second Anglo–Mysore War had neither been consistent with their promises nor with their pretensions.

Notes and References

[1] Sinha, *Haidar Ali*, pp. 233, 234.

[2] Wilks, *History of Mysore*, Vol. I, pp. 779, 785.

[3] When, in February 1778, Louis XVI declared war against England, hostilities in India also started between the English and the French. Although for a number of years grandiose schemes for the expulsion of the English from India had been worked out by the French adventurers patronized by the French colonial authorities, still, when the war came, the French were caught unprepared and before the year was out they had lost nearly all their settlements to the English (*Journal de Bussy*, Martineau (ed.), pp. 152 and ff.).

[4] *Journal de Bussy*, Intro., p. vii. d'Orves was at first the commander but after he died on 9 February 1782, Le Bailli de Suffren succeeded to the chief command of the French navy in Indian waters.

[5] Ibid., p. 114.

[6] Chevalier Cunat, *Histoire du Bailli de Suffren*, p. 118.

[7] *Journal de Bussy*, pp. 114, 115.

[8] Ibid., p. 116.

[9] Ibid., p. 107, de Launay to Bussy, dt. 22 March 1782; *Memoires du Chevalier de Mautort*, pp. 203, 204. Mautort also says that Duchemin was supplied with everything in abundance. He does not mention the scarcity of wheat. Wheat probably was scarce, because wheat is neither the main crop nor staple food of the Carnatic.

[10] Cunat, *Bailli de Suffren*, p. 149.

[11] *Journal de Bussy*, p. 120.

[12] Ibid., p. 288.

[13] Ibid., p. 116.

[14] Ibid., pp. 117–19. Haidar's three Brahman agents were Appaji Ram, Srinivas Rao, and Banaji Pundit.

[15] Ibid., pp. 120, 121.

[16] Secret Proceedings, 6 June 1782, Coote to Macartney, pp. 1921–23.

[17] *Journal de Bussy*, F.N., p. 288, de Souillac to Duchemin du 18 Janvier 1782.

[18] Beveridge, *History of India*, Vol. II, p. 503.

[19] At first Haidar had been very generous to the French. He promised them one lakh of rupees per month and regularly paid this sum for five months. He also gave Duchemin money to raise and equip two battalions of sepoys to be attached to the French army. But after he became disgusted with the French General he discontinued this financial aid. (*Memoirs du Chevalier de Mautort*, p. 218; *Journal de Bussy*, p. 290).

[20] *Journal de Bussy*, pp. 143, 287. Haidar called the French a nation very fickle, without character, and never keeping their engagements and their word. He also expressed some very harsh judgements regarding the discipline of the French army. Although Haidar said all this in a moment of anger, because one of his men had been murdered by a Frenchman, and afterwards apologised for it; nevertheless it reveals his real opinion of the French army under Duchemin.

[21] Ibid., Intro., p. xvii.

[22] Ibid., p. 97.

[23] Wilks, *History of Mysore*, Vol. II, p. 169. It was not de Cossigny, as mentioned by Wilks, but d'Hofflize who held the command of the French forces at this time.

[24] Innes Munro's *Narrative*, p. 308.

[25] Kirmani, *Tarikh-i-Tipu Sultan*, pp. 7, 8.

[26] *Journal de Bussy*, pp. 299, 300.

[27] Letter No. 398, Bussy to Marquis de Castries, dt. 18 December 1782; *Journal de Bussy*, p. 320.

[28] Ibid., Intro., pp. vii, viii.

[29] Ibid., p. 339.

[30] Ibid., pp. 339, 340.

[31] Ibid., p. 357.

[32] Letter No. 495 (Pondicherry Records). Tipu informed Bussy that he had left behind in the Carnatic 35,000 men. Bussy, however, maintained that the troops under Sayyid Sahib numbered 12,000–14,000.

[33] Letter Nos. 586, 603. Sayyid Saheb was unable to place at the disposal of Bussy abundant supplies because the Carnatic, owing to the devastations caused by the war, was plunged in famine. Sayyid Saheb did not possess sufficient supplies for his own troops. (See also *Journal de Bussy*, p. 350).

[34] Letter No. 497.

[35] *Journal de Bussy*, p. 356.

[36] *Mémoires du Chevalier de Mautort*, p. 274; Cunat, *Bailli de Suffren*, p. 281.

[37] Cunat, *Bailli de Suffren*, p. 281. The united forces of Haidar and the French had captured Perumukkal on 16 May 1782. Tipu, when leaving for the Malabar coast, had proposed to d'Hofflize he should occupy it. d'Hofflize had refused on the grounds that his already small army would be further reduced if he had to garrison the place. Tipu had, therefore, ordered the demolition of its fortifications. But as the demolition had not been completed, it could have formed a useful military post for the French, if Bussy had taken possession of it.

[38] Letter No. 402.

[39] Martineau, *Bussy et l'Inde Française*, p. 354.

[40] Ibid., p. 354.

[41] Innes Munro's *Narrative*, p. 321. Bussy in his letter to the Marquis de Castries, dt. 9 September 1783, says that the English army reached the banks of the river Pennar on 2 June (Letter No. 402). But this is wrong for Stuart did not take five days to reach south of Cuddalore. I have, therefore, accepted Innes Munro's version. According to de Mautort, d'Hofflize was also prepared to march with his brigade and some pieces of cannon to the opposite bank of the rivers and prevent the English from crossing it. But he was not given the permission. (See his *Mémoires*, pp. 281, 282).

[42] Wilks, *History of Mysore*, Vol. II, pp. 185–6.

[43] Letter No. 402; Wilks, *History of Mysore*, Vol. II, pp. 186–87.

[44] Mill, *History of British India*, Vol. iv, p. 192.

[45] Martineau, *Bussy et l'Inde Française*, p. 355.

[46] Wilks, *History of Mysore*, Vol. II, p. 195.

[47] *Mémoires du Chevalier de Mautort*, p. 296.

[48] Wilks, *History of Mysore*, Vol. II, p. 189.

[49] The French troops consisted of about 3000 Europeans and 2000 sepoys besides 8000–10,000 Mysorean troops (Letter no. 599). The English army, on the other hand, amounted to about 11,000 men: 1,660 Europeans, 8,340 sepoys and 1000 cavalry. But Munro's statement regarding the strength of the French army is not correct (Innes Munro's *Narrative*, p. 329).

[50] Mill, *History of British India*, Vol. IV, p. 192.

[51] *Mémoires du Chevalier de Mautort*, p. 298.

[52] Letter No. 402; Military Consultations, 24 June 1783, Vol. 90A, pp. 2724, 2725; Wilks, *History of Mysore*, Vol. II, p. 193.

[53] Letter No. 402.

[54] Ibid., the losses of the French were estimated to be 450, that of the British was small—1 officer killed, 3 officers wounded, and 20 rank and file,

principally Indians, killed and wounded (Wilson, *History of the Madras Army*, Vol. II, p. 81).

[55] Letter No. 402.

[56] Ibid.

[57] Letter No. 403.

[58] Secret Proceedings, 18 August 1783.

[59] Ibid. Tipu to Muhammad Ismail, his agent with Bussy; Martineau, *Bussy et l'Inde Française*, p. 379.

[60] *Estudos e Documentos sobre la Historia dos Portugueses na India*, Vol. I, Fasciculo ii (ed. Panduranga S.S. Pissurlencar), Letter No. 79.

[61] Martineau, *Bussy et l'Inde Française*, p. 385.

[62] Letter No. 532 (Pondicherry Records).

[63] Letter No. 704.

[64] Secret Proceedings, 4 September 1783.

[65] Ibid., 18 August 1783.

[66] Ibid.

[67] Letter No. 541 (Pondicherry Records).

[68] Letter Nos. 678, 713.

[69] Martineau, *Bussy et l'Inde Française*, p. 383.

5

Did Haidar Ali Turn a Defeatist in 1782?

D.S. Achuta Rau

olonel Mark Wilks wrote the first comprehensive history of Mysore.[1] His account is based mainly on English records and on some of the local accounts and oral information. He had little or no access to Marathi, French, Dutch, Portuguese and such other sources as have been brought to light in recent times. Naturally his account is often one-sided. A few inconsistencies and inaccuracies are visible in his account, particularly in his treatment of Haidar Ali and Tipu Sultan. He has spread certain erroneous views about Haidar Ali in his eager desire to glorify British arms and the achievements of his countrymen. Such a misrepresentation of facts is often set at naught by a study of the original sources both indigenous and foreign.

The years 1780–82 were eventful years in the annals of India. The principal Indian powers, indignant with the political faithlessness and intrigues of the English East India Company and awakened to the danger of their growing political and territorial ambitions, sank their differences and united for a common cause, namely the annihilation of the British power in India. The confederates drew up a plan of warfare which had for its aim an attack on English possessions simultaneously in every part of India. While Haidar Ali on his part endeavoured faithfully to carry out with vigour and determination the plan of the confederacy by invading the South, attacking Madras, and reducing the affairs of the Government of Madras to a critical position, the other coalitionist powers from whom he expected cooperation for the success of the enterprise had been prevented by their unexampled hesitancy and duplicity from pursuing the general plan.[2]

Though ultimately the Nizam, the Maratha chieftains, chiefly

Sindhia and Bhonsle, were won over and neutralized and Nana Fadnavis rendered inactive and helpless by the diplomacy of Warren Hastings, and Haidar Ali was left alone to wage the war, he was not one who would abandon himself to despair or think of a compromise. But Colonel Mark Wilks attributed to Haidar Ali a confession which is hardly consistent with his real attitude.

Wilks writes, 'It was about this time[3] that Haidar, being very much indisposed, left entirely with his Minister Purnaiah, addressed to him in the following words: "I have committed a great error. I shall pay dear for my arrogance. Between me and the English there were perhaps mutual grounds of dissatisfaction but no sufficient cause for war and I might have made them my friends in spite of Mohammad Ali, the most treacherous of men. The defeat of many Baillies and Braithwaites will not destroy them. I can ruin their resources by land, but I cannot dry up the sea and I must be weary of war in which I can gain nothing by fighting.... I ought to have reflected that no man of common sense will trust a Maratha and that they themselves do not expect to be trusted. I have been accused of idle expectation of a French force from Europe, but supposing it to arrive and to be successful here. ...."[4]

This statement attributed to Haidar Ali by Wilks must be considered a later invention and based on hearsay recorded more than a quarter of a century later. It hardly finds any corroboration in contemporary accounts. It glorifies the superiority of British arms and depicts Haidar Ali as a defeatist and is intended to convey how even such a formidable adversary as Haidar Ali realized his folly in entering into hostilities with the English, and soon realized the value of friendship with that nation. This observation of Wilks has unfortunately found currency in almost all later writings on Indian history whose authors had to depend solely upon the accounts of Wilks and Bowring for the history of Mysore, and it has done incalculable harm to the career and personality of Haidar Ali, one of the greatest statesmen and soldiers of the eighteenth century.

Haidar Ali was not a defeatist as Wilks' account would lead us to believe. He was a man of strong determination and unswerving purpose, a bold and enterprising general, skilful in tactics and fertile in resources, full of courage and never despondent in defeat. He strove his utmost till his death for the success of his undertaking even though he was deserted by his allies. He even spurned the Treaty of Salbai and the terms offered by General Goddard through his envoy and told the latter 'I have not entered the Carnatic and made war these two years for the purpose of going out as I came and if I choose to do so, there would be no need of waiting for your orders; rather than do that I will stay for two more years and I care not for the expenses.'[5] Earlier, when he became aware of the diplomacy of Warren Hastings to divide the allies, Haidar Ali despatched his envoys to Poona exhorting Nana Fadnavis not to come to terms with the English and assuring brighter prospects for his own affairs in the South.[6] It rebounds to the credit of Nana Fadnavis that when General Goddard was sent to him by Warren Hastings to secure the ratification of the Treaty of Salbai concluded with Sindhia, he refused to come to terms and explained to Goddard 'the sincere regard and friendship subsisting betwixt the Shrimant Pradhan and Nawab Haidar Ali Khan is more conspicuous and shining than the splendour of the sun. Therefore it is the wish of that friend whose heart is the residence of regard to settle the terms of a firm and a lasting alliance....'[7] Such was the lasting alliance of Nana and Haidar Ali and the latter still had confidence in his allies.

The following lines from the *Haidar-Nama*, a contemporary account in Kannada, and one of the most reliable sources for the history of Haidar Ali, reveals the true mind of Haidar Ali and at the same time his indefatigable will in carrying out his enterprise without harbouring any idea of surrendering his cause. 'Soon[8] Haidar Ali convened a council of war and consulted his principal generals on the best means of exterminating the English. He told them that it is not possible in spite of numerous defeats inflicted on the English to put down their powers by engaging them in one place for they have various places to draw resources like Madras, Bombay, Calcutta and above all England. If it is our intention to put down the English we should cause a great war in Europe between that nation and the French. The kings of Kandahar and Iran should be set up against Bengal and the Marathas against Bombay. Thereafter with a big army and with the help of the French and by the joint action of all of us they should be engaged in all places simultaneously so that one cannot come to the help of the other. The whole country should be plundered by our army in such a manner as to cut off their supplies entirely and thus to reduce them to starvation. Then alone will this country come into our possession.'[9]

Determined thus, says the author of *Haidar-Nama*, Haidar Ali sent his trusted official Appaji Ram with large sums of money to

51

muster 50,000 cavalry for the overthrow of the English.[10] What Wilks quotes as the confession of Haidar Ali revealing the futility of his war against the English, made in the presence of Purnaiah, might be a distortion of the above account preserved in the *Haidar-Nama*. It is probable that Purnaiah, who was the head of the commissariat service under Haidar Ali, was one of those who were present and listened to the exhortations of his master in the war council, and after the restoration of Mysore to the former ruling dynasty in 1799, Purnaiah in his advanced age might have recalled the vague memories of Haidar Ali's utterances and conveyed the same in a more or less different spirit to Colonel Mark Wilks to flatter the paramount power and to convey the idea that Tipu Sultan was a more inveterate foe of the English than his father Haidar Ali.

Notes and References

[1] *Historical Sketches of the South of India*, 2 vols., 1809–17.

[2] Forrest, *Bombay Diaries*, Vol. I, pp. 459–64; *Calendar of the Persian Correspondence*, Vol. VI, pp. 101, 116, 138, 189 and 203.

[3] December 1781 or January 1782.

[4] Wilks, *Historical Sketches*, Vol. II, pp. 373–4. Actually a French squadron early in 1782 under the command of Admiral de Suffren appeared in Indian waters and in the month of February next Duchemin came with 2,000 men under his command.

[5] Forrest, *Selection from Letters, Despatches of the Foreign Department of Government of India*, Vol. III, p. 393.

[6] *Calendar of Persian Correspondence*, Vol. VI, pp. 157, 189, 238.

[7] Forrest, *Bombay Diaries*, Vol. I, Letter from Nana Fadnavis to Brigadier-General Goddard; *Calendar of Persian Correspondence*, Vol. VI, p. 5, letter No. 7.

[8] January 1782.

[9] *Haidar-Nama*, Manuscript, folios 76–77.

[10] Ibid., folio 77.

Diplomatic History

6

A Conference between Tipu Sultan and Brigadier-General Macleod

Irshad Husain Baqai

ipu Sultan's success on the Malabar Coast forced the English to ask for a cessation of hostilities. Major Campbell drew up the terms of the armistice, which was signed on August 1783.[1] The Bombay Government had sent three small vessels with provisions, but these could not arrive in time. The vessel carrying Brigadier-General Macleod also could not leave Bombay earlier than August.

But the Madras Government was anxious for peace with Tipu Sultan. Lord Macartney had already twice made efforts in this direction. A treaty with Tipu Sultan was regarded as a logical consequence of the peace declared between England and France by the Treaty of Versailles, Tipu being an ally of the King of France.[2] The Commissioners of the Madras Government were therefore on their way to restart negotiations with Tipu.[3]

Brigadier-General Macleod thus had no alternative but to pursue the policy of peace when he arrived off Mangalore on 17 August 1783. Since he thought that the Bombay Government had borne the chief burden of the war on the Malabar coast, and therefore was more concerned in negotiating a peace with Tipu than the Madras Government,[4] he expressed a desire to see Tipu Sultan in a letter to Major Campbell, saying, 'I rejoice in the idea of a general peace as I shall get home happily to my little family. It would make me proud to see the warlike prince I once had the honour of fighting.'[5] He also wrote to Tipu Sultan for permission to land and interview him.[6] The permission seems to have been granted. The General landed at Mangalore and had an opportunity of seeing the 'warlike prince'. He has left an interesting record[7] of his conversations with the Sultan which took

55

place on 20–21 August 1783. In a letter to the Select Committee at Bombay, dated Mangalore, 2 October 1783, he describes his conversation with the Sultan as 'plain, but open and spirited', and he believed himself to have 'extinguished every idea in him [the Sultan] of renewing the war with the English and inspired him with a keen wish to have their friendship.'[8] The following is the account of this interview.

On 20 August Lieutenant-Colonel Campbell presented Brigadier-General Macleod to the Sultan. The usual darbar ceremonies were performed. Some general conversation took place which consisted mostly of enquiries from the Sultan about the engagement which the Brigadier-General had fought with the Maratha fleet.[9]

Tipu then asked if the General had anything particular to say concerning peace or war. After this the conversation continued in the following manner (as recorded by Brigadier-General Macleod).[10] Lieutenant Lighton acted as interpreter.

Brigadier-General Macleod: 'One of my greatest reasons for landing was that as there is now a prospect of peace I intend to return soon to Europe[11] and wish to have the honour of seeing the Nabob[12] that I may give my own royal master an account of the person of so famous a prince; I am also rejoiced to find by the cessation of arms which His Highness has concluded with Lieutenant-Colonel Campbell that there was likelihood of peace between our nation and him; I am desirous to strengthen the beginnings of it by confirming the cessation as Commander-in-Chief of Bombay, and if His Highness would allow me I would mention something to him which would prove it to be in his own interest to be a firm friend to the English and would pave the way to a peace.'

Nabob: 'I am sincere in my desire for peace with the English. I respect them and if they act fairly with me I will be their friend. I should be glad if the General would go to the King of England from me and tell him about me. I want to be a friend to him and his people and will send presents through the General to the King. I will be glad to see the General at my darbar tomorrow and to hear all he has to say. I will open my heart to him and he must act fairly with me, and I have a great opinion of him and Lieutenant-Colonel Campbell. They have shewed themselves good warriors and I wish to raise their name. I will see them tomorrow.'

Brigadier-General Macleod then writes:

During this conference Mr. Pierson de Morlat, the French envoy, came in. The Nabob told me that as the French had proposed the peace he had sent for him that I might see him in the darbar.

August 21st.

The Nabob sent for us in the evening. The Nabob asked me to proceed in what I had to say to him which I did as follows:

Brigadier-General Macleod: I always had a great respect for the Nabob and his family. His father was a great warrior and a great prince and every soldier admires him. The Nabob himself has great renown as a warrior and he has come to great power and fame at a much earlier time of life than his father. I know the wise means that he is taking to strengthen his army and discipline them. I wish him great increase of power and glory and if he will be a friend to our nation I should rejoice to see the House of Hyder as great as ever that of Temur was. But I will prove to the Nabob, if he will let me speak without taking offence, that if he hopes to be great and successful it cannot be by war with the English. (I was desired to speak freely and went on.) The Nabob is too well-informed a prince not to know that at the breaking out of this war with him the Government of Madras and their allies were not well prepared for war, that his father and he had taken great advantage of this and met great success at first; that notwithstanding this the English soon became equal in the field and at this moment the Nabob enjoyed recompense for all his great expense and trouble. The English were able to make this head against him when they were engaged in war with the French, Spaniards, Dutch and Americans[13] and with the Marathas in India. These wars employed all their resources of men, ships and money. Now we have peace with all these nations. The Nabob is our only enemy; all the force of the British Empire may now be employed against him. I assure the Nabob in the most solemn manner that the greatest preparations are being made against him. That ships and men are daily arriving from Europe and will continue to arrive till we have finished the war with him. I own that the Nabob is a great and formidable prince. But he cannot but think that the English, who were able to contest with all the greatest nations in Europe and with him and the Marathas in India at the same time, would have the advantage against him or any one of these enemies alone. The Nabob is too wise not to see that he can gain nothing by the war. The English may make conquests upon him and even if he was able to keep his ground and lose nothing he must at any rate lose his time, his money, and his best troops. His superiority in military talents would make him great against any other enemy, and as I wished well to his renown I wish him to choose some other enemy. Notwithstanding the advantageous situation of the English I am well convinced that it is their interest and inclination to have a firm friendship with him. Their principal interest is in Bengal and the Carnatic. The powers most likely to interfere with these possessions are the Marathas and the Nizam. The English would always wish him for their natural ally because it would be his policy to keep a watchful eye on those neighbours. Besides we do not want more territories but to enjoy peaceably what we have. We should, therefore, be glad to make peace with him. I have now spoken a long time. If what I have said is pleasing to the Nabob I shall be happy. I beg him to open his heart to me and tell me if I can be of any use to him by telling his mind to any of the governments in India. I will be rejoiced to be of service to so famous a prince.

Nabob: I am much pleased with what the General has said. I see he has good abilities. He has spoken sensibly and openly to me and that is the way I wish to be dealt with.[14] I am sincere in my desire to have a firm and solid friendship with the English, and the General and Lieutenant-Colonel Campbell have shewed themselves good warriors and I should be glad to make peace with them. I wish to exalt their names and to let their king know they are good servants. I will now say something about the war. Some time ago Muhammad Ali[15] borrowed above one hundred lacs of money from us and we assisted him with our army. In return he promised to give us Trichinopoly.[16] But he broke his word and would not pay us the money. He has done everything to shew himself our enemy. Being so near Madras he has poisoned the minds of the English against my father and me. He has even sent people to England to abuse us to the king and the people there. This is a bad usage from a man of our caste[17] and was the great cause of the war. Muhammad Ali is not true to the English. He has sent people to me to say that the English have taken so much money from him and made him so much in debt that the Carnatic would be no use to him if they remain there and that he would be glad to be friends with me and drive them out.

I desire to make peace with you and Lieutenant-Colonel

Campbell. What terms do you propose? Mr. Bussy and the French want to make the peace but I will do it myself and will not have them interfere. Make you the peace with me and I will make you great.

Brigadier-General Macleod: I most humbly thank His Highness for what he has been pleased to say of me and Lieutenant-Colonel Campbell and I wish to shew him my gratitude by doing everything in my power to serve His Highness consistent with my duty to my own master and my country. I am a military servant and General of the Bombay Force. I have no power to make peace. That must be done by the three Governors of Bengal, Bombay and Madras. All I can do is to confirm the cessation of arms and represent His Highness's sentiments in the most favourable way to the Governors.

Nabob: Why cannot the Sardars make peace? They are the proper persons to do it.

Brigadier-General Macleod: It is ordered by the King and Company that the Governors and Counsellors shall make the peace because they understand matters of revenue and trade better than the Sardars. I am happy to find that the Nabob is sincere in his desire for peace and I have no doubt that the Governors and Counsellors will conclude it with him to his satisfaction. If I should say anything against Muhammad Ali, who is a respectable prince, and a steady friend of the English, the Nabob himself would have a bad opinion of me. With respect to Trichinopoly I know that story very well. (I then related it as it is in Orme,[18] at which the Nabob and his minister shewed great surprise. They said I spoke the truth and they saw I knew affairs well). The Nabob must be sensible that the English never will give up Trichinopoly; his mentioning such a thing would stop all thoughts of peace. If he is so sincere, as he has done me the honour to say, I exhort him to begin by renouncing all claim to Trichinopoly that it may never appear again in dispute. As His Highness has commended me for speaking so freely I will add another advice, to give the English at once a proof of his goodwill and magnanimity by releasing all their prisoners immediately. This will strike all mankind with a high idea of his grandeur of soul. It will also be a noble token of his goodwill. I advise it for the sake of his renown as much as for the sake of the prisoners, for as a peace will certainly take place, a few months' longer captivity is of no great consequence. I will never deceive the Nabob. It would be presumptuous in me to propose terms of peace. I have no power to do so, though I believe the Governor of Bombay would trust me to make their share of the peace. I wish the peace equal for both sides and that it may be lasting.

Nabob: I praise you for what you say, I believe you speak truly and openly to me which I like. At your request and Colonel Campbell's I will release the prisoners—everyone of them—immediately. If you will go with me to Seringapatam I will deliver every man to you and you may send them to their different governments. Will you engage that if peace is not made these prisoners shall be sent back to me?

Brigadier-General Macleod: I engage my head for it exclusive of the common accident of death.

Nabob: Go with me to Seringapatam. I will give you the prisoners. Mr. Bussy shall not make the peace for me. You shall make it. I will send the terms with you to Madras on which I will make peace. Will you go?

Brigadier-General Macleod: I humbly thank your Highness for the great honour you do me in promising to give up the prisoners at my request and desiring me to make the peace for you. I will go most readily and your Highness will promise in case the peace does not take place to send me either to Tellicherry or Bombay as I shall choose.

Nabob: I do promise it. Let me know tomorrow what horses, palankeen and etc., you and your suite will want. Mangalore and other places will remain according to the cessation. I will give up all claim to Trichinopoly.

The above is a true account.

(Sd.) Norman Macleod, Brigadier-General.
(Sd.) John Campbell, Lieutenant-Colonel.

Subsequent events, however, took a different shape from what is suggested by the very cordial tone of the foregoing conversations between Tipu Sultan and Brigadier-General Macleod. While suspending hostilities Colonel Campbell had accepted very disadvantageous terms. He had agreed for instance to receive no supplies of victual by sea—the only way by which he could possibly receive them.[19] Thus the question of sending provisions to the garrison became the chief point of dispute between Tipu Sultan and the English army officers. Brigadier-General Macleod was keen on supplying as large a quantity of victuals as he could from Tellicherry or Bombay so that the garrison might not surrender, as the loss of Mangalore, he thought, would greatly affect the impending peace negotiations and would thus put Tipu into a more advantageous position. When Tipu put restrictions on the supply of provisions he was accused of violating the articles of the truce. A lengthy correspondence between Tipu Sultan and General Macleod took place which is characterized by Wilks as 'among the most remarkable in the history of diplomacy'.[20] The following two letters[21] are typical of many that passed between the Sultan and the English General. After his return from Tellicherry General Macleod wrote to Tipu Sultan:

> I have the honour to inform your Highness that I am returned to this place in order to know from you what are your intentions about Mangalore and whether you have allowed Colonel Campbell to receive one month's provisions according to the articles of cessation. I have brought with me one month's provisions, and I desire you to admit them into the Fort as you promised by the articles. If you do admit them peace will go on between you and the English, and they will love you as a great and good prince. If you refuse to admit them I will write immediately to all our Admirals and Generals and to the Governors of Bengal, Madras and Bombay that you have broken your faith and that your promises are good for nothing. You will soon be sorry; Sir Richd. Bickerton one of our king's greatest Sirdars by sea, and who always stands in his presence, is not here with the ships which you see. I wish to have your answer soon. Admiral Hughes will soon be here, and I will tell him what you say and do. I beg you to send the enclosed letter to Colonel Campbell.
>
> May God direct your mind to wisdom, truth and prosperity.

The Nabob's reply:[22]

Yours I receive. I am very glad you are come back, as well at the arrival of Sir Richd. Bickerton. The things which could be got in the country for the Fort's provision, I have ordered to be sold at proper price and they buy it every day. You have wrote me that you have with you a month of provisions for the Fort. In the articles it is not mentioned that you should bring any on the sea, rice and other provisions; look upon the articles then you will know when you were here last to oblige your friendship. I have let go into the Fort one month of arrack and other provisions at two different times, Which is not according to the article, which was come on the sea; if you go according to the article I will do the same.

What can I say more?

A true copy
(Sd.) Thos. Leighton, Secretary, Mangalore, Pettah, 24th Oct. 1783.

Thus the correspondence continued. The Sultan, however, did not give way. The lack of provisions made the condition in the garrison miserable. On 29 January 1784 Lieutenant-Colonel Campbell surrendered to the Sultan. In a letter[23] to the Select Committee of Fort St George, dated 6 February 1784, he wrote:

> With pain I have the cruel mortification of acquainting you that on the 29th of last month I found myself from the distress of the garrison in every respect under the disagreeable necessity of delivering up the Fort of Mangalore to the Nabob under articles the most beneficial I could ask for the garrison and which the Nabob has most hon'bly and strictly adhered to.

This was a serious loss for the English. They had decided not to surrender Mangalore till all English prisoners were released. But Tipu Sultan was not going to take any risks. Colonel Fullarton was at Tellicherry contemplating a march towards Seringapatam; Brigadier-General Macleod attacked the Bibi of Cannanore;[24] these facts had greatly influenced him. General Macleod never went to Seringapatam as was contemplated in his conversations with the Sultan. Instead, the Commissioners appointed by the Madras Government, Messrs. Sadler, Staunton and Huddlestone, negotiated with the Sultan the Treaty of Mangalore of 1784.

Notes and References

[1] Secret Consultations (Sec. Cons.) 14 Nov. 1783 No. 1 (Imperial Records Department).

[2] Appendix to Sec. Cons., 18 Aug. 1783.

[3] This treaty is known as the Treaty of Mangalore, concluded on 11 March 1784. Aitchison, 5th ed., p. 228.

[4] Letter from General Macleod to the President, Select Committee at Bombay, from *Morning Star* off Mangalore, Sec. Cons., 18 Aug. 1783.

[5] Sec. Cons., 14 Nov. 1783.

[6] Letter from General Macleod to Tipu Sultan, dated 19 Aug. 1783 (Sec. Cons., 14 Nov. 1783).

[7] Letter from General Macleod to Tipu Sultan, dated 19 Aug. 1783 (Sec. Cons., 14 Nov. 1783).

[8] Sec. Cons., 20 Jan. 1784.

[9] This refers to the capture of the English vessel, *Ranger Snow*, by the Marathas. General Macleod was on board the ship and took an active part in the fight and was seriously wounded. (Sec. Cons., 28 July 1783); see my paper, 'The *Ranger Snow* Episode', *Indian Historical Records Commission Progs.*, Vol. XVIII.

[10] A similar record is also available of a Conference of Srinivas Row, Wakil of Sir Eyre Coote, with Haidar Ali (Appendix to Sec. Cons., 26 Sept. 1762). Another conference is described in Forrest, *Selections from Foreign Dept. Records*, pp. 885–95.

[11] Sec. Cons., 16 Dec. 1783, No. I c.

[12] In the East India Company records Tipu Sultan is generally referred to as 'Tipoo Sahib' up to 1782. After his accession he is addressed as 'Nabob Tipoo Sultan Bahadur'.

[13] This refers to the war of American Independence in which the French and Spaniards were allies of the American colonies.

[14] Being himself bold and courageous the Sultan admired courage and frankness in others.

[15] Nawab Muhammad Ali Walajah of the Carnatic.

[16] The affair was a sore point with Tipu as with Haidar Ali. In his conversation with Srinivas Row, Wakil of Sir Eyre Coote, Haidar Ali is reported to have said, 'It was stipulated that I should have Trichinopoly and Madura made over to me; the paper of agreement, including a receipt for the money paid, is here ready, you may see it', and 'upon these are the signatures, both of Mahamed Ally Khan and a European named Saunders. You may see them here.' (Forrest, Selections from For. Dept. records, p. 889). Warren Hastings, while criticizing the Treaty of Mangalore of 1784, observed:

> 'It ought to be remembered that one ground alleged by the late Nabob Hyder Ally Cawn for commencing this war was that the Nabob Ali Wallah Jah had failed in the performance of the stipulation made about 30 years past for surrender of Trichinopoly with the Raja of Mysore, to which Hyder laid claim as the representative of that Government. This claim is personal and as it was an express cause of war, it ought to have been removed; on the contrary, it has acquired additional force by the past omission of it, and on the Nabob's refusal to assert his right by a renewal of the war.' (Forrest, *Selections*, p. 1093).

[17] Tipu means religion. It is of interest that Nawab Muhammad Ali always referred to Haider Ali as the son of a Naik. He called the Mysore rulers Haidar Naik and Tipu Naik.

18 This refers to Orme's *History of Indostan*. The description of this affair is in Vol. II.

19 *Cambridge History of India*, Vol. V, p. 288.

20 Wilks, *Historical Sketches*, Vol. II, p. 67.

21 Sec. Cons., 20 Jan. 1784, No. 29.

22 This is most probably the translation of the Sultan's letter by some army Munshi and there are therefore mistakes of language, grammar and punctuation.

23 Sec. Cons., 18 March 1784, No. 3.

24 See S.N. Sen, 'The Cannanore Incident', *Indian Historical Records Commission Proceedings*, Vol. XVIII.

7

Cornwallis and the Mysore–Maratha War, 1786–1787

B. Sheik Ali

Before the advent of Lord Cornwallis as the Governor-General of India, his predecessor, Sir John Macpherson, had adopted the policy of intervention in the Mysore–Maratha War of 1786–87. He offered to supply the Marathas with five battalions of troops to be employed anywhere either offensively or defensively.[1] He justified a revision of the earlier policy of neutrality on the ground that the Company's interests would be better served by joining a powerful party like the Marathas. Such a policy would reduce the military expenses of the Company and keep the Marathas on the English side should the French or Tipu cause any trouble to the English. The Home Government disapproved of such a policy, and wrote: 'You ought to have gone no further than to intimate to the Marathas that in the event of the French joining Tipu they might rely on the assistance of our troops'.[2] The authorities in England made their stand still more explicit when they observed, 'We are completely satisfied with the possessions we already have and will engage in no war for the purpose of further acquisitions'.[3]

When Lord Cornwallis took charge as the Governor-General in September 1786, he revised the policy of supporting the Marathas against Tipu. Macpherson's policy would have involved the Company in a complicated political and military situation. It would be a breach of the Treaty of Mangalore with Tipu, which had enjoined strict neutrality on both parties in case either of them was at war with other powers. If the English were to assist the Marathas directly or indirectly, Tipu would be provided with a just ground to join the French, whose exclusion from Indian politics was the principal objective of British policy. Moreover, it was contrary to the spirit of the Pitt's India Act just passed (1784), which was emphatic that the Company's servants in India should avoid unnecessary interventions in the disputes of the native powers. Accordingly, Cornwallis informed the Marathas and the Nizam that he had revoked the previous engagements and withdrawn the offer of help to them.[4] Cornwallis wrote to Dundas that Macpherson 'was guilty of a breach of an Act of Parliament in the offer, which he made of aid to Poona Government, and that he was guilty of basely degrading the national character, by quibbles and lies which he made use of to evade the performance of it'.[5] Cornwallis felt it difficult at first to extricate the Company from its commitments. He declared, 'We got in a very awkward foolish scrape by offering assistance to the Marathas; how we shall get out of it with honour, God knows, we out of it must get and give troops'.[6] On the pretext of strictly adhering to the subsisting treaties, he refused help to the Marathas and the Nizam.[7]

It is interesting to enquire what were the real causes for the stiff stand of Cornwallis. His policy was not out of any regard for Tipu, nor was he genuinely interested in maintaining the subsisting treaties, nor wedded irrevocably to a Pacific system. It was dictated purely as a measure of expediency. He too was as much conscious of the advantages to the Company of a war of conquest as Macpherson was, and wrote to the Court of Directors that the safety of the Company's possessions would best be preserved by letting the two formidable native powers engage in a war of exhaustion.[8] But he differed from Macpherson as to the suitable occasion for intervention, for the financial and military position of the Company was far from satisfactory at the moment. About the Company's military position he wrote, '... the European infantry on whom the defence of these valuable possessions may one day depend are in a most wretched state'.[9] The army was in despicable state. The financial position was still worse. Added to this, a war would involve the Company in diplomatic complications as well, for by the Treaty of Paris, England and France were prevented from participating in a war among the native powers. Cornwallis was afraid that English assistance to the Marathas might force Tipu to seek French aid, and thus the very purpose of going to war, namely to eliminate the French from the arena of Indian politics would be defeated. The effect of Macpherson's promise of aid to the Marathas had already brought the French and Tipu closer together, and the latter had applied for 4,000 Europeans to remain constantly in his pay.[10] These factors compelled Cornwallis to revise the decision of his predecessor.

Cornwallis adopted such a policy despite his full knowledge that it would disappoint the Marathas and invite their wrath on the Company. But he argued that British neutrality would shorten the war amongst the natives, and would render the European aid unnecessary. The Company would be relieved of the necessity of preparing for war.[11] Besides, such a policy was in accordance with the instructions of the Home Government who had frequently directed their servants in India to observe strict neutrality in the disputes of Indian powers, and to improve British relations with them by steady adherence to the subsisting treaties between the Company and them.

But Cornwallis did not stick to this policy of neutrality for long. The moment the Company's finances and military power improved, he began to envisage the reduction of Tipu's power, whose successes against the Marathas and the Nizam further excited the jealousy of the English. Cornwallis observed, 'Whether the Peshwa can place any reliance in Tipu's adherence to the treaty after dissolution of the compact between the Peshwa, Madajee Bhonsle, Tukojee Holkar and Nizam Ali Khan, is equally at present a subject of conjecture'.[12] On the pretext that Tipu might invade the Carnatic, Cornwallis directed Malet, the English agent at Poona, to enquire from Nana whether the Marathas were willing for an offensive alliance with the English against Tipu.[13] The basis of such an alliance was the appropriation of Tipu's territories, which were adjacent to the frontiers of the allies, after the conquest was completed.[14] Being apprehensive lest the Maratha response should be unfavourable in the light of earlier British refusal of aid to them, Cornwallis assured Nana that the English were sincere in their offer this time and that the Home Government had approved of such an alliance, the want of which alone had prevented them from cooperating with the Marathas in the past. Not only was Nana approached but an attempt was made by Cornwallis to win the other Maratha chieftains as well. Foster was authorized at Nagpur to invite Madajee Bhonsle to a defensive alliance against Tipu, and likewise Palmer was asked at Gwalior to induce Mahadji Sindhia to do the same.[15]

Thus there was once again a change in the English policy which was alternating between neutrality and intervention. It appears from the Records that every Governor-General was inclined to adopt a vigorous forward policy, but was sometimes restrained to do so only by the exigencies of the situation which would not every time guarantee success to the British arms. Tipu also actively tried to counteract these developments. He contacted Nana and prepared the ground for an Indian alliance to such an extent as to make Nana write to Sindhia, 'We must not only insist on the reparation of our wrongs but we must recover that part of the Carnatic conquests of the great Shivaji which is now occupied by the English'.[16] Tipu was in touch with the Nizam as well, who was interested in recovering the Guntur Sarkar. Before concluding any positive alliance the parties agreed upon a truce for three years and six months.[17] These developments indicate that the two parties, English and Tipu, were extremely suspicious of each other. There was some difference in the policies of these two parties. Whereas the English adopted an extremely flexible policy of either neutrality or intervention as it suited their convenience, Tipu was quite firm in his stand, and adopted a determined and consistent policy of opposition to the British. The Marathas and the Nizam had no such fixed policy, for they were motivated purely by their self-interest and joined any party that would advance their interest.

Notes and References

[1] Secret Proceedings Consultations (Sec. Proc. Cons.), 14 Feb. 1786.
[2] Poona Residency Records, Vol. II, No. 24.
[3] Sec. Desp. from England, 21 July 1786, Vol. I, p. 34.
[4] Poona Residency Records, Vol. II, No. 37.
[5] Forrest, *Selections from State Papers*, Vol. I, p. 103.
[6] Ibid., p. 22.
[7] Sec. Proc. Cons., 27 Sept. 1786.
[8] Secret Letters to the Court, 23, Jan. 1787.
[9] Ross, *Correspondence of Cornwallis*, Vol. I, p. 225.
[10] Sec. despatches to Court, 9 Aug. 1787.
[11] Sec. Proc. Cons., 26 Dec. 1786.
[12] Sec. Proc., 16 Aug. 1787.
[13] Sec. Proc. Cons., 14 Dec. 1787.
[14] Sec. Proc. Cons., 28 Aug. 1787.
[15] Sec. Proc. Cons., 18 Sept. 1787.
[16] Kincaid and Parasanis, Appendix A, Vol. II, p. 14.
[17] Mackenzie's Manuscripts, Vol. LXVI, pp. 56 and 119.

8

Tipu Sultan's Embassy to Constantinople, 1787

Ishtiaq Husain Qureshi

t is widely known that Tipu Sultan sent an embassy to the Sublime Porte (Ottoman court) in 1787. The objects which the Sultan had in his view and the reasons for his correspondence with the court of Constantinople are not so well known. When the mission reached Basrah, the English agents wrote, 'We have not been able to learn for a certainty the objects of their mission, but we have reasons to believe that the embassy to the Porte is for the purpose of obtaining firmaunds [sic] to establish factories in the Turkish dominions....'[1] Regarding the proposed visit of Tipu's agents to France and England, the same letter suggests that the aim was 'probably to engage the alliance of those powers against the Mahrattas and to prevail upon them not to join the Mahrattas against Tippoo'.[2]

It is true that Tipu had the intention of establishing trade relations with Turkey, but this object could only have been a secondary one because Tipu did not persist in it. Besides, a man of his acumen could not have been ignorant of the fact that it was useless to establish factories in Turkey without merchant ships and effective naval power to guard them. Nor could he have ignored the certainty of an impending conflict with the British who enjoyed supremacy in India and over the Arabian Sea. Similarly, the idea of Tipu's desire for an alliance with the French and the English against the Marathas is farfetched, because he was more desirous of winning Maratha friendship against the English. Tipu knew instinctively that the English were his natural enemies. Therefore, he consistently desired an alliance with the French

---

* This article was originally published under the title 'The Purpose of Tipu Sultan's Embassy to Constantinople'.

whom he considered to be his willing allies against the English. But he was not so afraid of the Marathas as to send representatives all the way to France and England to secure help. He defeated the Marathas in 1787, but he gave them generous terms because he did not want them to join forces with the British in the impending war.

The embassy naturally kept its real purpose secret and did not disclose it until it was necessary. Therefore, it is not proper to repose much confidence in the British report so far as the purpose of the embassy is concerned. Those writers who have taken their cue from such documents have failed to understand the real object of Tipu's mission to Constantinople. The significance of the embassy becomes quite clear if we take into consideration the political condition of South India.

Haidar Ali, the founder of the might of Mysore, had, by his foresight and ability, as well as judicious use of his great military capacity, become the most formidable power of South India. The British, who were not as indifferent to the possibilities of establishing their power in India as is generally made out by some historians, considered Haidar Ali to be the greatest obstacle in the achievement of their ambition.[3] This is borne out by the fact that Sir Eyre Coote, on hearing the news of Haidar Ali's death could not help writing 'on the many beneficial effects which may be expected to arise to our general interests in India by the important news of Hyder Ally's death—it opens to us the fairest prospect of securing to the Mother country the permanent and undisturbed possession of these Eastern dominions.'[4] Haidar Ali was not unaware of the intentions of the British, nor of their methods of acquiring territory. In a letter to Muhammad Iftikhar Khan, he wrote that 'the English first try to secure a footing in other territories by outward professions of friendship and then gradually they bring them under their full sway.'[5] In the same letter he says that the English have always been his inveterate enemy.[6] This animosity was natural between two powers which had the ambition of extending their dominions in the same area.

At the time of Haidar Ali's death, his enemies fondly believed that his newly built power would cease to be a dominant factor in South Indian politics. The natural anxiety at the death of a military commander and ruler like Haidar Ali was exaggerated by British informants. For instance, Murad Ali, an *amaldar,* wrote to Major General Stuart: 'The companions of the Naik are gone off to Tippoo to say,

"Collect your scattered forces at Colar and despatch a person with the letter of peace to the heads of the English army and if the Nawab Walajah desires anything as a recompense for the destruction of his kingdom, settle matters by agreement and live contented in your kingdom".' It is possible that some weak hearts advised Tipu to seek terms of peace, but the army seems to have had unbounded confidence in him. Fath Muhammad, a British sepoy, who had been able to visit the Mysore camp, reported that 'he could perceive that the army in general had the highest opinion of Tippoo's humanity and abilities to command them and were highly confident that they would succeed while he remained at their head.'[7]

This confidence reposed by the army in the capacity of Tipu was justified by later events, which very soon showed that he was a worthy successor of his father and could fulfil the role of an ambitious ruler. Thus, the fear which his father's success had aroused in the minds of the neighbouring chiefs and of the English were far from allayed when Tipu came to the throne and maintained the tradition of his father.

What were these fears? It was the open ambition of Haidar Ali as well as Tipu to be overlord of all the area south of the river Krishna.[8] This brought them into conflict with the Nawab Walajah, the ruler of Arcot. The Carnatic was contiguous to Mysore and its weakness offered a great temptation to the rising power of Mysore. There was nothing in the conditions of eighteenth-century India to damp these ambitions. The anarchy brought about by the rise of the Marathas and the weakening of the Mughal Empire had made it possible for new dynasties to establish and extend their power. Public opinion considered it natural in princes to seek aggrandisement at the expense of their neighbours. The Nawab Walajah wrote to Lord Cornwallis, 'There is a great difference between the politics of Europe and of this country. The Princes of India consider conquest as the means of increasing their prosperity, of securing an inheritance to their children and of delivering in [sic] their name to prosperity. They do not regard wealth and they never choose to enter into any alliance from which there are no expectations of gaining an increase in territory.'[9]

It should, however, be remembered that Haidar Ali turned hostile to the Nawab of Carnatic only by force of circumstance. In spite of Haidar Ali's desire to make friends with the English, they had seen greater advantages in entering into an alliance with the Nizam directed against Haidar Ali. Then the Madras government brought on itself his wrath by failing to honour its pledge to help him against his enemies. The Nawab of Arcot had had slight differences with Haidar Ali before, which need not have resulted in deep-rooted enmity. It was the hope of the Bombay government that the differences between the rulers of Mysore and Carnatic could be 'smoothed out'. But the hostility of the British and their failure to abide by their word ruled out any possibility of a reconciliation between Haidar Ali and Nawab Walajah. It was as the ally and protégé of the English that the Nawab of Carnatic suffered. Walajah, however, never realized that Haidar Ali's hostility was directed mainly against his own protectors and not against himself; and he became implacable in his hatred for the ruler of Mysore.

Haidar Ali and Tipu were both men of deep acumen and possessed a sound political instinct; they soon came to foresee that if the Indian powers did not unite against the British, the whole of South India would pass into British hands. It did not require a prophet to see that the power which was the protector of Carnatic as well as Haiderabad was on its way to claiming full overlordship of South India. English diplomacy was, however, too strong for them. Whenever they attempted to induce the Marathas and the Nizam to join hands with Mysore, they failed in securing the sincere co-operation of the two powers against the English. The ruler of Carnatic was not in himself of much importance because he was entirely dependent on the English.

The relations of the rulers of Mysore with their Muslim neighbours were further complicated by legal cobwebs. The legal position originally had been that the Nizam was the Viceroy of the Deccan. The Nawab of the Carnatic was the governor of the area further south, but subordinate to the Nizam. Clive's treaty of Allahabad with Shah Alam (1765) changed the position slightly in favour of the Nawab of Carnatic. He secured the title of Walajah and his traditional dependence on the Nizam came to an end.[10] Thus the Nizam as well as the Nawab Walajah both had excellent legal titles to their dominions. They were, for their territories, the representatives of the Mughal Emperor, still regarded as the legal sovereign. The Marathas had their *sanads*: the English had secured grants for the areas directly under their administration. The Hindu family of Mysore were tributaries of the Empire and thus nominally under the Nizam. The Rajah of Travancore was a tributary of the Nawab of Carnatic.[11] Where did the new House of Mysore come into this picture?

In the beginning, Haidar Ali was content to be a servant of the Rajah of Mysore who had legal title to his dominions. Haidar Ali extended his personal territory, but he kept on the fiction of being subordinate to the Rajah.[12] But this position was precarious and legally full of danger. As late as 1779, in a letter to Basalat Jang, Nizam Ali Khan refers to Haidar Ali as a mere *zamindar* or chief.[13] In 1768 when the Nizam had ceded the *diwani* of Mysore to the English; it was only Haidar Ali's valour which saved him from destruction and enabled him to dictate terms at Madras in the First Mysore War. In January 1782, Nizam Ali Khan again entered into an agreement with Mr Holland, the British Resident at Hyderabad, to invade Haidar Ali's dominions and to partition his territories.[14] The Nizam felt justified in planning the destruction of Haidar Ali because he considered him to be a mere usurper with no right to his territories.

Tipu ended this fiction of his dependence on the Hindu Rajah of Mysore which made his legal title even weaker. According to the legal ideas of the day, every Indian ruler had to acknowledge the supremacy of the House of Timur. This in itself would have been quite acceptable to Tipu, but as matters stood, he could get recognition only as a subordinate either of the Walajah or the Nizam. Both of these princes had shown inveterate hostility to his interests and planned his destruction. Besides, both the Nizam and the Walajah were dependent on the English who were by no means friendly to Tipu. Haidar Ali had once been appointed the Governor of Sira, a district of the Nizam's dominions, by the Emperor. Therefore, the Nizam was never tired of repeating that Tipu was his servant, though there was little reality in the claim.[15]

Tipu had never been under the control of the Nizam; he was a prince of greater authority and power; the Nizam, however, harped on his legal status. Legal subordination to Muslim courts which were jealous of the power and glory of Haidar Ali and Tipu, and which were under the influence of the English, was fraught with danger. It was possible for the English to use this position in their own interests by carefully playing on the jealousy and cupidity of the Nawab Walajah and the Nizam. If the Nizam chose to invade Mysore, or if Tipu found it necessary to fight the Nizam, Tipu could be branded as a rebel against the legally-constituted authority.

It may be argued that rebellion against legal authority was not considered such a crime in the eighteenth century, but this would be a superficial view to take. The Mughal Emperor had been a *roi fainéant* for some time when the East India Company, the Marathas and other powerful princes of India sought sanction for their power by securing grants from Delhi. Great was the hold on the public mind of legal propriety. The Muslims in particular who were by no means a negligible factor in the political life of the Empire, had great respect for legal forms, because their personal and religious law was inseparable from the political and legal theory of those days. The law still regarded the Mughal Emperor as the political and religious head of the Muslims in India; hence rebellion against him or his deputies was a sin. This aspect could easily be emphasized by interested parties and Tipu's Muslim soldiery was not immune to such propaganda. Tipu could argue that he had to engage in a desperate struggle against the British for his very existence. In the struggle, the Nizam and the Walajah were likely to be used by the British to cripple Tipu's resources and fighting capacity. Could he afford to be branded a rebel against legal authority and put a terrible strain on the loyalty of his Muslim soldiery?

The obvious remedy was to get sanction from the Mughal Court for his position as one of the princes of the Empire. The Mughal Court, however, was not favourably inclined. In 1783, in conjunction with the French, he made every attempt to get the grant of Arcot transferred to himself, but he was unsuccessful because of British influence at Delhi. Colonel Demonte had been sent on behalf of the French to Delhi.[16] In the beginning Shah Alam seemed to be favourably inclined toward the French.[17] Some other nobles supported Demonte and Tipu, but ultimately the British representative, Major Brown, was able to defeat the supporters of the French.[18] Nawab Majd-u'd-dawlah, the *na'ib wazir*, was the chief minister at Delhi at that time, because the nominal *wazir* was the Nawab of Oudh.[19] Majd-u'd-dawlah was a great supporter and friend of the English and swore that he could not betray their interests 'while he was alive'.[20]

The result was that Tipu failed to get even the customary *khilat* which was a mark of ordinary courtesy, much less a grant for Arcot.[21] This happened when the French made a real attempt to influence not only Delhi but also the Marathas, giving it out that the King of France had decided to turn the English out of India and when the Emperor Shah Alam was also not too pleased with them.[22]

If Tipu had failed at that time, what hopes could he have had of securing any recognition when the English power seemed supreme and English influence unchallenged at Delhi?[23] Besides, any move by him to secure a status independent of the Nizam would be opposed both by the Nizam and the Walajah. It was a hopeless position for any ruler, much more for an ambitious and spirited prince like Tipu.

The only way out of these difficulties seemed to be a declaration of independence. If his independence could gain recognition, at least the legal difficulties would vanish. For this purpose he had to attain the status of a prince, because it must be remembered that Haidar Ali Khan never claimed to be anything more than a *dalvoy* of his Hindu sovereign, the Rajah of Mysore. Tipu, forced by circumstances and the need to defend his position and patrimony, decided to dethrone the Rajah. This step was also necessary because the Rajah's family had continuously been intriguing against Haidar Ali as well as Tipu. Having secured his position at home, he, tired of the continuous intrigues of the Nizam and the Walajah, decided to proclaim himself an independent monarch. Basalat Jang had procured for Haidar Ali the government of the *suba* of Sira and the Mughal government had sent him the usual insignia of office along with a number of presents. But this position was of definite subordination to the Nizam, and Tipu had tried in vain to get a grant of an area from the Delhi court which would be independent of the Nizam's control. Hence there was no way out for Tipu except that of proclaiming his independence of the Mughal government. Tipu's subsequent diplomacy seems to have been directed towards gaining recognition for his newly-adopted title of an independent monarch. After his successful war against the Marathas and the Nizam (1784–87) he demanded that the two powers should recognize him as an independent monarch.[24] The importance of this demand can be gauged from the fact that he was not fully successful in his attempt. They, however, promised to address him in all future correspondence as Tipu Sultan and not as Fath Ali Khan, as the Nizam had insisted on calling him up to this time.[25]

The recognition he was not able to secure in India he tried to secure abroad. He corresponded with Zaman Shah, the ruler of Afghanistan, and Karim Khan Zand of Iran. Both these rulers addressed him as a brother monarch.[26] He was also in correspondence with France to strengthen the bonds of friendship with the French who were his obvious allies against the English and also to gain international status. Similarly, he corresponded with Salim, the Sultan of Turkey, with a similar end in view. He gained his object because the Sultan of

Turkey addressed him as an independent monarch.[27] On account of the British influence at Constantinople and the rapid progress of French arms in Egypt, the Turkish Court was not very eager to encourage Tipu in his attempt to challenge the British. Indeed the British succeeded in persuading the Turkish court to write to Tipu to forsake the friendship of the French and to ally himself with the English, a request which Tipu could not accept.

But Tipu did succeed in gaining recognition of his independence in spite of British machinations at Constantinople. The British news reporter wrote: 'Golaum Alley Beg [Tipu's envoy] died in that country and another man returned having accomplished his means [sic] and he also procured from the Sultan the title of king and permission to hold [sic] a mint and to have the Khutba read in his name'.[28] This caused a great stir in political circles in India and efforts were made to prove that Tipu's claim was baseless. The British recognized that recognition of Tipu's independence was a source of great danger. It was felt that 'people will begin to consider his usurped title of king as derived from an authority held respectable among Mohamedans'.[29]

Why were the British so upset by this recognition? The reasons were obvious. The old Mughal Emperor could be bought off: they could go on increasing their power without arousing the suspicion and fear of the Muslims who were continuously administered the illusion that the English were after all the servants of their Emperor. Sultan Tipu provided a new nucleus for Muslim resistance—conscious of the fact that the English were stealing the sceptre from the hands of the effete Mughal court. This was the plea which Tipu had advanced for his attitude towards the English as well as the Emperor.[30] If Tipu succeeded in rousing the Muslims, the British would have to face much greater difficulties in subjugating India. Besides, Tipu's letters were drawing the attention of the Muslim powers in India. What was more, he had schemes of cooperation in political and economic spheres which would create a new hindrance for the British because it was Tipu's suggestion that Muslim countries should have trade relations, factory establishments, new arms and naval power.[31] An independent, live centre of Islamic renaissance in India could not suit British interests.

Hitherto religious feeling could have been aroused against Tipu by branding him a rebel, a destroyer of the unity of the Mughal Empire. But the Sultan of Turkey had a better right to recognize the position of Tipu, because the Empire of Turkey still enjoyed great prestige as the foremost political power of Islam in spite of its decay. The Sultan claimed to be the Caliph of the Muslim world. It is true that the Mughal Emperors claimed to be Caliphs in their own dominions but the Turkish Sultans were the 'servants of the sacred shrines' and they had been given that office by the House of Abbas. The Nizam could no longer harp on his legal superiority, because the Sultan of Mysore now had a better title to his kingdom than the viceroy of the Deccan to his viceroyalty. It is not surprising, therefore, that the English decided to crush Tipu and directed all their attention to his destruction. The Sultan's ideas were dangerous: hence Wellesley's high-handed treatment of him even when he had ceased to be an effective power. In the light of these factors one understands the jubilation over the fall of Tipu Sultan and the systematic propaganda against that brave, pious and high-souled martyr which English historians employ to hide British iniquity and intrigue.

Notes and References

[1] Sec. Cons., 3, 5 Jan. 1787. 'Firmaunds' is a corruption of *farman*.

[2] Ibid.

[3] 'The value of the prize for which they (the English) were competing was even then perfectly known'. Sir Alfred Lyall, *The Rise and Expansion of the British Dominion in India*, (1919 ed.), p. 19.

[4] Cons., 18 Jan. 1783.

[5] O.R. III, Tr. 14.

[6] Ibid.

[7] Intelligence received 18 Dec. 1782.

[8] Sec. Cons. 9, 12 Nov. 1787, Intelligence received from Malharjee at Hyderabad, 21 Sept. 1787.

[9] Sec. Cons. 17, 2 Oct. 1787.

[10] *Cambridge History of India*, Vol. V, pp. 275, 276.

[11] Sec. Cons. 7, 12 Nov. 1787.

[12] For a full discussion of this question, see Indian Historical Records Commission Proceedings, Jan. 1942, Pt. II, pp. 301–3 (D.S. Achuta Rau, Haidar Ali, His Relations with the Crown').

[13] O.R.112 Persian Records, Letter from Nawab Nizam Ali Khan to Nawab Basalat Jang.

[14] O.R. 9, Persian Records.

[15] Sec. Cons. 10, 12 Nov. 1787, Letter from the Nizam to Mons. Consigny.

[16] O.R. 86, 88 (Persian records).

[17] O.R. 88.

[18] O.R. 93.

[19] O.R. 84.
[20] O.R. 84.
[21] O.R. 92.
[22] O.R. 86.
[23] *Calendar of Persian Correspondence*, Vol. VII, p. 8.
[24] Sec. Cons., 23 May 1787, No. 9.
[25] Letter from Mir Muhammad Hussain, received 21 June 1787, No. 42.
[26] Zaman Shah's letter to Tipu Sultan and Tipu Sultan's letter to Karim Khan Zand, included in various histories of the period; see *Tarikh-i-Saltanat-i-Khudadad*, pp. 554–58.
[27] Salim's letter to Tipu Sultan included in W. Kirkpatrick and in *Tarikh-i-Saltanat-i-Khudadad*.
[28] Mir Muhammad Hussain's letter received 21 June 1787.
[29] Sec. Cons., 12 Nov. 1787, No. 9.
[30] Letters to Sultan Salim and other Muslim monarchs.
[31] Ibid.

9
Relations between Travancore and Mysore in the Eighteenth Century

A.P. Ibrahim Kunju

aking the cue from English political and military writers of the period, even Indian writers have generally held that the Mysorean invasion of Travancore was an unwarranted act of hostility. But if we look closely into the records of the period, it will be clear that the activities of the king of Travancore were so provocative that it is a wonder that the Mysorean rulers actually invaded Travancore only as late as 1790.

From the time Haidar invaded the petty kingdoms of northern Kerala, his one aim was the subjugation of the whole west coast. It would not only have strengthened his position by providing him with the facilities of the western ports but also secured for him the more vulnerable western flank of his dominions. After his conquest of the Malabar kingdoms and the submission of Cochin, only Travancore remained outside the Mysorean political orbit. Consequently, the subjugation of Travancore was one of the major objectives of Haidar.

From the very moment of the conquest of the Malabar kingdoms, Travancore had loomed large in the political settlement of the area as it had given shelter to the dispossessed chieftains of Malabar. These chiefs not only had a haven of refuge in Travancore, but they used Travancore as a safe base of operations against the Mysorean rule in Malabar. When the Mysorean army concentrations were withdrawn from Malabar, the rebels returned from Travancore and created fresh troubles. The help rendered to these rebels against the Mysorean government was thus a standing complaint of Haidar against Travancore. In helping these rebels against Mysore 'the Raja of Travancore was not only animated by a generous desire to help the refugees, but he recognized their political value in creating trouble for Mysore forces, if Haidar Ali should try to carry out his own design of attacking Travancore. The Mysore generals also realized that their hold on Kerala would never be safe so long as Travancore provided an asylum for the dispossessed chiefs.'[1] Therefore Haidar was determined to bring Travancore under Mysorean control by any means. But his attempts to bring about this desired end were thwarted by the several wars in which he was engaged with the English, the Nizam and the Marathas.

Meanwhile Rama Varma, the king of Travancore, was actively assisting the enemies of Haidar to overthrow his power. He continued to incite rebellions in Malabar, through the dispossessed chieftains. He also gave free passage to English troops through Travancore in 1778 to attack the French port of Mahé, which was under Haidar's protection. The Madras Select Committee wrote to the Court of Directors on 13 March 1779: 'The Raja of Travancore afforded the troops sent to attack Mahé a free passage through his country and amply supplied them with provisions.'[2]

During the Second Anglo–Mysore War, the Travancore Raja assisted the English troops in their march through Travancore to attack Mysorean possessions in Malabar. Regarding this affair Van Angelbeck, the Dutch Commandeur at Cochin, wrote to the Raja of Cochin: 'It is understood that the Senior Raja of Travancore is inclined to send his own men, along with the English soldiers who had arrived from Tinnevelly, to the north and reinstate the chiefs of the Zamorin's country. We trust that he will not do so.... If the chiefs of the Zamorin's country are assisted, it is certain that he and his subjects will suffer greatly through the hostility of Nawab Haidar Ali to the Trppappur Svarupam. Even for his alliance with the English, the Nawab is greatly incensed at the Raja.'[3]

The Raja of Travancore was aware that he was courting the hostility of Haidar Ali by actively assisting his enemies. Realizing that sooner or later Haidar would attack Travancore, he prepared for resistance by strengthening the Travancore Lines. He sought closer ties of friendship with the English and assisted them in their endeavours to overthrow the power of Haidar. During the Second Anglo–Mysore War, the Raja sent two battalions of sepoys in support of the English army under Colonel Macleod at Ponnani. It was their assistance that saved him from the desperate position at Ponnani, and later made it possible for him to penetrate to Bidnur and thereby save the Carnatic.

In view of these commendable services to the Company, the Bombay Government instructed the Peace Commissioners to Tipu to insist upon including the Raja of Travancore as the ally of the Company. Consequently, the Raja of Travancore was included as a 'friend and ally to the English' in the Treaty of Mangalore (11 March 1784), and Tipu engaged himself not to 'make war upon the friends or allies of the English'.

To secure his country further from a possible invasion by Tipu, Rama Varma strengthened the northern defences of his country. With the connivance of the Raja of Cochin, Rama Varma seems to have tried to extend the Travancore Lines into the Vaipin Island by constructing an earthen outwork and bastions and it was the opposition of the Dutch that prevented the design. For we find the Dutch Commandeur at Cochin protesting to the Raja of Cochin against the attempted extension of the Lines by men of the Raja of Travancore.[4]

After the death of Haidar, the Raja of Travancore continued to assist the Malabar chieftains against Mysore. Tipu repeatedly warned the Raja against assisting his enemies. But these warnings were unceremoniously rejected. This attitude of defiance was probably the outcome of the promise of assistance which the Raja had received from the Madras Government. In 1788, the Raja had agreed to pay for the maintenance of two battalions of the Company's native infantry, in view of the threatening attitude of Tipu. It was provided in the agreement that should any additional force be required to meet the designs of an enemy, it was to be furnished at the Company's cost. With this promised support, Rama Varma cast prudence to the winds and began to egg on the dispossessed Malabar chieftains to create disturbances in Malabar.

Tipu came to believe that the activities of the Raja of Travancore were a menace to the security of his possessions in Malabar. He felt that it was the Travancore Lines that were creating over much confidence in the mind of the Raja of Travancore. Therefore Tipu demanded the demolition of that part of the Lines which were erected in Cochin territory. He contended that the Lines cut him off from two-thirds of the Cochin territory which lay to their south. But Rama Varma refused to comply with the demand on the grounds that the Lines had been constructed some twenty-five years earlier and before the Raja of Cochin became tributary to Mysore.[5]

Besides his refusal to demolish the Lines, the Raja of

Travancore further provoked Tipu by purchasing the two Dutch forts of Cranganore and Ayakkotta. Ayakkotta is situated on the northern extremity of the Vaipin Island, and 2½ miles to the north-east, on the mainland stands the fort of Cranganore. These two forts being strategically important to his possessions in Malabar, Tipu had been negotiating with the Dutch for their purchase. When the Raja of Travancore came to know of these negotiations, he decided to acquire them for himself. He asked the advice of the Madras Government regarding the purchase. Sir Archibald Campbell, who was then Governor of Madras, dissuaded him from entering into the transaction. Similarly Hollond, the succeeding Governor, also urged the Raja 'to be extremely cautious in his conduct during the present critical situation and on no account afford Tippoo Sultan a pretext for invading Travancore country.'[6] But this piece of advice was unheeded, and the Raja began secret negotiations for the purchase of the two forts. When this news reached the ears of Hollond, he instructed Powney, the English Resident at the court of Travancore, to dissuade the Raja from 'making purchases from the Dutch of lands and forts which they hold under the Raja of Cochin, a tributary of Tippoo, as likely to have the appearance in the eyes of that Chief, of collusive transaction', and to warn the Raja that 'the Government of Madras would not support him in any contest in which he might engage, beyond the limits of his own possessions'.[7] But before this letter reached the Raja, he had concluded the agreement for the purchase of the two forts, on 31 July 1789, for three lakhs of 'Surati' rupees.

On receipt of the news of the purchase of the two forts, Hollond wrote to the Raja reprimanding him: 'I cannot approve of your having entered into a treaty with the Dutch for the extension of the territory without the consent of this Government. This very impolitic conduct makes you liable for forfeiture of the Company's protection; for you cannot expect that they will defend a territory of which you were not possessed when their troops were sent into your country, and which have since been obtained without their assent.' The Raja was asked to return the forts in question to the Dutch so that the *status quo ante* might be restored. Even Lord Cornwallis wrote, strongly disapproving the conduct of the Raja and observed, 'Should he provoke Tippoo by making. collusive purchase of forts or places in the territories of one of his tributaries ... he will justly draw Tippoo's

82

resentment upon himself and at the same time forfeit all right to the Company's friendship or interference in his favour.'[8]

Rama Varma, who was greatly upset by these developments, tried to justify his action. He wrote on 3 September 1789 that Sir Archibald Campbell had approved his plan of purchasing the forts, that he had ascertained before purchasing the forts that the Dutch held them independently of the Cochin Raja and that they were essential for the security of his country.

But none of these assertions were correct. When the claim about his approval of the purchase of the forts was referred to Sir Archibald Campbell, he denied it, saying: 'When Major Bannerman signified to me that the Island of Jayacottah which the Dutch were inclined to dispose of to the Raja, appeared to him to be the fittest situation for a cantonment on the northern frontier of Travancore country, and gave various reasons in support of it, I differed entirely from him in that opinion.'[9]

Secondly, the assertion that the Dutch were in independent possession of the two forts is not correct. It is true that the Dutch conquered the two forts from the Portuguese, but the Portuguese used to pay tribute to the Raja of Cochin for these possessions.[10] Therefore the Dutch had no independent possession over them. What is more surprising is that, in spite of his assertion that he had enquired about the title of the Dutch to sell the forts previous to the purchase, the Raja of Travancore made enquiries in this regard only afterwards. We find in a letter of 23 December 1789, the Raja enquiring of the Commandeur at Cochin details regarding the Dutch rights over the place.[11] It is obvious therefore that the Raja started these enquiries only after Lord Cornwallis instructed the Government of Madras to enquire into the title of the Dutch Company to part with these forts in question.

Thirdly, that the sale of the two forts to the Raja of Travancore was a collusive act between the Dutch and the Raja, is clear from the letters which the Raja of Travancore wrote to the Dutch Commandeur at Cochin. In a letter received at Cochin on 25 July 1789, the Raja wrote: 'We have sent Kesava Pillai there to impress upon the Admiral the necessity to do the needful in the interests of both parties in the matter of Cranganore and Munampam (Ayakkotta). As long as these two places are in the possession of the Company, the Nawab (Tipu) will proceed against them, instead of against us. Without Tipu proceeding against us our ally, the English Company, may not move in the matter. If these two places are in our possession, he (Tipu) will not proceed against them; even if he proceeds (against them), the English will proceed against him on the ground that he had broken the treaty with them. It is on this account that we are writing to the Admiral.'[12] It is clear from this letter that the transfer of the two forts was designed to involve the English in a war with Tipu.

Thus it is clear that Tipu had sufficient cause for an invasion of Travancore. When he found that a peaceful accommodation of the points at issue was not possible the Mysorean troops were moved to the vicinity of the Travancore Lines, in the hope that it would induce the Raja to make an accommodation. On the night of 28 December the Mysorean troops are said to have attacked the Lines at Melur and carried a considerable portion. The Travancore troops retreated until they reached a square enclosure, where they checked the advance of the enemy. When reinforcements arrived they attacked the Mysorean forces from the right and left and compelled them to retreat with heavy losses.

This incident has been exaggerated by English historians as a 'wanton attack' by Tipu upon Travancore. Tipu described it as a frontier incident and disavowed any knowledge of it. The Madras Government itself regarded it only as a 'minor affair and not regular hostilities'.[13] But historians have taken it for granted that Tipu himself was present during the action and in the course of the panicky retreat, he fell into the ditch and received severe contusions on the leg which occasioned 'the lameness which occasionally continued until his death.'[14] On reaching the camp, he is said to have sworn in a paroxysm of humiliation and rage that he would not quit the place until he carried 'this contemptible wall'. His palanquin, his seals, rings and personal ornaments fell as trophies into the hands of the enemy.[15] But these accounts are based on hearsay only. There is no reliable evidence to prove either that Tipu had taken part in the attack or that he received any injuries which lamed him for life. With regard to the trophies of war reported to have been captured by the Travancore troops, the Travancore Records mention only two stands of colours and one small bell.[16]

When Tipu found that peaceful accommodation of the differences between himself and the Raja of Travancore was not possible, he decided to coerce him into submission. From 12 April, the

Mysoreans began a regular cannonade of the Lines, as a result of which a considerable portion of it was carried. The Travancore troops became panic-stricken and fled. All attempts to rally them failed. The auxiliary force provided by the Company took no part in the fighting, on the plea that they had received no instructions. Finding themselves too weak to hold their position at Cranganore, they retired to Ayakkotta. The Mysorean forces immediately occupied the Cranganore fort and razed the Lines to the ground. They overran Travancore territory up to the northern bank of the Periyar.

As soon as the 'frontier incident' was brought to their notice, the Supreme Government issued explicit orders to the Madras Government that the incident was tantamount to a declaration of war against the Company and, therefore, war must be declared on Tipu. By that time, the negotiations for a coalition against Tipu initiated by the English with the Nizam and the Marathas had proved successful, with the result that the English were confident of victory in any coming struggle. Lord Cornwallis wrote to Meadows, the Governor of Madras, in March 1790; 'At present we have every prospect of aid from the country powers, while he (Tipu) can expect no assistance from France.'[17] Thus, the Governor-General felt that this was the most favourable opportunity for enhancing his country's 'honour' and promoting its 'interest'. Taking Tipu's attack on the Travancore Lines as a pretext, he declared war against Mysore in May 1790. To protect his country from the threatened invasion, Tipu withdrew from Travancore on 24 May. The rest of the story is too familiar to require narration at length.

Notes and References

[1] K.M. Panikkar, *A History of Kerala*, 1960, p. 348.
[2] Quoted in ibid., p. 363.
[3] Cochin State Records, Van Angelbeck's Letter to the Cochin Raja, dated 1 Feb. 1782. Misc. Corr. List., LXII, No. 17.
[4] Ibid., No. 31.
[5] Military Cons., 1 Jan. 1790, Vol. 133A, p. 5.
[6] Military Cons., 26 May 1789, Vol. 129C., pp. 1447–48.
[7] Ibid., 28 Aug. 1789, Vol. 131A, pp. 2373–75.
[8] Ibid., 29 Sept. 1789, Vol. 131B., pp. 2659–61.
[9] Panikkar, *Kerala*, p. 374.
[10] Misc. Corr., List., LXIA., No. 10.
[11] Kozhikode Collectorate Records, Vol. III, No. 47.

[12] Ibid., No. 44.
[13] Military Desp. to Court of Directors, 16 Sept. 1790, Vol. 20, p. 69.
[14] Wilks, *History of Mysore*, Vol. II, p. 145.
[15] Ibid.
[16] Matilakam Records, Churuna, 1308, pp. 154–56.
[17] Pol. Proceedings, Cons., No. 4.

10

Tipu Sultan's Projected Confederacy against the British, 1790

N. Kasturi

In 1779, Haidar Ali of Mysore built up a 'terrible confederacy' with the help of the Nizam and all the Maratha chieftains, except the Gaekwar of Baroda, to destroy British power in India—a calamity that was averted by the Treaty of Salbai (May 1782) and the Treaty of Mangalore, with Haidar's son, Tipu Sultan, in March 1784.

That treaty was never accepted as final by Tipu who was even more ambitious than his father and, as yet, lacked the chastening influence of misfortune. In a letter to the Padshah at Delhi on 23 June 1785, he writes, 'This steadfast believer with a view to the support of the firm religion of Mahomed, undertook some time since the chastisement of the Nazarene tribe, who unable to maintain the war waged against them, solicited peace of me in the most abject manner.... With Divine aid and blessing of God, it is now again my steady determination to set about the total extirpation and destruction of the enemies of the faith.'[1] From the palsied hands of His Imperial Majesty, the Mughal Emperor, Tipu solicited mandatory letters calling upon the Nizam and other Muslim chiefs of the Deccan to join him in the Holy War.

Nizam Ali Khan, the Subedar of the Deccan, was in no mood, in 1785, to listen to these calls for a confederacy. He was disposed to ally himself with the Marathas in another campaign against Mysore, to keep the unruly upstart from crossing the Tungabhadra. He sent an army, late in 1785, under Mushir-ul-Mulk, Mughal Ali and Sham Sher Jang to cooperate with the Marathas in the defence of Badami, Adoni, Nirgund and other forts; but, as a result, it is said, of Tipu's timely bribe of Rs 20,000, Mushir abandoned Adoni and retreated to the North. The Marathas, thereupon, concluded a separate treaty with

Mysore, by which they received thirty lakhs of rupees in cash and the promise of another fifteen lakhs, after a year. As Colonel Read writes, 'The Marathas rather regarded the Nizam as an auxiliary vassal that demanded their protection than in the light of a respectable ally.'[2] He was justly exasperated at this breach of diplomatic etiquette and harboured strong resentment against the 'Brahmins' of Poona.

The Guntoor Circar affair, long a thorn in the side of the Nizam, also became more alarming at this time. The territory was of great importance to him as the only outlet to the sea; it was equally valuable to the English, who had acquired a contingent right over it by the Treaty of 1768, because it lay between Madras and the Northern Circars. The Nizam was striving his utmost to retain the Circars, and even Lord Cornwallis wrote to Dundas, on 5 March 1787: 'The Business of the Guntoor Circars is a very delicate one and requires the most mature reflection. There are several reasons which make it very doubtful whether this would be a proper time for us to call on the Nizam to settle accounts and to deliver it up.... Our demand of the Circars from the Nizam in the hour of his distress would not only appear ungenerous, but would undoubtedly hurt him in the negotiations for a peace with Tippoo.'[3] In spite of this, early in 1788, Captain Kennaway was sent from Calcutta to Hyderabad with instructions that, if he found the atmosphere not propitious for the demand of the Circars, he should, 'instead of declaring the real object of your mission, confine yourself to the general expressions of friendship and assurances of our earnest desire to cultivate a good understanding between the two Governments.' Captain Kennaway did not discover anything unfavourable and, when he pressed for the cession, the Guntoor Circars were peaceably and quietly 'delivered up to the servants of the Company'.[4]

Colonel Alexander Read, who was watching on behalf of the Company the vicissitudes of native powers in the Deccan and writing instructive reports to the Governor of Madras, had advised against this step. He had written: 'It will be mortifying to his pride to part with it as calling to his and his people's recollection the great change of affairs in the Deccan since the death of Nizam-ul-mulk'.[5] According to Kirmani[6] this colonel, the Darogha of the Intelligence Department, had an uncanny way of 'discovering the secret intrigues of the country powers by sending clever spies and able moonshis at great expense'. Among his papers, collected in the Mackenzie *Mss* Vol. 46, there is much evidence of the nervousness with which the Guntoor affair was broached and the warnings which Colonel Read himself thought fit to administer. He says: 'I believe it is a received opinion among the Princes of India that we have a desire to enfeeble every power in connection with us and that consequently every one who is tenacious of his independency is wary in trusting to our support.'[7] 'If aroused by danger or a sense of honour, we do not know what he (the Nizam) would do.' Nizam Ali Khan, now more or less in the same mood as in 1779, began negotiations with Tipu Sultan. Colonel Read says that the 'Nizam was desirous to get back his lost possessions; dissatisfied with the Marathas; jealous of the English and in dread of Tipu.' Ambassadors were sent to Seringapatam in the strictest secrecy, ostensibly from the Nizam's brother-in-law Imtiaz-ud-daulah, but really to negotiate a treaty. They reached Tipu's capital in November 1787.

Tipu also wrote: 'My father, Hyder Ally Khan, gave many proofs of his friendship for Your Highness. It is sufficient to remind you of those he manifested during the Carnatic War, in which Your Highness was engaged and since that period, in being the principal cause of the English restoring to Your Highness the Guntoor Circar. I am sorry to observe that you seem to have forgotten those services, when without provocation you joined the infidel Marathas, invaded my country and desolated the land of Mussalmans. Notwithstanding such treatment, my reducing Adoni has been my only retaliation. But, let the past be lost in oblivion, both on account of the union that as true Mussalmans ought to subsist between us and of the last advice given me by the Nawab (who has received mercy). I am desirous of entering into a firm alliance with Your Highness and, to show how earnest I am in it, request you will appoint a time and place for a personal conference that all matters relating to our respective interests may be taken into consideration and a treaty concluded for our mutual advantage.'[8]

It is significant also that the embassies from Hyderabad were ostensibly from Imtiaz-ud-daulah, because one of the articles of the treaty by which an offensive and defensive alliance was formed, stipulated that the daughter of the Nizam's sister (married to Imtiaz-ud-daulah) should be given in marriage to Tipu Sultan. In another place, Colonel Read says that the embassy, on their return, brought a casket of jewels for the intended bride, there mentioned as the daughter of the Nizam. Kirmani, too, is not very definite whether a niece or a daughter was indicated, for he speaks merely of 'the mention of a matrimonial connection'.[9] There were comings and goings for months therefore, and Colonel Read writes that for about two years there were constant rumours of the matrimonial alliance, as the basis of a political confederacy.

Meanwhile, discussions proceeded apace and it was agreed that Tipu was to restore to the Nizam all the territory in his possession that appertained to the Deccan in the time of Nizam-ul-Mulk. 'It was even said that, in consequence of this, the Mutsaddies of the Revenue Department were actually employed in drawing out an account of the countries that were formerly under the Subah's jurisdiction. All differences which subsisted between His Highness and Tipu Sultan have been accommodated and friendship established, by Hafiz Fariduddin.'[10]

Tipu also evinced a desire to include the Marathas in the alliance, and the Nizam himself was found by Colonel Read sending Sooraji Pandit, the Poona Vakil at Hyderabad, with a letter to Nana Fadnavis 'to prevail on the Pant Pradhan to enter into a conference with His Highness, Tipu Sultan and the French against the English'. Nana Fadnavis, at that time embroiled in complications between Sindhia and Holkar in the north, was inclined 'to dissemble with Tipu', and shared 'a disposition to promote his views on the supposed Confederacy as a likely means to preserve peace with him'. Nana Fadnavis must have thought that this was a good enough way of keeping up the struggle against the English, for, as he wrote in a letter to Madhava Rao Sindhia, his sentiments were: 'We must not only insist on the reparation of our wrongs but we must try to recover that part of the Carnatic of conquests of the great Shivaji which is now occupied by the English'.[11]

Tipu, therefore, ordered the Maratha Vakils and Hafiz Fariduddin Khan to attend him at Coonattoor and, about the middle of September 1789, Colonel Read was able to report that the basis of the negotiations there, though strictly confidential, was the following:

1. A firm and lasting union between Nizam Ali Khan and Tipu Sultan in all matters in which they mutually engage for the good of their two States.

2. His Highness to join Tipu in a war against Marathas, at any time that nation shall oppose their views.

3. The Guntoor Circar to be made over to Tipu for the usual rent and His Highness to break all connection with the English.

4. His Highness to give his daughter to Tipu's son in marriage.

Besides this, a truce was agreed upon with the Marathas for a period of three years and six months. Colonel Read wrote on 15 September 1789 that Shivaji Rao, the Maratha Vakil, was in Tipu's camp and that it was currently reported that the Marathas had entered into engagements to assist Tipu in the event of war with the English. This engagement was further corroborated by the discovery by Colonel Read of the following events. (mentioned in his despatch dated 4 January 1790). 'The Wallajah (Nawab of Arcot) has sent an agent to Poona to persuade the Marathas to invade Tipu's country, to which the minister has replied that they have made a treaty for three years and three months with the Sultan and could not, without breaking their engagements, commit hostilities against him.'[12] Colonel Read also gives evidence to show that some Mysore Sowcars proceeded to Poona with money to enlist 30,000 Maratha horsemen and that they were encouraged by the friendly disposition of the Poona Government.

Meanwhile, the Nizam had other irons, too, in the fire and was awaiting replies from other capitals. He had sent an Amir to the Wallajah asking him to suggest the likeliest means of getting Guntoor back from the English. He had despatched Abdul Cassim (Qasim) to Calcutta to negotiate for substantial financial payments (if not the surrender of the Circars) and for positive military help. And, indolently, he awaited the turn of events. Lord Cornwallis had written on 7 July 1789 very favourably on both issues promising him two battalions of sepoys and six pieces of cannon manned by Europeans whenever he wanted to employ force against Tipu Sultan. This letter liberated him from all fear on his Southern Frontier and gave him also a respectable rent from the Guntoor Circars. Malet, the British ambassador at Poona, also strove hard against the formation of the new Confederacy and corrected the impression of duplicity that Lord Cornwallis had given, when, as soon as he assumed office, he had cancelled his predecessor's offer of three battalions of British troops.[13]

Tipu's Vakils at Hyderabad were given a rather cold audience on 2 January 1790, and they were sent back in April of that year, 'without any apparent mark of friendship from the Nizam'. They also carried with them a definite refusal, in rather insulting terms, of the marriage proposal. Kirmani is very touched by this rebuff and he writes, 'Considering the term Naik which belonged to the Sultan's forefathers as discreditable and relationship with him a disgrace, according to the advice of his foolish women, he [the Nizam] turned his face aside from the true path.... Good God! Is it possible that on the strength of worldly power and distinction, low fellows boast of their noble descent and men of the dregs of the people, falsely claim to be Shaikhs and Syeds and consider no one equal to themselves. "Low birth is hidden by wealth and station!" "The Golden Veil conceals the ugliness of the old courtesan!"'[14]

Meanwhile, by his attack on Travancore, Tipu had invited the wrath of the Company on his head and Lord Cornwallis had, by conciliation and compromise, gathered together once again the broken threads of diplomacy. On 5 July 1790, a treaty of offensive and defensive alliance was concluded between the Company, the Marathas and the Nizam. Tipu could vent his wrath against his Muslim brother on the Hyderabad throne only by insulting references to him in letters as Hajam Ali, instead of Nizam Ali and by painting a detestable animal, beneath the picture drawn by order of his father, of the Nizam marching with the Mysore troops in the old days of 1780! To-day on the walls of the Daria Daulat Bagh Mansion on our right as we enter, we can see the pathetic perpetuation of Tipu's wrath, at the break-up of his projected Confederacy.

Notes and References

[1] Kirkpatrick, *Letters of Tippu Sultan*. No. LXXI.
[2] Mackenzie, MS No. 46, India Office Library, p. 51.
[3] Ross, *Cornwallis Correspondence*, Vol. I, p. 252.
[4] Briggs, *Nizam*, Vol. I, Appendix, p. 251.
[5] Mackenzie, MS No. 46, p. 62.
[6] Kirmani, *Nishan-i Haidari*, trs. Miles, p. 174.
[7] Ibid., p. 58.
[8] Ibid., p. 53.
[9] Ibid., p. 149.
[10] Ibid., p. 55.
[11] Kincaid and Parasnis, Vol. III, App. A, p. 141.
[12] Ibid., p. 119.
[13] Ross, Vol. I, p. 22.
[14] Kirmani, *Nishan-i Haidari*, pp. 149–51.

11

The French and the Third Mysore War: Testimony of the Mauritius Records

B. Sheik Ali

Threre are certain records relative to Tipu Sultan in the Archives of Port Louis, Mauritius. He, being desirous of securing foreign aid, was actively in correspondence with the French authorities both in India and overseas. The records in Mauritius which reveal the French policy towards the Third Mysore War consist of the letter of Cossigny to the Governor of Pondicherry, de Fresne, dated 28 April 1791, and the reply of Governor Cossigny to two letters of Tipu dated 7 June 1791, one addressed to the French commander at Pondicherry and the other to Tipu directly.

Despite the fact that Tipu had strongly urged the French to assist him in the war, they remained neutral. According to these records, he had initiated a war against the English at a wrong moment. Cossigny wrote to de Fresne, 'The Prince is badly counselled but he will take profit to good advice that we will give him.'[1] The advice the French gave to Tipu was to win over the Marathas at all costs. The French Governor at the Isle of France urged him neither to spare money nor energy in dissolving the Confederacy. Tipu had written him two letters requesting for a force of 5,000 troops.[2] In reply Tipu received a letter dated 7 June 1791 which said, 'Do not engage in big battles, but attack your enemies as often as possible to fatigue them. Do not allow them to have food or *fodder*.... Write to the Marathas and the Nizam; tell them your interests, that your enemies are also theirs.... The time has come to get rid of all those enemies. Otherwise they would put all the princes in jail as they have done before.... Make big monetary sacrifices, trust in what I tell you.... What is the use of money?... I hope your fame will surpass your father's. Your father showed the way to Delhi. It is for you to go there and show yourself full of glory to the whole of Asia.'[3]

The French Governor thus evaded the main issue of assistance to Tipu and indulged in advising him that no efforts should be spared to win over the Nizam and the Marathas. Tipu was informed that the French were also doing their best to disengage the two other Indian powers from the coalition. 'I have got news from the Marathas and Nizam Ali Khan. I answered them according to your interests.'[4] The Governor did not categorically refuse to help either. He mentioned: 'The French are making big preparations of war since one year. I cannot now tell you everything about it but be sure that they (the French) have understood what you told me.'[5]

The reason given in these records for the evasive policy of the French is their awareness of the fact that Cornwallis commanded the resources of three Presidencies besides those of his confederates. Even though they were conscious of the military abilities of Tipu, the two sides were greatly unequal. Cossigny wrote (28 April 1791) about Tipu, 'He is quite intelligent and knows quite a lot of things, but he is ambitious and longs for glory. He is quite gifted for war and takes his position in a country he knows very well. He works hard and detests pleasure. This is quite all right, but Cornwallis also is a big man and he has gathered at this instance the strength of four Presidencies. It is very much against the prince who has recently established his power, who is more feared than loved and who is of a different religion from most of his subjects. In his position I think he must be afraid to commit his fort to the hazard of a battle.'[6]

These were the considerations that weighed with the French, seeking to avoid entanglement in the war. They knew that Tipu would lose the war and they did not like to join the losing side. Hence the only solution they thought of was to urge Tipu to detach his Indian neighbours from the war at all costs. They did not think that it was a very difficult task; according to them, the dissolution of a confederacy was quite an ordinary Indian trick.[7]

Another cause of French indifference towards Tipu was their belief that he was not very keen on securing their aid. Cossigny felt that Tipu knew the French position well and that he had nevertheless made a request for help only to frighten the Marathas and the Nizam. He wrote (7 June 1791) 'In a way, I am sure that he (Tipu) does not positively expect such help, and since I know the politics of the Sarkar of Tipu, I think he has dictated those letters with emphasis in his darbar and copies of them must have been sent to the Marathas and the Nizam and to all other Indian princes. If it was otherwise, it would be a big mistake to imagine that the demand would be so easy to execute.'[8] Therefore the French authorities at Mauritius did not expressly deny the help but replied that they had reported to their superiors at Paris and that there was some hope that the French King would consent to his request.[9] Cossigny wrote to Tipu, 'If I get some orders, I will not lose any time, but it is impossible for me to leave the post which is entrusted to me. Though there are some troops in Mauritius, I cannot dispose of them at my own will. Moreover, the difficulty of the transport of troops over such a long distance prevents me from taking any positive step.'[10] Tipu was further informed: 'You must be sure that one cannot prepare for the war in a day. If the king were to act very quickly, the forces could not be sent before one year. Until that time resist the English and make sacrifices to win over the Marathas to your side.'[11] But the progress of the revolutionary upsurge in France did not permit these promises to be fulfilled and Tipu was later informed that the French would remain neutral.

Notes and References

[1] Cossigny's letter to the Governor of Pondicherry, No. 93, Series A, Vol. 8, 34.

[2] Ibid.

[3] Cossigny's letter to Tipu Sultan, 7 June 1791, No. 101, Series A.

[4] Ibid.

[5] Ibid.

[6] Cossigny to de Fresne, dated 28 April 1791, No. 93, Series A, Vol 8.

[7] Ibid.

[8] Cossigny to de Fresne, dated 7 June 1791, No. 98, Series A, Vol. 8.

[9] Ibid.

[10] Ibid., No. 101.

[11] Ibid.

12
Tipu Sultan and Sir John Shore

B. Sheik Ali

Sir John Shore, who succeeded Cornwallis, was interested in the conservation of the Company's power and not in its extension. He was guided in his policy by the Charter Act of 1793 which stipulated: 'To pursue schemes of conquest and extension of dominions in India are declared to be measures repugnant to the wish, honour and policy of the nation.'[1] The affairs of the Company were well settled at this time with its vast resources, sound finances, devoted allies, humbled enemies and disciplined forces. As for Tipu Sultan, it was a period of preparation for his last struggle. He utilized the time between 1792 and 1798 in repairing the ravages of the Third Mysore War. Apparently the two powers were on friendly terms but in reality the deep-seated suspicions and jealousies were not removed. The English were aware that Tipu was secretly preparing for a war to recover his losses. Cornwallis had already taken precautions, thinking that Tipu had not reconciled himself to the humiliations of 1792. Immediately after the departure of the allies from Srirangapatam, the Governor-General tried to conclude a general Treaty of Guarantee against Tipu for the defence of the new acquisitions. It stipulated that if Tipu attacked unprovoked any of the confederates, the other two should join to punish him. This treaty aimed at keeping Tipu in perpetual isolation but it was never signed as it excited the jealousy of the Marathas. The secret negotiations of Cornwallis offended Tipu and destroyed the chances of any possible Anglo–Mysore accord. The English further offended him by the forcible occupation of Wynaad, contrary to the terms of the Treaty of Srirangapatam. Its strategic situation and rich plantations prompted Cornwallis not to surrender it, despite Tipu's repeated protests and clear stipulation in the Treaty. Even the Bombay Government admitted the justice of Tipu's claims but the Governor-General refused to surrender it. Wynaad was not the only place thus denied to Tipu. Corrumbala, Amara and Sulya were also unjustly retained by the English. When Tipu strongly protested against the British breach of faith, a commission was appointed to enquire into the matter. Even after the Commissioners established the claim of Tipu to Amara and Sulya, the English did not restore them on the plea that they were already in the possession of the Coorg Raja.

This was the state of affairs at the time Sir John Shore succeeded to power. His first act of importance on assuming office was the restoration of the Mysore princes held as hostages to Tipu. In March 1794 they returned to Mysore accompanied by Captain Doveton. The next step was to fix the English policy towards the Malabar chiefs and their relations with Tipu. The situation was getting tense over the question of Wynaad and Corrumbala. Sir John would neither restore the places to Tipu nor would he specifically declare his real intentions. As a compromise, he framed a policy of four points.[1] Firstly the Company was not to assert its own indisputable right over the two districts, Wynaad and Corrumbala, which might force a rupture with Tipu. Secondly, if Corrumbala was occupied by Tipu's officers with his sanction, no opposition was to be made. Thirdly, if they proceeded beyond the limits of these two districts, the English should interfere and repel them. Lastly, if Tipu's officers without his knowledge committed predatory incursions, Tipu was to be informed of their conduct. Accordingly, instructions were issued to the Bombay Government warning them not to offend Tipu by asserting the Company's claim to the districts. He confessed that the Company's claim was so weak that the Nizam and the Marathas would not be sufficiently convinced to support it in case of war.

Politics in the Deccan underwent a great change after 1795 which helped Tipu to play an important part. The defeat of the Nizam, the humiliating convention of Kurdlah, the death of the young Peshwa Madava Rao II, and the consequent war of succession, helped Tipu to revive his power. The old Triple Alliance was completely broken. Sir John Shore declined to support the Nizam either against Tipu over the question of Kurnool and in his ill-fated war against the Marathas. His policy towards Tipu was not to provoke a war with him but to remain prepared if it became inevitable. He did not expect that Tipu would

take the offensive: 'The defalcation of his territories and the depriva-
tion of his property will impose silence on his resentment and restraint
upon his ambition.'[2]

However, Tipu's relations with the English deteriorated after
1795. Rumours spread that he was preparing for war. He was in touch
with the courts of Hyderabad and Poona for an offensive alliance
against the English. Imtiaz-ud-Daulah, the nephew of the Nizam and
highly influential in the Hyderabad court after the captivity of Azim-
ul-Umrah, was in league with Tipu to destroy British power. Tipu's
agents, Medina Saheb, Sakka Ram and Qadir Hussain Khan were
employed for the some purpose.[3] Tipu had sent an agent, Abdullah
Baig, to the Sindhia to secure his military assistance.[4] He repaired the
inner rampart of the fort of Srirangapatam and even solicited the aid
of Zaman Shah.

These reports perturbed the Governor-General who believed
that the losses of 1792 had only moderated the hostility of Tipu which
might be roused to a just resentment over the wrongs suffered by him
if an opportunity presented itself. Sir John Shore observed that the
ambition of Tipu has more and stronger motives for action than that
of the Marathas and that 'the consolidation of our alliance with the
latter is an object of importance to us'.[5] British suspicions were further
increased by the rapid economic recovery of Tipu's dominions and
the Company's own unsatisfactory military position in the Deccan.
The number of European troops had been reduced to 3000.[6] They were
widely dispersed on the coast to counteract Dutch designs. The revolutions in Poona, the imprisonment of Azim-ul Umrah and the increasing influence of the French at Hyderabad had tilted the balance of
power in favour of Tipu.

As a precaution, Sir John Shore took certain measures. He
ordered the Company's troops to be prepared for war, and despatched
them to certain strategic points. He sent reinforcements from Bengal
and instructed the Madras Government in detail over the course of
action to pursue.[7] If a considerable number of Tipu's troops were to
march towards Malabar, it should be deemed an indication of war.[8] A
mere remonstrance over Tipu's hostile activities was not judged proper
unless supported by a threat of war. Such remonstrance might provoke
Tipu to war, if he really meant peace. But if he was assisted by a large
number of troops from outside, war was to be declared.[9] Thus the
policy of Sir John was to remain prepared for war at all times: 'We may

assume it as an undeniable principle that to impose peace on our neighbours by strength of a military establishment, ready at all times for active or extensive exertion, is not only the wisest, but the most economic system.'[10]

Sir John took another step to frighten Tipu. He sent a joint note signed by all the three confederates complaining of his military preparations and calling for an explanation.[11] It was to convince Tipu of the existence of the old alliance, that it had not been dissolved either by the revolutions at Poona or by the Nizam–Maratha War. Tipu in reply expressed his surprise at the remonstrance and denied all charges. He assured them that he would remain peaceful. These assurances did not satisfy the English. They called these evasive and deceitful and their relations were strained with him. But Sir John did not precipitate a war and restrained the passions of those who wanted it, even though he believed that 'subversion of the British power as opposing the firmest barrier to his ambition, must naturally be the object which he has most in view'.[12] Nevertheless, he thought that Tipu could not implement his designs immediately as 'his obvious policy is to wait until events produce a disunion amongst the confederates and to foment it if he can'.[13]

Notes and References

[1] *Secret General Letters to Court Secret Letters*, 15 May 1794.

[2] *Poona Residency Correspondence*, Vol. II, no. 223.

[3] *Secret Letters*, 31 Aug. 1796, para 24.

[4] *Military Sundry Book*, Vol. 102, 8 Apr. 1798, para. 324.

[5] *Secret Proceedings*, 18 Feb. 1795, Minute of the G.G.

[6] *Secret Letters*, 15 May 1794.

[7] *Secret Proc.*, 17 Nov. 1796.

[8] *Letters to Court*, 30 Sept. 1796.

[9] *Secret Cons.*, 12 Sept. 1796, p. 900.

[10] *Secret Proc.*, 18 Feb. 1795.

[11] *Secret Cons.*, 20 Sept. 1796, G.G. to Tipu.

[12] *Political Proceedings*, 18 Feb. 1795.

[13] Ibid.

13
The Seringapatam Correspondence and the Carnatic Nawabi

C.S. Srinivasachari

On 7 April 1800, the Governor-General forwarded to Madras certain letters and papers relating to a correspondence between Nawabs Muhammad Ali and Umdatu'l-Umara with Tipu Sultan, which were found among the papers at Seringapatam. The Governor-General asked Lord Clive, the Governor of Madras, to conduct an inquiry into the circumstances, of which the papers appeared to afford indications, as to the exhibition of treachery on the part of the two Nawabs towards the English. Mill says that the Governor-General himself had prejudged the issue of the inquiry and suggested that Lord Clive prejudge it in a similar manner; that 'the evidence resulting from the whole of these documents has not only confirmed, in the most unquestionable manner, my suspicions of the existence of a secret correspondence between the personages already named, but satisfied my judgement, that its object, on the part of the Nabobs Wallajah and Omdut-ul-Omrah, and especially of the latter, was of the most hostile tendency to the British interests'. He asked Lord Clive to proceed immediately to make arrangements preparatory to the actual assumption of the Nawab's administration, 'which now appears to have become inevitable', though his wish was to delay the actual assumption till the inquiry should be complete. The Governor-General was frank enough to add, 'While those orders lately conveyed by the Hon'ble Court of Directors relative to the Company's connection with the Nabob, were under my consideration, a combination of fortunate circumstances revealed this correspondence'.

The papers thus sent as the basis of inquiry consisted of certain letters between Tipu Sultan and his two Vakils, Ghulam Ali Khan and

Ali Reza Khan, who accompanied in 1792 the two hostage sons of the Mysore ruler to Madras, a letter from a subsequent Vakil of Tipu at Madras, and another held to have been written by Nawab Umdatu'l-Umara under a fictitious name. In these letters there was not much to prove, which itself is proof that they had not been 'fabricated for the purpose of proving'. Tipu's Vakils were required to communicate among other matters secret intelligence including an account of the defence works of Fort St George and they were furnished with a cipher for carrying on the correspondence. The Vakils gave in their letters a description of the deportment of the Nawabs towards the hostage princes. The Nawab Muhammad Ali had been, according to the evidence of one of the letters, very intimate with Tipu Sultan.[1]

Besides the reports of the Vakils there were the letters of Tipu which did not contain anything more than 'a return to the civil expressions of the Nabob; vague declarations of good-will couched in a similar style'. The key to the cipher found among the records at Seringapatam shows that Nawab Walajah was designated by the term 'friend of mankind'; Tipu Sultan as the 'defender of the faith', the Marathas as 'despicable', the English as 'new-comers', the Nizam by that of 'nothingness', etc. The cipher was in the handwriting of one of the *munshis* of Tipu.

A Commission composed of Messrs. Webbe and Close was constituted by the Governor-General to investigate into this affair. Ali Reza, one of the two Vakils of Tipu, who was then residing at Vellore, was examined first. Of him the Commissioners say that 'we discovered an earnest disposition to develop the truth.' They accused Ghulam Ali, the second Vakil, who was residing at Seringapatam, of efforts at concealment. Both testified that the expressions of good-will made by the Nawab Walajah or his son, in their hearing, were never understood by them as being other than complimentary; Ali Reza said they were much exaggerated as it was customary with the Vakils 'to heighten the expressions of the regard which fell from Lord Cornwallis or the Nabob Wallajah for the purpose of gratifying the Sultan.' The secret intelligence which the Nawab is said to have conveyed through the Vakils was for the preservation of peace between Tipu and the English which was greatly desired by the latter at the time and Walajah advised Tipu, after having learnt that suspicions were caused by some negotiations between Seringapatam and Poona, to suspend those negotiations at least during the administration of Cornwallis; also having learnt that Pondicherry was about to be attacked by the English the Nawab advised the Sultan to withdraw his Vakil from Pondicherry and to stop his correspondence with the French.[2]

The lack of civil expressions and regard in reference to the English found in the correspondence of the Vakils was probably due to their knowing that such a display of lack of courtesy would be agreeable to their master. The formula, 'the affair you know', which frequently occurs and which the English people conjectured as indicative of a great many deeply-laid plans on the part of the two Mussulman leaders, was after all learnt to refer to a proposed marriage alliance between the Carnatic and the Mysore families. The Nawab's secret meetings with the Vakils prior to their departure, his offer to establish a cipher for the purpose of private communication which was not utilized by Tipu, the further letters from the later envoys Muhammad Ghiyas and Muhammad Ghaus in the years 1795–97 do not reveal anything more than a mere exchange of compliments.

There are 21 letters published in the appendix to the declaration of the Governor-in-Council of Fort St George, dated 31 July 1801. The examination of witnesses in Vellore and Seringapatam by Messrs. Webbe and Close in the month of May 1800 was ordered to be printed by Parliament on 21 June among the Carnatic papers. The Commissioners did not record the evidence of Munshi Habibullah and Diwan Purniah as their testimony did not establish any fact of consequence. Mill is emphatic that the evidence of the letters and of the subsequent examination of the Vakils did not and could not afford any proof of any criminal correspondence of the Nawab with Tipu and he significantly adds: 'but the total inability of the English to produce further evidence, with all the records of the Mysore government in their hands, and all the living agents of it within their absolute power, is a proof of the contrary; since it is not creditable that a criminal correspondence should have existed, and not have left more traces of itself'.

The Report of the Commissioners was drawn up and signed at Seringapatam on 18 May 1800. It was not till over a year after that date, during which the Governor-General was occupied by other matters, particularly the subsidiary treaty with the Nizam of October 1800, that he wrote a long Despatch to Lord Clive with an enclosure to the Nawab. In the Despatch, he said that the negotiations with the Nizam rendered it politic for the postponement of the Carnatic question for the time. But the delay enabled him to receive the opinions of the Board of Control and the Court of Directors on the subject of the Seringapatam Correspondence. He learnt with pleasure that these opinions accorded entirely with his own and with those of Lord Clive. He wrote that he confidently inferred from the evidence of the correspondence and the examination, 'the existence of a criminal correspondence between the Nabob and Tipu'; and he had consequently resolved on the dethronement of the Nawab and the transfer of his sovereignty to the Company. He had desired Webbe to go to Calcutta and convey to him all the personal knowledge that he had on the subject, and with that additional knowledge he had carefully revised the examination of the evidence. But he would still make an attempt to persuade the Nawab to acquiesce in the proposed arrangement through a treaty; and he asked Lord Clive to let the Nawab know that all the proofs of his correspondence with Tipu Sultan were in the English possession, and at the same time offer him the inducement of a generous provision of a sum of three lakhs of pagodas annually for his personal expenses. The Governor-General was convinced of 'the criminal purpose, and of the actual endeavour of the late and present Nabob of Arcot to establish an union of interests with the late Tippoo Sultan, incompatible with the existing engagements between the Nabob of the Carnatic and the Company, and tending to subvert the British power in the peninsula of India'. He was specific in the direction to Clive that if the Nawab should refuse to acquiesce in the proposal, the Madras Government was to assume the civil and military government of the Carnatic and exercise its full rights and power. If the Nawab should appeal to the Court of Directors against this proposal, because the Secret Committee had already assented to the proposal for the extinction of his sovereignty, the Nawab's appeal should not be admitted and he should not have the right of a formal investigation of his conduct. Thus the Governor-General decided, *ex parte* upon the basis of evidence furnished by the English themselves, and examined only by themselves and for themselves and upon which they could put any construction they pleased, without admitting the accused to offer a single article of counter-evidence or to sift the evidence brought to condemn him.

The argument that Mill puts forward, that the Nawab was a sovereign ruler who stood in treaty relations with the British power is controverted by Wilson, who says that the Nawab had never been a sovereign prince; but the Ministers of the British Crown had most *impolitically and mistakingly* taken him as such. But the history of his relations with the Company was a clear refutation of this assumption. Wilson added that the Nawab was nothing more originally than an officer of the Nizam of the Deccan, appointed and removed at his pleasure. It was the English that secured him independence of the Nizam and it was to them he owed his security. 'He was their creature and not their equal.' The dispute lay not between two potentates of equal status, but between master and servant, between sovereign and subject. It was the mistake of the English to have perpetuated in their own attitude the pretensions of the Nawab to sovereign rank. In Wilson's opinion, even Wellesley was generous and weak-minded in this respect, because he chose to treat the Nawab, not as a refractory dependent but as a sovereign prince in alliance with the English. Wellesley wrote in his despatch: 'The case requires that we should act as against a state, on the basis of the general law of nations, and that we should employ the power of the British empire in India to demand, and if necessary, to enforce an adequate security for our rights and interests against the machinations of a faithless ally, who has violated the fundamental principles of a public alliance to the extent of placing himself in the light of a public enemy.' But even Wilson has got to modify his standpoint.[3]

'The English people held at one convenient time that the Nawab was an independent sovereign prince. On another occasion they were at pains to prove his independence of the Nizam of Hyderabad and declare that his power was derived directly by grant of the Mughal Emperor. On a third occasion the Company condemned his attempt at equal correspondence with King George III, and now Lord Wellesley conveniently holds up his definite subordination to and dependence on the Company in political status.'[4]

To resume our narrative: Lord Wellesley put forward the high-sounding plea of imperialism, viz. that the Company was justified, in the interests of the people of the Carnatic, in seizing the administration from the Nawab's hands, because 'in proportion as the feelings of millions are of more value than the feelings of an individual' and because even if the English should only retain the administrative and judicial system of the Nawab, bad as it was, the people would suffer less than they would if it continued to be administered by the Nawab's officials. Likewise the Company held that in the short period when they enjoyed undivided power over the Carnatic, though their administration had been marked neither by skill nor by success, some efforts had been nobly intended and would be undoubtedly followed by more judicious expedients. Lastly, Mill thus puts the coping stone on the arch of the Company's move to take over sovereignty of the Carnatic: 'Yet I believe it will be found that the Company, during the period of their sovereignty, have done more in behalf of their subjects, have shown more of good-will towards them, have shown less of a selfish attachment to mischievous powers lodged in their own hands, have displayed a more generous welcome to schemes of improvement, and are now more willing to adopt improvements, not only than any other sovereign existing in the same period, but than all other sovereigns taken together upon the surface of the globe.'[5]

When the Governor-General's instructions reached Lord Clive the Nawab Umdatu'l-Umara was suffering from the illness that was to prove fatal. The Governor was generous enough not to agitate his mind with the communication of the despatch. But as above noted, he posted an English force at the gates and in the grounds of the Nawab's palace, on a requisition by Colonel Barrett, who reported that some of the armed peons who accompanied Husamu'l-Mulk Bahadur from Trichinopoly, perhaps at the instigation of Sultan-u'Nisa Begum, with plans of a possible usurpation of power for her son, might create a tumult and effect a revolution in the succession. The Governor concluded that these peons were brought to Madras for some evil purpose and anticipated it by occupying the palace himself. He had also suspected that the Nawab had accumulated a considerable treasure which interested persons might try to remove. The Nawab himself, according to Muhammad Karim, had consented to Barrett making the requisition for English troops. But a paper of Taju'l-Umara to Messrs. Hall and Johnston with the request that they might present their petition for his installation on his rightful throne, says that the posting of English troops was advised and adopted without any communication either with the Nawab or with his ministers until the very moment of its execution on 5 July.[6]

Notes and References

[1] The Vakils reported in their letter to the Sultan, dated the 16th of Jaffree of the year Shir, 1220, corresponding to 4 August 1792, that when the Nawab was told that the Sultan had addressed him as a prince, and 'that your

Majesty [had] added, God preserve the Nawaub Walajah, who is a prince, and one of the Leaders of the Faithful, and a pillar of the Faith'—then, at the term, "a pillar of the Faith", the Nawab could not suppress his tears. He said, 'I am what I know myself to be. Tell the Sultan, that he is the pillar of the Faith; and may God preserve him and grant him a long life, since I and all Mussulmen derive support from him; for otherwise the state of affairs here is evident—"That which is evident does not require explanation"... and he further added:

'You are not acquainted with the state and order of affairs here. Consider me from my heart your well-wisher and sincere friend; and at all times be assured, that in whatever I may be able to effect your benefit either by word or deed, I will not decline my exertions. What I said and wrote to his Lordship upon the subject of making peace, God well knows who was then or is now desirous of it. His Lordship, however, possessed uncontrolled authority, was a man of wisdom, and listened to the advice of others, and my observations made no impressions upon him.... [I] had accordingly suggested pacific measures, the expediency of which he urged in a thousand ways; they [the English] were so displeased that they went away without partaking of the entertainment, nay, that to their animosity might be attributed the assumption of His Highness' country. That when the orders were received from the king of England to restore the country, they framed the presence among themselves that His Highness was too much attached to Tippoo Sultan; and that the restitution of his country would consequently be an impolitic measure; but his Lordship maintained his opinion singly, and, disregarding the animosity of all the others against His Highness, delivered to him (His Highness) the country, agreeably to the directions of His Majesty.'

Tipu wrote in one of his letters that the Nawab was the chief and principal of the professors of Islam. To Umadatu'l-Umara he made similar professions and was proud of the sincere friendship and cordiality existing between them.

Mill says of these letters that nothing could be extracted from them 'but declarations of friendly sentiments in a hyperbolical style'. In the letter quoted above there was a fabricated remark of Colonel Doveton, which tends to weaken the validity of all their reports. The Persian translator Edmonstone himself says that 'if the evidence upon the Nawab's conduct rested solely upon these letters of the Mysore Vakils, the proof might be considered extremely defective and problematical.'

[2] The Vakils' Report contains only these words regarding two matters: 'What, in the judgement of this well-wisher, now appears expedient is this, in a short time his Lordship will go to Europe; the Princes, please God, will soon return, and the kists are in a course of payment; after his Lordship's departure the liquidation of the kists and other points, whatever may be His Highness's (Tippoo's) pleasure, will be right and proper; at present it is better to be silent upon everything, because at this time His Highness's honour would at all events be called in question.

'Although a friendly connexion has long subsisted with the French on the part of the Ahmedy Sircar (Tipu's government), yet, considering the circumstances of the times, it is not advisable [that is to maintain an epistolary correspondence with the French]; should there be any points of urgency to communicate, there is no objection to do it verbally.'

[3] 'This means, it is to be presumed, that a sovereign who is an enemy, and who is too weak to resist, may be deprived of his sovereignty; but even if this doctrine were generally true, which it is not, the public hostility to the Nawab of the Carnatic had not been so decisively manifested as to justify such extreme punishment. The inconsistencies and unsoundness of many of our attempts to vindicate our political measures in India are undeniable. It would have been more honest and honourable to have confined ourselves to the avowal that the maintenance of the British dominion in India was the mainspring of all our policy. It might also have been safely asserted, on this occasion at least, that the interests of the people demanded the separation of the double administration of the affairs of the Carnatic, and an end being put to the misgovernment of the Nabobs of Arcot.'

[4] Even on the first day of the Conference between the Commissioners of the Madras Government and the Regents of the boy-prince, Taju'l-Umara, on the very day of the demise of the Nawab, the former declared that disputed points between independent powers could be decided 'only by the means possessed by each party respectively to provide for its own security', and in the present case 'the most abundant proofs were in possession of the British Government of the violation of the alliance between the Company and the late Nabob, and particularly the express stipulations of the Treaty of 1792; and the British Government being satisfied of the sufficiency of those proofs, had no intention of constituting itself a judge of the conduct of its ally; but being prepared to appeal, if necessary, to the established maxims of the public law of Nations, it had resolved to demand from the late Nabob Omdut-ul-Omrah satisfaction for the violation of the alliance and security for its rights and interests against the future operations of His Highness's hostile Councils' (Paper No. 4—Carnatic Affairs—House of Commons, Papers 128 of 1801–02.)

[5] Mill, *History of British India*, Vol. VI, p. 331.

[6] No. 18; Papers concerning the late Nabob of the Carnatic, ordered to be printed on the 21st and 23rd of June 1802.

Intercommunal Relations

14
Tipu's Endowments to Hindus and Hindu Institutions

A. Subbaraya Chetty

Writers on Tipu can be said to belong to three schools. The first school, led by foreign writers like Wilks, asserts that Tipu was an unmitigated Muslim fanatic like Aurangzeb or even worse. To the second school of writers belongs Mr S.N. Sen who, commenting on Tipu's letters to the Swami of Sringeri Mutt writes, 'Tipu tolerated the practice of Hindu Religion within his own territory and became popular with all his subjects, but the same tole-ration was not allowed to the population of the enemy countries by the zealous Mohammedan ruler of Mysore.'[1] Writers of the third school say that since his letters to the Sringeri Mutt date from 1791, Tipu came to have a certain amount of faith in Hindus in the later part of his reign only as a result of his faith in the efficacy of Hindu cere-monies of incantation, etc., to destroy his enemies which became from 1791 his one obsession.[2]

But these writers have not gone deep enough into the matter. If they had done so, they could have found out that Tipu from the very beginning of his rule was as sympathetic and faithful to the Hindus as to the Muslims. The numerous charities and endowments he made to several Hindus and Hindu institutions are given below:

1782 (i) An order directing Haridasayya, *Amildar* of the Baramahal Territory to resume for the Sarkar all the lands and franchi-ses, except Devadayam and Brhamadayam (Temple and Brahmin Endowments). (See Baramahal Records (B.R.), Section V, p. 39).

(ii) Grant of Kothanuthala, a village in the present Cuddapah district, to one Ramachar, son of Komachar, for the *puja* of the Anjane-yaswami temple of Gandikota (Local Records (L.R.), Vol. IV, p. 434).

111

(iii) A *sanad* in Marathi issued to his *Amildar* Konappa directing him to allow the Swamiji of Pushpagiri Mutt to enjoy the revenues of Thongapalli and Golapalli. (L.R., Vol. IV, p. 474).

(iv) A *sanad* ordering the continuation of the usual worship of Venkatachalapali temple and restoration of the discontinued puja of Anjaneyaswami temple at Pulivendla in Cuddapah district (L.R., Vol. IV, p. 280).

(v) Grant of Gattupet Agraharam as 'Serva Manayam' for the expenses of Narasimhaswami temple of that place at a lesser rate than in his predecessor's time (L.R., Vol. IV, p. 289).

1783 (i) An Agraharam grant to Himakuntala Lakshminarasimha Somayyaji and five other in the south of the village of Potladurthi, Kamalapuram *taluqa* (L.R., Vol. II, pp. 294–95).

1784 (i) A *sanad* granting Venktampali Agraharam to Venkatachala Sastri and a number of Brahmins, requiring them to dedicate their time praying for the length of his life and prosperity (B.R., Vol. V, p. 135).

(ii) On Baba Budangiri, there is what is called Dattatreya Peetah, an inscription referring to Tipu's restoration of twenty villages given originally by the Kings of Anegondi to the Pettah (*Mysore Archaeological Report (M.A.R.) of 1931*, p. 21).

1785 (i) A grant to the Naraswami Temple of Melukote of 12 elephants sent through the *naik* Srinivasachar (S.R. 77, *Epigraphia Carnatica*, Vol. 3).

(ii) Grant of Chintagunta to Krinampatu (L.R., Vol. 3, p. 32).

1786 (i) Grant of kettledrum to the temple of Narasimhaswami of Melkota (M.A.R., 1916, p. 39).

(ii) A Sanskrit verse in the Canarese script recording the grant of lands to the temples and Brahmins on the banks of the Tungabhadra (L.R., Vol. 24, p. 16).

(iii) Grant of village of Ramakrishnam Botlupalli as *shotryam* to Ramakrishnam Botlu (L.R., Vol. 3, pp. 31–32).

1787 Grant of permission for the construction of a mosque on the side of a Hindu temple got from the Brahmins with their goodwill (M.A.R., 1935), p. 61, and Miles' *History of the Reign of Tipu Sultan*.

1788 (i) A Marathi inscription ordering Asuf Mohamed to continue the enjoyment of the villages of Oballapet and Koppolu to Rangacharlu and Sumati Srinivasacharlu together with other allowances. (*Inscriptions of Madras Presidency* by Rangachari, Cud. 364).

(ii) Continuation of all *manyams* to Chennakeswaraswami Temple of Machunur (L.R., Vol. 2, p. 275).

(iii) A *sanad* of Tipu granting a hereditary annual pension of ten pagodas to one Narasimhajoshi, a *panchangi* (B.R., Section 18, p. 98).

(iv) Continuation of grant of life pension to Rama pandit, physician (B.R., Section 18, p. 98).

1789 Grant of pension to Venkannachari and Srinivasa Moorthi Achari (B.R., Section 18, p. 111).

1790 (i) A Canarese inscription recording Tipu's grant as Inam of Kamalapuram to Lakshmikanthachari (L.R., Vol. 10, p. 258).

(ii) An order of Tipu to Haridasayya, *Amildar* of Baramahal, directing the restoration of the land attached to the Devasthanam of Chandramowliswara in the village of Kaveripatti for the purpose of Paditharam and Dhiparadhanam on the representation of the fact by Sankarayya Pujari of Salem District, with all the produce that may have been collected from it in the interim, agreeable to the established custom. (B.R., Section 5, p. 116).

1791–1799 Letters to Sringeri Mutt. 1. (1792) Supply of men and money necessary for the reconstruction of the Saraswathi idol pulled out during the Mahratta raid on Mysore (M.A.R., 19 [sic], p. 74).

1793 Letter to Sringeri Swami requesting him to live in his [Tipu's] country only and to pray to God for the increase of his prosperity.

1782–92 Directing that 1/64 of the grant made to Anandabhatt Gopalabhat of Anayampettah must be used for the maintenance of Lakshminarasimha Pagoda of that village (B.R., Section V, p. 10).

(ii) Presentation of a Dutch bell (carried from the Christian churches of Malabar) to the Venkaramana Temple of Nagar (N.R. 78, *Epigraphia Carnatica*, Vol. VIII, Part II).

(iii) Presentation of a silver jewelled cup to the Srikanteswara Temple at Nanjangud.(*M.A.R.*, 1918).

(iv) A proverb in vogue in Kanakala of South Canara District—'Tipu Sultan Ale Ruppe', referring to the silver jewels that Tipu presented to Veera Hanuman Temple of Kanakala.

(v) Babayya Durga at Penukonda and the Durga of Sayyad

Salar Masul Sahib near Tonnur (*Mysore Archaeological Survey Report of 1939*, Part II, p. 27).

(vi) Pervali Kyfit—During the rule of Tipu, at the temple of Sri Ranga of that village all the daily, annual and other periodical pujas, festivals, processions, worships, with all facilities and privileges provided for everyone connected with that temple according to traditions and all the court officials personally supported all the performances of the *pujas* (L.R., Vol. 40, pp. 462–63).

(vii) In Tipu's time, the idol was installed in the Prasanna Venkateswara temple in Uratur in Kommaditima and provision was made for the expenses of daily worship and *inam* lands were granted to the Archakars and other servants of the temple (L.R., Vol. 10, p. 180).

(ix) On Bababudangiri there is what is called Dattatreya Peetah an inscription referring to Tipu's restoration of twenty villages given by the kings of Aregundi to the Mutt (M.A.R., 1931, p. 21).

(x) Tipu's *sanad* for an annual allowance of 85 *chakras* to the two Pagodas of Lakshminarayana and Somasundaraswami of Doulatabad (B.R., Vol. 22, p. 8).

Notes and References

[1] S.N. Sen, *Indian Antiquary*, Vol. 48, p. 102.

[2] S. Krishnaswami Iyengar, 'Sidelights on Character of Haidar Ali and Tipu', *The Hindu*, Madras, 2 April 1939.

15
Tipu Sultan as Defender of the Hindu *Dharma*

B.A. Saletore

One of the later Indian rulers to whom scant justice has been done by historians is Tipu Sultan of Mysore.[1] This is not surprising when we note that Sultan Tipu stood apart from his illustrious father, Nawab Haidar Ali Khan, and also from the enemies against whom he waged incessant wars, especially the English. Sultan Tipu's implacable hatred of the English is perhaps not a little responsible for a judgement like the following passed on him by modern English historians: 'His fierce Muslim bigotry did not prevent him from having recourse to Brahman prayers in time of danger, or even from making gifts to Hindu temples.'[2] Smith does not substantiate this ungenerous statement concerning one aspect of the character of Sultan Tipu, which it is the object of this article to elucidate on the basis of contemporary letters and inscriptions.

This particular aspect of the character of Sultan Tipu related not to times of danger, as Smith maintains, but to times of peace, and not to any political exigency but to matters of conviction and precedent. If historians were to judge rulers only by the destructive actions which they committed, it is very doubtful whether we could find in any age or country a monarch who could escape condemnation. That Sultan Tipu was prone to excesses and that, in this regard, he justified the apprehensions of his great father cannot be doubted.[3] But in spite of his weaknesses, Sultan Tipu's special claim to recognition at the hands of posterity is the honest endeavours he made to further the cause of the Hindu *dharma* in his kingdom. This will be evident when we study (a) his great care to preserve religious usage in a monastery which is now the State monastery of modern Mysore; (b) his gifts to

115

Hindu temples; and (c) his genuine concern for the prosperity and status of one of the most celebrated religious centres in India.

a. *Sanad regulating religious practice.* Tipu Sultan's role as a legislator in Hindu religious matters is illustrated by a *sanad* preserved in the Sri Parakala Matha in the city of Mysore. It is written in Kannada, a language which, together with Persian and Urdu, as Smith writes, Sultan Tipu could speak fluently.[4] The *sanad* is addressed to Kuppayya, the Manager of the State Temples in the Kingdom (*srimatu devasthanadasime-parupatyagara Kuppayyanige*). That it has been written and sent to Kuppayya is evident from the next line: Order which had been written and despatched (*barasi kaluhida nirupa*).

It has a seal in Persian characters with the name of Sultan Tipu and is dated 1186 H/1772–73. The second line of the *sanad* contains merely the Hindu cyclic year and the month and the day (*Siddhartha saum. Bhadrapada ba. 5*) which corresponds to 15 September 1783.

The order relates to the manner of reciting certain invocatory verses in the well-known temple of Melukote or Yadavagiriksetra in the State of Mysore, and situated on the bank of the Kalyani river. The order deals directly with the question thus:

That it is heard that the official (of Sultan Tipu) by name Ance Samayya had hindered the old usage prevalent in the temple of Melukote (*Melugote-devasthanadalli purvarabhya nadadu barutta yiddaddannu Ance Samayyanu addimadi yid[d]hanante*) concerning the singing of the invocatory verses (of the Srivaisnavas); that it was now ordered that both the forms of invocation which begin with Ramanujadayapatra and Srisailadayapatra were to be used according to old usage (*purva-prakarakke Ramanujadayapatra-Srisailadayapatra saha-nadadu baruvahage nemaka-madisi-kaluhisi-i[d]dhitu*); that the Manager of the State Temples, Kuppayya, was to do justice to both the sections called Vadagale and Tengale of the followers of the temple, who would be chanting the two styles of invocation according to the time-honoured custom (*prakarabhya nadadu bandu yiruva prakarakke Vadagale-Tenkale ubhaya-pak-savannu sariyagi-nadasikondu barutt*); that the same high official Kuppayya was to remove the image of Pula Lokacar (i.e., Pillai Lokacarya, a Tankalai saint) from the place where it had been recently brought to its original place (at Melukote) (*nutanavagi tandu yiruva Pula-Lokacarannu modalu yidda balige kaluhisi*); and that the same high official was to take the *tirunaksatra*, the god, in a procession to the Kesavasvami

116

mandapa and other *pandals*, and to cause to be distributed, according to the old custom, the consecrated food offered to the god (*prasadam*) and the holy water (*tirtha*) and conduct the services of God with the usual pomp (*Tirunaksatrakke Kesavasvami munttada mantapagalige Devarannu bijumadisi tirtha-prasada saha praku merege kodisutta Svami-seveyannu sambrahamadalli agu-madisuvadu*).

A copy of the order was to be preserved in the Register of the State Accountant (Sanubhaga), and the original preserved (lit. pasted) in the *matha* of the Jiya (Head) of Prakala (*nirupa prati Sanu-bhagara rekhakke barasi Parakala Jiyara mathadalli kattisivudu*).[5]

The particular interest of this order of Sultan Tipu relating to the chanting of certain invocatory verses in the temple of Melukote lies in the fact that it rectifies an omission in an order passed by a previous (Hindu) ruler of Mysore, king Kanthirava Narasa Raja Odeyar, concerning the privilege granted to one of the two sections mentioned above. According to a *sanad* issued by king Kanthirava Narasa Raja Odeyar, also preserved in the same *Matha*, and dated only in the cyclic year Virodhi, the 13th lunar day of the dark half of Jyestha (24 June 1709), the privilege of appending the invocatory verse (*Taniyan*) of Ramanujadayapatra in the temple of Melukote, while reciting the Tamil hymns called the *Prabhandhas*, had been granted only to the Vadagai or Vadagale section of the Srivaisnavas.[6] This privilege was now thrown open by Sultan Tipu to the other section called the Tenkalai or Tangale.

A few remarks are necessary in order to appreciate the order passed by Sultan Tipu in regard to a purely religious matter. First, this order, like all those which will be examined in this article, was written in the language of the people—Kannada, thereby showing that the ruler, in spite of the fact that he was an adept in Persian and Urdu, and in spite of the fact that he could trace his descent to a line that was non-Indian in origin, yet preferred to identify himself entirely with the interests of the people, and to use their own language even in official orders. Further, this order is assignable to September 1783. By April of that year, Sultan Tipu had concluded his swift Bednur and Mangalore campaigns.[7] According to Smith, Mangalore was ceded to Sultan Tipu by June 1783, by the Treaty of Versailles.[8] The *sanad* is dated three months later, when he was not in any fear of enemies. Further, the *sanad* not only remedies the injustice done by his own official, but also rectifies an omission made by a previous Hindu ruler of Mysore. And, finally, it embodies regulations relating to certain details of daily worship, and especially those relating to the well-known Right-Hand and Left Hand sections of the people. This shows that Sultan Tipu was aware not only of the details of worship in Hindu temples, but, what is equally interesting, that he was alive to the delicate differences which have for generations together marked these two sections of the people concerning privileges and honours in temples.

b. *Gifts to Temples*. Let us now turn to the next point—his gifts to temples. Four different temples in four different parts of his kingdom received the privilege of royal gifts. These were the Ranganatha temple at the capital Srirangapattna, the Narasimha temple at Melukote, the Narayanasvami temple also at Melukote (Srirangapattna *taluk*), the Laksmikanta temple at Kalale (Nanjanagud *taluk*) and the Srikanthesvara temple at Nanjangud itself. The well-known Ranganatha temple at Srirangapattna was presented with seven silver cups and a silver camphor bearer by Tipu Sultan Pacca (Badshah), as is evident from the inscriptions on them.[9]

To the Narasimha temple at Melukote, Sultan Tipu presented a kettledrum which contains the following inscription (in Persian) which in English reads thus: 'Oh Impetuous! The second piece of the victorious drum of Ali, finished under the excellent supervision of the Haidari Government. Date of completion, 1215 of the *Mauludi* era (1786) Weight, atl (ritl) and 37-½ dak (*dang*).'[10] It is true that the name of the Sultan does not occur in the record; but according to the tradition current in Melukote the drum was the gift of Sultan Tipu to the temple.[11]

The gifts of that ruler to the Laksmikanta temple at Kalale comprised four silver cups and a silver spittoon (*padiga*); to the temple of Narayanasvami at Melukote, a silver spittoon;[12] and to the temple of Srikanthesvara at Nanjangudu, a jewelled silver cup.[13] These various articles contain inscriptions informing us that they were given as gifts to the respective temple by Sultan Tipu Badshah. Without other evidence it would be difficult to say whether they were gifts made during times of peace or war.

But in all likelihood such gifts were not the outcome of fear on the part of Sultan Tipu. I think they bespeak a genuine desire on the part of that monarch to show marked favour to those temples in the welfare of which he may have taken some personal interest. There are two considerations which make us believe that Sultan Tipu was sincere in his motives when he made gifts to Hindu temples. First, the policy of making presents to temples had already been set by his illustrious father. Thus an inscription on a silver cup belonging to the Gopala-krsna temple at Devanahalli informs us that the silver vessel was a gift to the temple from Nawab Haidar Ali Khan Bahadur. The inscription is dated about 1760.[14] Secondly, Sultan Tipu's policy of giving gifts to Hindu temples was followed by his Muslim officials. Thus for example, Japara Kana Bommani (Ja'far Khan Bommani), the Amildar of Badshah Tipu Sultan, presented the Siddhalingesvara temple at Edeyur, Kunigal *taluk*, with two bells. The gift was made, according to the inscription on the two bells, to (the god) Siddhalinges-varasvami by that Muslim official.[15]

   c. *Patronage to Hindu Religious Centre.* That Sultan Tipu was not unaccustomed to look to the spiritual needs of his vast Hindu subjects is proved beyond doubt by the third and the most important consideration relating to his attitude towards the Hindu *dharma*. This concerns Sultan Tipu's relations with the celebrated Hindu seat of learning, the Sringeri Matha, which form a very interesting chapter of Hindu–Muslim concord in the annals of India.

   But here it is worthwhile remarking that the tradition of maintaining the most cordial relations with the Hindu centres of spirituality had really been begun by Sultan Tipu's wise father, Nawab Haidar Ali Khan Bahadur. It was this monarch who had set a precedent which his son faithfully followed.

   Three letters decorated with gold illumination, written in Kannada, and preserved in the Sringeri Matha amply corroborate our assertion. They were letters written under orders from Nawab Haidar Ali Khan Bahadur to the head of that Matha. One of them begins thus: 'To the illustrious Svami of Sringeri (*Sri Sringeri-svamigalavarige*).' The Svami is not mentioned by name in the letter which then proceeds to narrate that Nawab Haidar Ali Khan gave his salutations to the Svami of Sringeri.[16] The date is given thus: '*Caitra ba. 8 Niruddhakke*', which evidently, as the late Rao Bahadur Narasimhacharya rightly conjectured, is an error for Virodhikrita, in which case the cyclic year Virodhikrita would correspond to 1769. Nawab Haidar Ali Khan next proceeds to relate that he himself was well, and that the Svami was to give orders frequently for the continuance of the glory of the Svami's spiritual empire (*Tamma-sambrajya-vaibhavatisayagalige agagi kattu madisi-kaluhisuvahage madisabeku*). The Nawab next acknowledges the receipt of the information sent by Balaji Pant through Venkata-ramanayya (*adagi* [lit. thence] *Balaji Pantaru Venkataramanayyana sangada saha kattu madisi kaluhistanttha abhipraya sakalau tiliya-layitu*).

The letter then has the following interesting details:

> You (the Svami) are a great and holy personage. It is nothing but natural for every one to cherish a desire to pay respects to you. As Saheb Raghunatha Rao has desired me to send you to him so that he may pay his homage to you, I request that you will accordingly undertake the journey and pay him a visit. For your journey I have sent by Ramaji one elephant, five horses, one palanquin, and five camels; gold cloth for the goddess, five pieces of silk cloth for the (Sringeri Matha) standard (*nisani*), a pair of shawls for your use and ten and a half thousand rupees for expenses. Two pairs of cloth have also been sent (*Tau doddavaru yiddhiri sakalarigu tamma darsana tegudu kollabekemba apeksa yiratakkadu sahajave... rri yi-Saheba Raghunatha-rayaravaru sandarsana nimityavagi sagisi kalaha [kaluhi] sabek embahage helikaluhisiddarinda ade merege tavamnnu sagi hogi sandarsana kottu sagi baruvahage madisatakkaddu melala vivarav ella Balaji Pantaru Venkataramanayyana saha sruta madalagi parammarisatakkaddu tamma painada bagge ane 1 Kudure 5 palaki 1 vante 5 saha Ramaji sangada kaluhisi yiddhitu devarige niraji sire 1 nisani bagge tapta 5 tamage salu 2 vecchakke hattuvare savira rupayi saha kaluhisi yiruvadarinda parammarisikomba hage madisabeku dhotrada jodugalu 2 nnu kaluhisiyiddhitu baranodisatakkaddu*).[17]

One special point of interest in the above letter is the reference to Raghunatha Rao, the prominent rival of the Peshwa (Balaji Rao) of Poona. Here we have proof of the marked regard which the Mysore Sultan Nawab Haidar Ali Khan showed to Raghunatha Rao in spite of the occasional political conflicts which the Mysore State had with the Marathas of Poona. The Svami of Sringeri in the above letter is not mentioned by name, but he was Abhinava Narasimha Bharati, who ruled over the Sringeri pontificate from 1767 till 1770. He is mentioned by name in the next letter of Nawab Haidar Ali Khan Bahadur, which is also found in the same Sringeri Matha. This second letter is not dated. It acknowledges the Svami's benedictory letter (*asirvada patrike*) and the Svami's presents to the Nawab, and assures the Svami of the continuance of the gifts of land (*inams*), etc., to the Matha, and requests him to go and reside happily in the Matha as before. A request is also made to the Svami to receive the present sent.[18] The assurance that the Svami may return to his spiritual seat and reside there happily is to be interpreted to mean that that *guru*, as the late Mr. Narasim-hacharya maintained, was probably living somewhere outside the Sringeri Matha.[19] The cause of this voluntary exile of the guru is not known, but it is not improbable that it may have been due to the unsettled political conditions of the times, and especially due to the Maratha raids into the neighbourhood of Sringeri itself, about which we shall presently give some details.

The third *nirupa* (order) of Nawab Haidar Ali Khan Bahadur is dated 1780. It is addressed to all state officers directing them to see that no obstructions are caused to the representatives of the Sringeri Matha when the latter went about their official duties of collecting the ecclesiastical fees like *sricarna-kanike, diparadha ne-kanike,* etc. This order has at the top a seal containing the name of Nawab Haidar Ali Khan and the Hijra date.[20]

Thus, from 1769 till 1780, Nawab Haidar Ali Khan Bahadur had made it clear that a new chapter had been opened by him in the history of the relations of the Muslim rulers of Mysore with the head of the Hindu seat of spirituality at Sringeri. This is the background against which we may now proceed to place the facts concerning Sultan Tipu's relations with the same Hindu centre of spiritual learning.

The sources of information for this part of our narrative are about thirty letters written in Kannada by Sultan Tipu to the *guru* of the Sringeri Matha. These letters may be studied under the following heads: their peculiarities; their subject matter; and importance.

Their Peculiarities

The letters bear a round royal seal at the top, the paper being invariably of a red colour. They range from 1791 to 1798, the dates being given in the *Mauludi* era which begins with the birth of the great Prophet Muhammad. The Muslim years and months according to the *abtas* system introduced by Sultan Tipu are given, in most cases, with the corresponding Hindu cyclic years, months and *tithis* or lunar days. They differ in their modes of salutation and address. When addressed to the Sringeri *guru*, they begin thus:

> To Sacchidananda Bharti Svami of Sringeri, possessed of the usual

121

titles (of) *Srimat-paramahamsa* and such other titles, the *salam* of Tipu Sultan Badshah';

and when addressed to others, thus:

'Jalla wa ala huw-al-Malik-ul-Manna—Tipu Sultan Badshah-i-Ghazi, khallad-allahu mulka-hu wa saltanata-hu.'[21]

Of special interest to us in the twentieth century is the fact that in all these letters, Sultan Tipu never even once refers to the divergence which existed between his own religion and that of his numerous Hindu subjects; and that throughout the letters he identifies himself entirely with the country which he governed. That is to say, Sultan Tipu realized that his existence was not apart from that of his people.

Their Subject Matter and Importance

The subject matter of the letters covers three items—an attack on the country by three groups of enemies; the raid on the Sringeri Matha by the Marathas, and purely personal affairs concerning the welfare of the Sringeri *guru* and some items of a civil nature. It is no doubt true that, while referring to the three groups of enemies, Sultan Tipu wishes for their destruction by the performance of some religious ceremonies like the *sata-candi-japa* and the *sahasra-candi-japa*. Thus, in the letter dated the 2nd of the Month of Haidari (Bhadrapada) of the year Mauludi 1219, Sultan Tipu acknowledges the receipt of the information sent through Gopaladasa that it is proposed to have the ceremonies of *sata-candi-japa* and *sahasra-candi-japa* performed for the destruction of the traitors, and requests the Svami to have these ceremonies performed, so that the three groups of enemies—evidently the English, the Marathas and the Nizam (*yi-rajadalli bandu upadra-maduva tri-vargarrigu nasavagu[va]hage*)—might be vanquished, and to send him the details of expenses to be incurred. The letter was written by the Huzur Munshi Narasayya.[22]

That the Sringeri *guru* complied with the behest of the Mysore ruler is evident from two letters dated in the month of Khuradali (Asvija) of the year Zabarjad (Virodhikrita) of the *Mauludi* era 1219 (1791), and from four letters dated in the month of Dini (Kartika) of the same year. In the first set of two letters, Sultan Tipu acknowledges the receipt of the details of expenditure to be incurred for the ceremonies mentioned above, and expresses pleasure at the Svami's

122

decision to have the latter ceremony performed for the welfare of the country and the destruction of the enemies. Tipu then intimates that orders have been issued to the *asaf* (local governor) to supply everything that may be necessary for the ceremonies, that the *Amildar* of Koppa *hobali* and Triyambaka Rao, the *Mutasaddi* of the Nagar *asaf-kacceri*, have been ordered to go to Sringeri, store all the necessary things and supply them to the Matha as required, and requests the Svami to have the ceremony performed according to the prescribed rites, after making gifts to the Brahmans who might be engaged in their performance, and after feeding 1,000 Brahmans every day. In another letter of the same year 1791 (Virodhikrita), Sultan Tipu asks the Svami to keep Gopal-joyisa with him till the ceremony is finished, and then to send him on to *huzur* (i.e. the royal presence).

In the next set of letters dated in the month of Dini, Sultan Tipu expresses pleasure on hearing that the ceremony of *sahasra-candi-japa* was begun on the 12th lunar day of the dark fortnight of Asvija; that, as desired (evidently by the Sultan), a *parwana* had been sent to Muhammad Raza to see that no disturbance was caused by mischievous people during the performance of the ceremony; and that the Sultan had despatched a fine palanquin for the Svami's use through Chobdar Faqir Muhammad, and asks the Svami to send Gopala-joyisa to the royal presence on the conclusion of the ceremony.[23]

On the strength of the above letters, it would be unwise and incorrect to conclude that Sultan Tipu, as Smith asserts, had recourse to Brahman prayers only in times of danger. In the first place, offering prayers in temples for the success of the king's army was a custom prevalent in ancient days in India, and not uncommon even in our own times. Witness, for example, the occasions when during the course of World War I (1914–18), prayers were offered in temples, mosques and churches throughout India for the success of British armies in the West. Even during World War II, prayers were offered by the followers of different religions throughout India for the success of the Allies, which evidently meant for the destruction of the Axis powers. It would be absurd for a future historian to deduce from this that the British Government in India had recourse to 'Brahman prayers' only in times of danger! If this is allowed, it cannot be made out how or why Sultan Tipu was at fault because he requested the *guru* of Sringeri to offer prayers and perform certain ceremonies for the destruction of the three enemies, one of whom were no doubt the English!

Moreover, in the letters cited above, Sultan Tipu never says that prayers were to be offered and ceremonies performed for his sake. He expressly says that the three groups of enemies were 'harassing the country'. Indeed, in a letter dated in the month of Jafari (Sravana) of the same year, 1791, Sultan Tipu requested the Svami to offer prayers to God so that the harassers may perish and the country prosper.[24] This is further proved by another letter addressed to the Svami, dated the 30th of the month of Rabbani (Phalguna) of the year Seta (Sadharana) of the *Mauludi* era 1218 (1791). This letter says the following:

> We are punishing the hostile armies that have marched against our country and are harassing our subjects. You are a holy personage and an ascetic. As it is your duty to be solicitous about the welfare of the many, we request you to pray to God along with other Brahmans of the Matha, so that all the enemies may suffer defeat and take to flight and all the people of our country live happily, and to send us your blessings.[25]

In another letter dated the 16th of the month of Tame (Jyestha) of the year Zabarjad (Virodhikrita) of the *Mauludi* era 1219 (1791), the Sultan refers to the same national calamities, and entreats the Svami to pray for the destruction of the enemies and the welfare of the country.[26] Never did any Indian monarch so clearly identify the interests of the people with his own as Sultan Tipu did when he wrote these letters to the Sringeri *guru*.

Much more important than the above aspect in the career of that stalwart ruler of Mysore is the one relating to the terrible havoc which the Marathas had caused in and around the Matha of Sringeri. It is here that we see Sultan Tipu as the real Defender of the Hindu *Dharma*, not in the manner of a political profiteer who made use of the confusion that existed in the Hindu ranks, but in the light of a saviour of one of the greatest spiritual centres of learning which belonged to a religion other than the one which he professed. The events mentioned here concern the activities of the formidable Maratha general, Parasurambhau, who was attempting to join hands with the English in the western parts of Sultan Tipu's dominions. This was in the years 1791 and 1792. I have discussed these events elsewhere in greater detail.[27] In June 1791, General Parasurambhau proceeded in the direction of Chitaldroog, which he failed to conquer. He laid waste the country around it, and in the month of December of the same year, attacked Shimoga which fell into his hands. He remained in the neighbourhood of Shimoga till the middle of 1792, when he proceeded to Bednore. From here his main concern was to join hands with Lord Cornwallis, who was now besieging Tipu's capital, Seringapatam.

We are concerned here with the activities of the Maratha general, Parasurambhau, especially in regard to Sringeri, and the consequent action which Sultan Tipu took to repair the immense loss which the Sringeri Matha suffered as a result of the Maratha raids. The Sultan's letters give a most gruesome account of the havoc committed by the Marathas in the Matha itself. Led by their general, Parasurambhau, they despoiled the *sanctum sanctorum* of the Matha, pulled out the sacred image of the goddess Sarada from her pedestal, and robbed the Matha to the extent of sixty lakhs of rupees.

The letters deserve citation in detail. Three letters dated in the month of Samari (Asadha) of the *Mauludi* era 1219 (1791), give us the following information:

Maratha horsemen had raided Sringeri, killed and wounded many Brahmans and other people, pulled out the image of goddess Sarada, carried off everything found in the Matha; the Svami having consequently left Sringeri was living with only four of his disciples at Karkala (now in the South Kanara district of the Madras Presidency). He wrote to Sultan Tipu informing him of these happenings, requesting him for Government aid as it would not be possible for the Svami to reconsecrate the image of the goddess Sarada without his help.

Sultan Tipu's answer to this appeal truly befits the spirit of a devout Hindu ruler. The Sultan replied thus:

> People who have sinned against such a holy place are sure to suffer the consequence of their misdeeds at no distant date in the Kali age in accordance with the verse: *Hasadbhih kriyate karma rudabhih anubhuyate* (Those who commit evil deeds smiling, will reap the consequences weeping). Treachery to *gurus* will undoubtedly result in the destruction of the line of descent. An order is enclosed to the *asaf* of Nagar directing him to give on behalf of Government 200 *rahati* in cash and 200 *rahati* worth of grain for the consecration of the goddess Sarada, and to supply other articles, if desired, for money. You may also get the necessary things from the *inam* village. Having thus consecrated the goddess and fed the Brahmans, please

pray for the increase of our prosperity and the destruction of our enemies.[28]

In one of the letters dated in the month of Jafari (Sravana) of the same year 1791, also addressed to the Svami, Sultan Tipu again alludes to the Maratha raid on Sringeri thus:

> We will also send an elephant from *huzur.* Wrong-doers to *gurus* and country will soon perish by the curse of God. Those who took away elephants, horses, palanquins, and other things from your Matha will be punished by God. Cloth for the goddess has been sent through Narasimha Sastri. Please consecrate the goddess, and pray for our welfare and the destruction of our foes.[29]

The Sultan, in one of his letters dated in the month of Dini (Kartika) of the same year 1791, asks the Svami to send a *takiti* (order) to Parasurama (General Parasurambhau) asking the latter to return the articles worth sixty lakhs carried off by him from the Matha; and the Sultan requests the Svami to have the ceremony of the *sahasra-candi-puja* referred to in the preceding paragraphs conducted according to the rules for one *mandala* or forty-eight days, and informs him that orders have been sent to Nagar to forward a palanquin for the goddess, and that another will be sent from *huzur* (Tipu's head-quarters) for the Svami's personal use.[30] Further, the Sultan asks the Svami in his letter dated in the month of Rahimani (Pusya) 1792, to get information from Narasimha Sastri, who had been sent in search of General Parasurambhau (who was reported to have died) and requests the Svami to pray to God three times a day (morning, noon and evening) for the ruler's welfare and the destruction of the three groups of enemies who had entered the country.[31] The Sultan's great anxiety concerning the depredations committed by General Parasurambhau and the latter's whereabouts is evident in his letter dated in the month of Ahmadi (Caitra) of the year Sahar (Paridhavi) of the *Mauludi* era 1220 (1793). In this letter the Sultan acknowledges the receipt of the Svami's letter to the effect that, as no reply had been received from the party sent to Parasurama, he (the Svami) himself intended to go as far as Poona, and requests the Svami to pay a visit to Seringapatam, so that the Sultan might have an occasion of paying homage to him, and also to visit Nanjanagud and other places, and then to proceed on his intended journey.[32]

The letters of Sultan Tipu to the Sringeri *guru* also delineate another side of that ruler's character, that relating to his genuine solicitude for the welfare of the *guru* of Sringeri and for the advancement of the cause of knowledge. In every letter addressed to the Sringeri Svami, Sultan Tipu gives expression to the high regard in which he held the former, and entreats him to pray for the welfare of the ruler and of the kingdom and to send him his blessings. In one of the letters dated in the month of Samari (Asadha) of 1791, Sultan Tipu acknowledges receipt of the *prasadam* (consecrated food offered to God) and shawls, and advises despatch of a cloth and bodice for the goddess and a pair of shawls for the Svami; while in another letter, dated also in the same month and year, the Sultan addressed the officers, directing them not to obstruct the representatives of the Matha when going to, or returning from, their disciples.[33] Further, for the personal safety of the *guru* and for the safety of the property of the Matha, the Sultan in one of his letters dated in the month of Zakari (Margasirsa) of 1791, informs the Svami that the Amildar of Koppa *hobali* had been ordered to see that no disturbance was caused by the Sukaligas, and that some Barr Sepoys would be despatched from the *huzur*,[34] evidently to help the Amildar. Moreover, the State officers were directed by the Sultan in a *rahkari* dated in the month of Haidari (Bhadrapada) of 1792, to receive the Svami with due honours, and to attend to his requirements. In another letter dated in the month of Dini (Kartika) of 1793, the Sultan requests the Svami to let him know about the latter's whereabouts.[35]

The next letter dated in the month of Razi (Magha) 1793, informs us in what high esteem the Sultan held the Svami. After acknowledging receipt of the Svami's letter, the Sultan writes thus:

> You are the *jagadguru*, Preceptor of the world. You are always performing penance in order that the whole world may prosper, and that the people may live happily. Please pray to God for the increase of our prosperity. In whatever country holy personages like yourself may reside, that country will prosper with good showers and crops. Why should you live so long in a foreign country? Please finish your work soon and return.

This letter was written by the *huzur-munshi* Subbarao. The letter in the original is as follows:

Seal without the legend. Srimat *paramahamsadi-yathotktabirud-*
ankitar-adantha-Sringeri-Sri-Sacchidananda Bharati-svami-
galavarige Tipu-Sultan-Padasaharavaru salam tau barasi kaluhisita
patrikeyinda sakala-bhiprayavu tiliyalayitu tau jagad-gurugalu sarva-
lokakku ksemav-agabeku janadalli (janaralli?) svasthadalli yirabek
embadagi tapassu maduttale yiddhiri sarakarada ksemau uttarottara
abhivardhamana aguvante trikala tapassu maduvalliyu Yisvara-
prarthane madutta baruvadu tammantha doddavaru yavadesadalli
yiddhare a-desakke male-bele sakalau agi subhiksav agi yiratakkad-
addarinda parasthaladalli bahala divasa tau yatakke yirabeku hoda
kelasa vannu ksipradalli anukulapadisikondu sthalakke sagi baruvante
madisuvadu tarikha 29 mahe Rajisala sahara sanna 1220
Muhammada Paridhavi samvatsarda Magha ba (hula) 14 lu khatta
Subbarava Munasi hajura (Signature of Sultan Tipu).[36]

In yet another letter dated in the month of Rabbani
(Phalguna) of 1793, the Sultan informs the Svami that the festivals of
the gods at the Sringeri Matha are being conducted according to the
scale newly laid down by him, and that the *asaf* of Nagar has been
directed to see that the feeding (of pilgrims, etc.) is satisfactorily carried
out at the *chatra* (or rest-house) and requests the Svami to keep on
writing to the Sultan every now and then about his welfare.[37] This
personal interest which Sultan Tipu took in the welfare of the Svami
Sacchidananda Bharati is further proved by three other letters. In the
first of these dated in the month of Ahmadi (Caitra) of the year Rasaji
(Ananda) of the *Mauludi* era 1222 (1794), the Sultan acknowledges
the receipt of the letter from the Svami stating that he will start on the
5th lunar day of the bright fortnight of Magha, and requests him to
bring Narayana Bhatta with him. The letter dated in the month of Razi
(Magha) 1795, relates that the Sultan had received information about
the Svami's ill-health, and that he was sure that the Svami's illness
would soon disappear by the grace of God, and advises despatch of a
rahdari for the Svami's return journey. Despatch of the *rahdari* to the
Svami is again assured in another letter dated in the month of Jafari
(Sravana) of the Harasat (Nala) year of the *Mauludi* era 1224 (1796),
and the Svami is requested in his letter to pray to God for the welfare
of the Sultan in the holy place which the Svami would visit.[38]

The Sultan's keen desire to add to the intellectual progress of
the land is shown in a letter addressed by him to the same Svami, but

dated in the month of Razi (Magha) of the year Saz (Pingala) of the *Mauludi* era 1225 (1798). The Sultan advises despatch of a *pancanga* or calendar newly prepared under order of the Government for the Kalayukta year, requests the Svami to make use of it, and give the Sultan his blessing. The Sultan seems to have been very eager to meet the Svami. This explains why in a letter dated in the month of Dini (Kartika) of the year Sadab (Kalayukti) of the *Mauludi* era 1226 (1796) he invites the Svami to *huzur*, and advise despatch of a *rahdari*.[39]

The numerous letters cited above prove beyond doubt that Sultan Tipu, whatever may have been his deficiencies in other respects, was certainly a great benefactor of one of the most renowned places of Hindu worship and that, whether in peace or in war, he was prepared to place his country above his own self even in the matter of prayers. People have indeed reason to be grateful to him for the prompt measures he took to resuscitate the cause of Hindu *dharma* in the great seat of Shankaracarya, when it was eclipsed by political calamity.

Notes and References

[1] Long after I had typed a major portion of this article my younger brother Dr R.N. Saletore, who chanced to go through my MS, told me he had written an identical article in the *New Review* of Calcutta some time ago. I have not seen this article on Sultan Tipu written by Dr R.N. Saletore. I believe it covers the same ground as mine, but from a slightly different standpoint.

[2] Vincent Smith, *Oxford History of India*, ed. S.M. Edwards, Oxford, 1923, p. 585.

[3] Cf. B. Ramakrishna Row, *The Annals of the Mysore Royal Family* (Kannada), Mysore, 1916, Vol. I, pp. 234–35.

[4] Smith, *History of India*, p. 585.

[5] *Mysore Archaeological Report* [M.A.R.] *for the year 1938*, pp. 124–25.

[6] Ibid., pp. 113–15. On p. 115, Dr Krishna, to whom we are indebted for the discovery of these *sanads*, has a useful note on the verse itself.

[7] See the anonymous author M.M.D.D.T.'s *History of Hyder Shah alias Hyder Ali Khan Bahadur, and his son Tippoo Sultan*, revised by H.H. Prince Ghulam Mohammad, the only surviving son of Tipu Sultan, London–Calcutta, 1855, pp. 266–69.

[8] Smith, *History of India*, pp. 545, 554.

[9] *M.A.R. 1912*, p. 53. The late Rao Bahadur R. Narasimhacharya, who was the first to notice these and other inscriptions on bells and other gifts made by Sultan Tipu, writes that three of the cups and the camphor-bearer also bear additional inscriptions in other parts, informing us that they had been presented by a chief of Kalabe by name Kantayya; and that they may have been carried away by Sultan Tipu but regranted by the latter 'at the prayer

of the devotees of the temples with his inscriptions newly engraved.' Ibid., pp. 58–59.

[10] This is only a supposition which is not supported by any evidence. I think that Sultan Tipu merely caused his own inscriptions to be inscribed on the same articles without having forcibly removed them from the temples. It was a custom for one or more inscriptions to be inscribed on the same object, as the veteran Mysore archaeologist himself says in his next sentence relating to the 'additional label Sri-Krsna' appearing on another silver cup, showing that it was a gift of king Krsna Raja Odeyer III (ibid., p. 59).

[11] *M.A.R., 1916*, pp. 73–74.

[12] *M.A.R., 1917*, p. 59.

[13] *M.A.R., 1918*, p. 60.

[14] *M.A.R., 1913–14*, pp. 50–51. Evidently this is the birthplace of the great Haidar, for, according to the anonymous French author of his life cited above, 'Haidar Ali was born in "Devanelli" (Devanhalli), a small fortress or castle between Colar (Kolar) and Oscota (Hosakote) in the country of Benguelour' M.M.D.D.T., *History of Hyder Shah*, pp. 33–34. The birthplace of Nawab Haidar Ali Khan is not mentioned in the *Annals of the Mysore Royal Family*, Vol. I, pp. 176–77.

[15] *M.A.R., 1919*, p. 42.

[16] The intervening lines *hakikata nariphata mangalate* are not quite clear. Perhaps they mean 'through mutual correspondence'.

[17] *M.A.R., 1916*, pp. 41–42 and 73.

[18] Ibid., p. 73.

[19] Ibid.

[20] Ibid.

[21] Ibid.

[22] Ibid., pp. 42, 75.

[23] Ibid., pp. 74–75.

[24] Ibid., p. 74.

[25] Ibid.

[26] Ibid.

[27] See my *Maratha Dominion in Karnataka*.

[28] *M.A.R., 1916*, p. 74.

[29] Ibid.

[30] Ibid.

[31] Ibid., p. 75.

[32] Ibid.

[33] Ibid., p. 74.

[34] Ibid., p. 75.

[35] Ibid.

[36] Ibid., pp. 43, 75.

[35] Ibid., p. 75.

[36] Ibid., pp. 75–76.

[37] Ibid., p. 76.

16

Muslim Rulers of Mysore and Their Christian Subjects

George M. Moraes

t the time of its conquest by Haidar Ali, Kanara possessed a
well-established and flourishing community of Christians
made up, for the most part, of emigrants from Goa. These
were reinforced by a sprinkling of Portuguese traders, and accessions
made from among non-Christians by missionary labours. Under the
encouraging protection of Portuguese arms the Christians grew in
numbers and power until at length they could count 27 settlements,
each with a church served by a vicar and the whole under a Vicar
General, himself subject to the Archbishop of Goa.[1] The exact nature
of their privileges may be gathered from the terms of a treaty which,
after a successful campaign the Portuguese imposed on the feeble
Nayak of Ikeri. The contracting parties agreed on that occasion that
disputes arising among Christians or between Christians and Hindus
should be settled by the Portuguese Factor and the Vicar, and where
recourse to the Factor was not possible, by the priests who may be
found at the ports or in the district of the Raja of Kanara. Any appeal
from their decisions was to lie with the Government of Goa, and under
no circumstances were the local governors and *thanadars* to take
cognizance of these matters in cases of alleged injustice. Further, any
Christian woman known to lead an immoral life was to be surrendered
to the Factor for deportation to Goa, there to undergo due punishment. No trafficking in Christians was to be permitted either on the
part of the Raja or on that of his subjects. Christians were to be exempt
from imprisonment for debts. The Raja of Kanara was not to suffer
any Christians either from Goa or from other Portuguese dominions
to cohabit with Hindu women, and should permit the priests,

whenever such a case occurred, to seize the culprit and deport him to Goa without themselves being liable to molestation from local authorities. In the factory and town of Mangalore and wherever there might be Christians, the Portuguese were to be allowed to erect churches. Priests were empowered to punish laxity in or hostility to religion among Christians, according to their own law, for which the Raja was expected to render every assistance; and whenever any of them happened to pass through Kanara to take their abode there or in another country, they were to be free from all molestation by the local *thanadars* and governors, and also exempt from tax in respect of any luggage they carried, save on goods for sale.[2]

The Christians had thus come to acquire an honoured and autonomous position, very nearly forming a 'state within a state'.

When Haidar Ali wrested this province from the Nayak of Ikeri, he confirmed the Christians in the enjoyment of all the time-honoured privileges.[3] By a *parvana* issued in 1776, he granted 2,440 *fanams* yearly to the Catholic Church at Calicut, together with the property belonging to it and the Church at Parappanangadi, and recognized the jurisdiction of the clergy over Christian delinquents. 'Every one of the Christians', says the *parvana*, 'that may commit any guilt or crime, the justice thereof belongs to the padre and the Factor.' The fact was that Haidar being beset by formidable enemies was loth to antagonize the Portuguese.

In 1768 an incident occurred which had an adverse effect on the fortunes of the Christians in Haidar's dominions. The latter had declared war on the English and was sweeping the board in the Carnatic, and the English General Staff decided upon a diversion on the west coast to relieve the alarming situation in Madras. Accordingly, the Government of Bombay sent an expedition under Admiral Watson to seize Mangalore. One Ramys Havaldar, who had formerly been in the employ of the Cannanore Government and a 'Moorsman' (Muslim) commanding Haidar's fleet at Onor were to be approached to secure a betrayal of their powerful master.[4] The appearance of the English squadron at Mangalore created a delicate situation for the Portuguese Factor. On the one hand the two nations were bound by an age-long alliance albeit commercial rivalry; on the other, in consequence of the extraordinary rights which they exercised in Kanara the Portuguese were morally bound to support the local power against any aggressor. In this dilemma, the Portuguese Factor declared his intention to remain strictly neutral and warned the invaders to take care to respect the Portuguese jurisdiction which included the churches, the Portuguese concession and the Christian community in general.[5] The officers of Haidar naturally expected the Portuguese Factor to stand by them in this critical hour, for their best efforts would avail them little if the Portuguese Factory and fortification, commanding as they did the entrance to the river, were not to go into action against the invaders. When, however, despite their repeated entreaties the Portuguese Factor persisted in his strange and unreasonable attitude, they formed a plot to entice him away from the fort and themselves take possession of it. This plot was betrayed by the captain of the artillery which was manned by Christians. The Factor summoned all Christians to take shelter in the factory, including those in the service of the government. And when he heard on the next day that Haidar's troops were intending to storm the fortress he invited the English to assist him in the defence of the fort. The Christians constituted the mainstay of the defence of Mangalore, and with their defection, the resistance collapsed, and the English easily gained their objective.[6]

Haidar Ali was incensed at the treacherous behaviour of the Christians. He summoned the Portuguese priests and questioned them as to what punishment such treachery merited. And when answered that death was the penalty for betraying one's sovereign he preferred to be lenient and had them clapped behind prison bars.[7] The Portuguese records however also speak of priests who suffered incarceration on this occasion. Father Sebastian de Faria, Vicar Vara of Honavar, was taken with two more priests to Hydernagar; and there were at least five others who were then arrested.[8]

Haidar had hardly settled his scores with the English, when he was threatened by the Marathas. Naturally enough, while he dealt with this new peril, he wanted his dominions in Kanara to be secure from the depredations of his immediate neighbours, the Portuguese. Accordingly he forced the English to accept a humiliating treaty and opened negotiations with the Portuguese for an alliance. With famine staring them in the face in consequence of the stoppage of supplies or rice from Kanara, the Portuguese jumped at this opportunity of reconciling themselves with the master of the granary of the west coast, as Kanara was then known. A treaty was forthwith concluded. The factory was restored with all its rights, the vicars and the Christians who had been taken prisoner were released, and the Church was allowed its old untrammelled jurisdiction over Christians in matters of justice.[9]

The amicable relations between the two powers thus resumed continued undisturbed till 1776 when Haidar imprisoned the Portuguese Factor of Mangalore, and almost dismantled the Portuguese fortifications. The reason seems to have been that Haidar had now become so powerful that he was unwilling to allow the Portuguese to levy their accustomed tribute and customs. He could moreover no longer be content with mere passive help on their part, but wished that they should help him with six hundred European troopers yearly to serve in his campaigns.[10] The Portuguese government showed itself reluctant to comply with these demands and, after protracted negotiations lasting four years, a second treaty was signed. It was agreed that the Portuguese should be permitted to levy tribute and collect customs as heretofore, and continue in possession of their factory in Mangalore, on condition that they should defend the town against any enemy, and the further concession that concerns our subject, that the clergy should be allowed the exercise of their religion unembarrassed.[11]

But Haidar's peace with the English could not endure long. Each party distrusted the other, and if the English made no attempt to retrieve their honour earlier, it was not from want of a desire to try conclusions with the Muslim adventurer. Though all along 'casus belli' multiplied fast, it was not till 1782 that the parties decided on a call to arms. But Haidar, whose health had been declining for some time, died on 7 December 1782[12] and the English, taking advantage of the situation, made a landing in Kanara a week later. Under General Mathews the entire littoral from Karwar to Kundapoor was secured, and thanks to the good offices of Shaikh Hayat, who was acting as Governor in the absence of Tipu, they obtained possession of Nagar, the capital of the kingdom, and of Mangalore the royal port.[13] This success of the English was short-lived, for, as Father Joaquim Miranda, an eyewitness, observes, while they were engaged in rapine and plunder, Tipu hurried from Arcot with a third of his powerful army and recovered the entire country including Nagar (Bednur) and Mangalore.[14]

Wiser from experience, the Portuguese on this occasion chose for themselves the role of passive though not uninterested spectators. The Viceroy reports that Tipu was pleased with the action of the Portuguese in refusing asylum to Shaikh Hayat at Goa, at the suggestion of the English, after their discomfiture in Kanara.[15] Some of the Christians, however, in their enthusiasm for the English cause, imperilled the fortunes of the entire community. Writing in May 1783 from Mangalore, Major John Campbell informed the President in Bombay, 'There are a number of native Christians here who had been formerly attached to the Artillery; 34 of them are taken in the same service here, and Francis Pinto, late an ensign in the 'Bombay Natives', whom General Mathews had promised to employ and give Ensign's pay and *batta*, I have appointed to take charge of them with the same rank, pay and allowance as he had formerly.'[16] This is supported by a statement of Scurry, who was a prisoner for a long time at Seringapatam, to the effect that General Mathews had borrowed Rs 33,000 from the Kanara Christians.[17]

This was sufficient to provoke the wrath of Tipu who had long been burning with fanatical hatred against the Christians. As a prince, he had advocated a thorough-going persecution when the Christians of Kanara had gone over to the English, leaving the defence of Mangalore to collapse.[8] Now he openly accused them of being principally responsible for the ease with which the English conquered this part of his kingdom 'acting as guides and facilitating their communications'.[19] He charged the priests with having brought all this trouble on him and his people, fined them three lakhs of rupees and had them expelled from his dominions.[20] He then conceived the project of stamping out Christianity from the land altogether and unleashed a sanguinary persecution.

A laconic description of what followed is given in a letter to the Secretary of State by the Portuguese Viceroy, who observes, 'No sooner did he (Tipu) find himself free from the English with whom he had concluded peace, than he gave open demonstration of his tyranny and hatred towards the Christians.... He exterminated the Christians of all those places, who should total forty thousand souls. Compelling them to cross the Ghats, he took them to Seringapatam, where he circumcised many and obliged them to follow the sect of the Moors. He sent me thirteen vicars, expelled from his dominions, writing to me to say that out of consideration for me he had refrained from inflicting on them greater punishments and greater monetary fines.... These priests reached Goa in great misery, and I replied to his letter protesting the justice of their cause and that of Christians.'[21]

The Viceroy had reason to protest. He was convinced that the whole body of Christians could not be charged with connivance at the success of the English invading force, for in those days the Christians followed the lead of the Portuguese in such matters, and the latter, as we have seen, had remained strictly neutral. Consequently, while condemning outright the action of such of the Christians as made common cause with the English against their own sovereign, we must admit that Tipu in making the entire community pay for the crimes of a few of their number was guilty of a high-handedness for which no justification can be pleaded.

Notes and References

[1] Buchanan, *A Journey from Madras through the Countries of Mysore, Canara and Malabar,* III, p. 24.

[2] Braganca Pereira, *Arquiro Portugues Oriental,* III, pt. II, pp. 98–99.

[3] Pissurlencar, *Antigualhas,* A decree of Father Joaquim Machado, Vicar General of Kanara, issued some time before 1766 regulates the procedure for appeals against the decision of parish priests: 'From today onward in order to maintain the peace and tranquillity of this Christian realm and avoid hatreds and litigation in cases already decided before the said parish priests and Vicar Varas, whenever they may have to appeal on the same matter in case the decision has been unjust, they shall do it within the time limit of 30 days before the Superior of the Mission, and in his absence before the said Vicar Varas, and after the lapse of this period no case shall be admitted a second time to judgement, so that in this way justice may be observed and perpetual litigation prevented, and the said parish priests who may accept for decision suits already settled before their predecessors in office and their referees I hereby declare suspended and the respective parties condemned, whether the suit be one for money or for anything valuable, to pay one-third of the value of the subject matter which will be devoted to the use of the *fabrica* (revenue destined for the repairs and maintenance of a church), being at the same time deprived of any further right of appeal' *Mitras Lusitanas,* p. 29.

[4] Public Department Diary, 1768, No. 52, p. 32.

[5] Pissurlencar, *Antigualhas,* Fasciculo I, No. 12, p. 167.

[6] Ibid., Nos. 12 and 13, pp. 167–70.

[7] Op. cit., pp. 384–85.

[8] Pissurlencar, *Antigualhas,* Fasciculo I, No. 30, p. 196 (A letter of the Archbishop of Goa to the Governor of Goa dated 17 November 1771, commending the efforts of 'Lingao do Estado' Sadasiva Camotim on behalf of the priests).

[9] Ibid., No. 23, pp. 185–86; No. 36, p. 200. The treaty was actually signed on 25 January 1771.

[10] Ibid., Fasciculo II, No. 50, pp. 220–23.

[11] Ibid., No. 63, pp. 258–59.

[12] Wilks, *Historical Sketches of the South of India,* II, p. 413.

[13] Pissurlencar, *Antigualhas,* No. 74, p. 301, No. 79, pp. 305–6; also authorities mentioned in Moraes, *Mangalore, a Historical Sketch* (Bombay, 1927), p. 48, note 1.

[14] Pissurlencar, *Antigualhas,* No. 79, as above.

[15] Ibid., No. 77, p. 303.

[16] Saldanha, *The Captivity of the Canara Christians under Tipu Sultan,* p. 18 note b.

[17] Scurry, *Captivity,* p. 103.

[18] Pissulencar, *Antigualhas,* No. 79, p. 306.

[19] Ibid., No. 77, p. 304.

[20] Ibid., No. 75, p. 302, and No. 81, p. 314.

[21] Ibid., No. 81, p. 144. See also No. 80, Muhammad Shafi's letter, in which captivity is referred to. For other accounts of the imprisonment and sufferings of the Christians see Moraes, *Mangalore,* pp. 62–68; Moore, *The History of the Diocese of Mangalore,* pp. 36–63, and Saldanha, *The Canara Christians under Sultan Tipu.*

17

An Unpublished Letter of Tipu Sultan to a Muslim Divine

K. Sajan Lal

This original letter, 13.1″ x 7.6″ in size, on silver-sprinkled paper with enclosures (a note and list of presents), has a wrapper with a small seal bearing the name of Tipu Sultan in Nasq with 5121 in figures.[1] Its wrapper has two dates: 20th Ramzan 1209 A.H. (10 April 1795) and 23rd Shawwal 1209 (12 May 1795).[2] It is difficult to surmise the name of the addressee, because its 'kamarband' has been lost. But from the contents of the letter, one could say that it was addressed to a venerable religious person.

As for the two dates on the back of the letter, I presume that one, viz., 20th Ramzan, 1209 A.H., is the date of despatch, and the other, 23rd Shawwal 1209 A.H. is the date of receipt at its destination.

For the interest of readers, I give a free translation of this Persian letter:

> In the name of God, the Merciful, the Compassionate, the advent of your esteemed letter, which contained an acknowledgement under grateful obligation for the regard manifested by your venerable self towards me. Such consideration tends to cement the ties of mutual friendship. May the Almighty always protect and lengthen the life and prosperity of such magnanimous elders. Similar prayers are perpetually observed for your noble self by the entire Muslim population during the daily five-times prayers as well as in the Juma (Friday prayers) in this Darul Islam (Metropolis of Islam).
>
> It is, however, incumbent on every orthodox Muslim to reciprocate for his religious brother an identical treatment which he adopts for himself. It is a matter of great satisfaction that all the

138

commendable qualities are assembled in your good self which do not call for any elucidation.

It is earnestly expected that you would consider me always sincere well-wisher and afford me occasion for cheerfulness by favouring me with communications of your welfare.

Here in the Khudadad Factory[3] cloth is woven by Muslims, who commence their daily work in the name of Allah and other rehearsals. A few pieces are herewith forwarded, although these not worthy of your good self, but in view of the sacred rehearsals, it is believed you will render me grateful by accepting them.

In a letter to Nizam Ali Khan, Tipu uses the same phraseology:

The advantages and benefits of unity and harmony among the followers of Islam are certainly exposed to your full view. I am sure that your blessed mind is ever engaged in adopting measures to increase the power of Islam and the splendour of the faith of Muhammad as indeed befits the world of leadership and your good name. You will please suggest ways and means for affording protection to the honour, life and property of the people who are dependent on Muhammadan Chiefs who in fact constitute a unique trust for God, the real Master.[4]

A short note with a list of articles which accompanied the letter has twenty-five items of interest such as (1) turban cloth, one white and four Burhanpuri pieces; (2) cloth for shoulder woven in gold borders, five pieces; (3) striped sheets, ten pieces; (4) Gujarati brocade with a gold and silver flower design, five pieces.

It is significant to note that all the above articles were manufactured by the *khudadad* (official) factories which specialized in textiles.

Notes and References

[1] I have seen a number of letters addressed to the Nawab of Kurnool bearing the impression of this very seal. In our Arts College Persian MSS Library, one Registered No. 576, called the *Kulyat-i-Mulla Urfi*, possesses a number of seals, of which two are of Tipu Sultan, of the same type as found on the wrapper of this letter.

[2] I found the impression of this very seal with the figure 5121 on another important MS, the *Fatehul-Mujahideen-i-Askari*, written by Zainul-Abideen, the Mir Munshi of Tipu Sultan. This is also found in our Persian

MSS Library, Registered No. 818. These facts prove the genuineness of the seal. The figure 5121 on the seal perhaps relates to the year of his accession.

3 Literally, 'God Given,' a title adopted by Tipu Sultan for his Government. Tipu Sultan had established a large number of factories, which were known as those of *Sarkar-i Khudadad.* Cf. Mohibbul Hasan, *History of Tipu Sultan,* pp. 344–48.

4 Cf. ibid., p. 254. But these appeals to the Nizam's humanity and religion, in the words of Mohibbul Hasan, 'fell on deaf ears.'

Towards
Modernization

18

Tipu's Drive towards Modernization: French Evidence from the 1780s

M.P. Sridharan

During his lifetime, Tipu was a topic of unfading interest to his contemporaries, as much to republicans in the United States of America as to monarchists and revolutionaries in France.[1] Two hundred years after, the bibliography on Tipu betrays no signs of aridity; at least one historical novel[2] woven round hitherto unknown accomplishments of the Mysore Sultan compels historians to undertake more painstaking research into the history of Mysore in the eighteenth century. However, the exposition of the political events and the materials on which the historian has to lean have been so loaded with preconceptions and prejudices that the rule of Tipu has remained a matter of interest to the political historian.[3] Some pioneering attempts[4] nonetheless have been initiated to assess the assets and liabilities of Mysore in Tipu's times and to arrive at some tentative understanding of the economic resources and technological levels of the period.

Most of the letters sent by Tipu to French employees which are found preserved in the Archives Nationales in Aix-en-Provence are written on silk. The material is embellished with floral designs woven into it at random in gold brocade, suggesting an advanced level in textiles. The language used in most letters is Persian but there are a few written in Telugu too.[5] Almost all these letters were exhibited in original at the Section Historique of the Exposition Coloniale in Paris during 1931, with a separate explanatory booklet published on them.[6] The correspondence reveals that some of the princes and courtiers of Mysore of the period were also familiar with French.

Along with his three ambassadors to the court of Louis XVI[7] Tipu had sent two interpreters, Pierre César and Hallé, who were both

143

of Portuguese descent but the French authorities do not appear to have quite trusted them.[8] They attached their own interpreter, Russin, to the ambassadorial party but his performance turned out to be disappointing because of his limited Persian and Arabic vocabulary. La Luzerne, the French Minister of Marine in 1788, was greatly impressed by two young men in the ambassadorial entourage, the son of Akbar Ali Khan and the nephew of Usman Khan[9], both of whom were quite at home in French. Tipu had suggested in one of his letters that one of his sons should be sent to France for his secondary education but he linked it up with a demand for a French boy to be sent to Mysore on a reciprocal basis. The correspondence turned out to be sterile on this count as on many others, but it reveals that Tipu's desire to have one of his sons educated in France was more a recognition of the need for cultural exchange than an admission of French superiority in the field of education.

The material found in the French Archives (of which the letters of French officers constitute only a small segment) number over two thousand, some of which extend to a score of foolscap pages in length. About a quarter deal with the embassy that Tipu sent to Louis XVI in 1788. Tipu's original plan, which he discussed with Pierre Monneron at Mysore, was to send a party of four hundred men in one of his own ships and bearing his own standard on the high seas. The French did not accept the proposal on the grounds of financial stringency. Nineteen lakhs of rupees had been lent by Tipu to the French a decade earlier which the French had been evading repayment. In the course of the negotiations of 1787, the Sultan magnanimously wrote off the debt hoping that his action would persuade the French to accept his terms and conditions for the despatch of the embassy to France. But the French had other constraints too. Four hundred Indians in eighteenth-century France would have been too many charges on hand. Although Monneron opined that 'his ships will produce a great effect in Europe because it will be the first Indian ship to appear in European waters'[10] the French authorities in Paris did not desire a ship of Tipu's to sail into a French port for fear of offending the British and the Treaty of Paris of 1783. Another constraint on the French that would not allow them to accept Tipu's proposal to send 400 men to France was that they did not have boats that could undertake the long voyage with 400 on board. Tipu had arranged a ship that could convey 400 men to Europe but after weary negotiations, he settled for a party of which 35 were to be servitors. The ship that the French finally launched for the Embassy was 'L'Aurore' which could provide for just 70 including the crew. The available evidence suggests that ship-building had made considerable headway in Mysore in the eighteenth-century and was no longer a matter of building the small *paroes* which the Maraikkars of Calicut and the Mammalis of Cannanore had employed in their naval engagements against the Portuguese two centuries earlier.

Tipu had enjoined his ambassadors to recruit some artisans and professionals from France and also to collect some plants and instruments from France. He was interested in barometers, thermo-meters, spectacles, clocks and the printing press.[11] The French supplied most of what he asked for, especially those articles which he sought repeatedly. The cypress trees in Lal Bagh where his body was laid to rest alongside his father Haidar's, were obtained from France, through his ambassadors. Just before leaving France in October 1788, the ambassadors had drawn up contracts of appointments in Mysore for a number of French professionals, almost all of whom reached Mysore and took up their assignments.

One of those recruited was a French surgeon, Benard, whose services were terminated soon after he joined. Benard complained to the Pondicherry Governor, Conway, about the breach of contract and about 'the inequities' heaped on him by Tipu Sultan. Conway was one of Tipu's bitterest critics and used the French surgeon's complaint as a strong weapon to run down Tipu's reputation in French circles; but the correspondence that was exchanged on this topic of the French surgeon shows Tipu at his persuasive best. He argues that the services of the surgeon were terminated because he brought no new skills or methods in medical treatment to Mysore. Evidence in favour of Tipu's arguments is quite weighty especially in the light of the records maintained by the hospitals in French Indian settlements at the time which show that the French depended heavily on ayurvedic medicines, bonesetters and physicians.[12]

Tipu took great pride in presenting coins to French governors and commanders, displaying the quality and sophistication of his numismatic issues. On 21 September 1787, Cossigny, then Governor at Pondicherry, received a letter from Tipu, written in Telugu by Seshayya, announcing the glad tidings of the birth of a son.[14] Along with the letter, he sent two gold rupees, five pagodas[15], two gold *fanams*, five silver rupees, five half-rupees, five quarter rupees and five one-eighth rupees. The French officers were duly impressed by the coins, which according to the evidence were minted in Mysore from metals mined locally. The highest denomination of French coins at this time was the *livre* which stood at 2.5 to 1 with the Mysore silver rupee in 1788.

Cossigny's letter from Pondicherry dated 5 July 1786[16] refers to a musket 'produced by Tipu Sultan's workers' presented to him by Tipu. In his comments on the musket he grades it equal to any produced in Europe. Nagar is the town identified by Cossigny as the centre of Tipu's munitions industry. Tipu presented two pistols manufactured in Mysore to Louis XVI[17] which were judged by French experts to be of excellent quality. On one occasion, in November 1787, Tipu sent back 500 muskets forwarded to Mysore by Conway for the reason that they were inferior in quality to those produced in Mysore.[18]

In March 1785, the French authorities at Pondicherry drew up a general military and economic review of Tipu's Mysore.[19] This balance sheet itemizes Mysore's natural resources: 'pepper, sandalwood, cardamom, cotton textiles, rice, other grains and lacquer; its expansive forests offer products for the maritime powers: leather, coir, iron, ink, muslin, and voiles which are manufactured there. At Seringapatam, where they manufacture ten muskets per day, there are ammunition depots; also at Bangalore and Nagar where they prepare ammunition for their artillery. The Nabub also has foundries in these places for the manufacture of bronze cannons. There are gold mines in his country in the ranges of Coorg; the rivers there carry gold grains sometimes as big as a pepper pea.'[20] This evaluation is endorsed by another report drawn up later in the year.

Notes and References

1 H.C. Rice, *Thomas Jefferson in Paris*, Princeton, 1976, Ch. 8, pp. 95–96; J.P. Boyed, *The Papers of Thomas Jefferson*, Princeton, 1976, Vol. 12, pp. 502–04, fn; Vol. 13, pp. xxx–xxxi; K.A. Antonova, 'Tipu Sultan and the French', *Central Asian Review*, Vol. XI, No. I, 1966.

2 Bhagwan S. Gidwani, *The Sword of Tipu* (New Delhi, 1976).

3 S.N. Askari, 'Some Letters of Tipu Sultan', *Indian Historical Records Commission*, New Delhi; Sethumadhava Rao, *Eighteenth Century Deccan* (Bombay, 1980).

4 G.P. Taylor, 'The Coins of Tipu Sultan', *Indian Antiquary*, Vol. XVIII; J.R. Henderson, *The Coins of Haidar Ali and Tipu Sultan* (London, 1936).

[5] Archives Nationales Depot d'Outre Mer (ANDOM), Aix-en-Provence, Inde-F.V. 3237; also Archives Nationales, Paris, Colonies C2-166.

[6] E. Gaudart, *Catalogue de quelques documents des Archives de Pondichery* (Pondicherry, 1931). Some of the original documents here referred to have been microfilmed and deposited with the Department of History in the University of Calicut.

[7] Mohibbul Hasan, *History of Tipu Sultan* (Calcutta, 1971), pp. 115–24. See also M.P. Sridharan, 'Some South Indians in 18th Century France', *Proceedings of South Indian History Congress*, Trivandrum, 1980.

[8] Archives Nationales (AN), Paris, Colonies C2-189, p. 23.

[9] Ibid., p. 47, also C4-73, C2-174.

[10] ANDOM, Colonies, Inde, F.V. Nos. 878 to 1125, No. 4535 to 5361.

[11] AN, C2-179 lines 10, 11.

[12] Ibid., pp. 87, C2-181.

[13] *ANDOM*, Colonies, F.V.N. 2438.

[14] *AN*, C2-180–150.

[15] According to a glossary drawn up in Karaikal (AN, C2-178, pp. 53–9), pagodas were gold coins because of the effigy of a Bhagwati which they carried. *Fanom* is the French variant *Panam*, five gold *fanoms* being equivalent to a gold rupee.

[16] AN, Ce.177, pp. 167–77.

[17] Ibid., C2-174, C2-179, C2-189.

[18] Ibid., C2-185, p. 28.

[19] Ibid., C2-174, p. 3.

[20] Ibid.

19

The Regulations of Tipu Sultan for His State Trading Enterprise

Iftikhar A. Khan

I offer here a translation of some of Tipu's commercial instructions and regulations contained in *The Hukmnamaha-i-Tipu Sultan*, 'Orders of Tipu Sultan', a manuscript copy of which is preserved in the India Office Library, London. I have used a photocopy at the Centre of Advanced Study in History Library at the Aligarh Muslim University, Aligarh. These were translated, with much abridgement and error, but some useful explanations, by William Kirkpatrick, an English official of the East India Company in his *Select Letters of Tippoo Sultan*.[1]

What William Kirkpatrick has translated and annotated in his *Select Letters of Tippoo Sultan* is just a small fragment of the state papers of Mysore which he obtained for his book from Colonal Ogg of the East India Company's Madras Establishment. He duly acknowledges the help given by Colonel Ogg and expresses his appreciation for his keen interest in the collection and preservation of the state records of Mysore for their public use.

The Persian manuscript of Tipu's commercial regulations and a collection of papers and ordinances was obtained by the East India Company from Colonel Ogg. The orders and ordinances on various commercial issues were issued by Tipu Sultan in two sets: one on 25 March 1793 (14th of Ahmadi of the year 1221 AH) and the other on 2 April 1794 (3rd of Ahmadi 1222 AH).[2]

Now that the original Persian text is available to us, one should no longer rely on Kirkpatrick's defective summary and commentary, as has been largely done till now.[3]

These regulations show how in the 1790s Tipu, shorn of half

148

his kingdom in the Third Mysore War, was trying to develop commerce within his kingdom and to establish profitable lines of commerce with other territories in India and with West Asia. He was obviously copying the organization of the European East India Companies with only this difference that the capital raised for his 'Company' was from the state treasury, though as the regulations show, profits were expected to add to it. Kirkpatrick observed: 'It may, indeed, be reasonably doubted, whether either the resources of his country, or his genius, were equal to the realization of so bold a plan, but it is as well perhaps, that he was not allowed time for the experiment.'[4]

Indeed, whether Tipu was equal to the task or not, the very fact that he seriously endeavoured to build up a 'public-sector company' like the one these regulations envisage sets him far above other contemporary Indian rulers, who were totally unmindful of such possibilities and indifferent to any modernization of economic life.

Tipu's regulations contained in the *Hukmnama* show that he tried to maintain a considerable personal control over the affairs of his 'Company' and its commercial factories within and outside Mysore. He wished to further the export of merchandise and encourage imports of treasure like any good bullionist. His emphasis on shipbuilding and the enlargement of his merchant fleet not only again puts him above his peers, but shows that his commercial enterprise was backed by investment in the ship-building industry. He personally wrote to some prominent foreign merchants and invited them to Mysore. He had many innovative plans in his mind[5] which did not fructify owing to his destruction by the English in 1799. Kirkpatrick, a critic of Tipu, pointed out, 'the circumstances surrounding the Sultan did not allow time for the experiment'.[6]

Translation of Select Regulations
In The Name of God,
Most Gracious, Most Merciful
(Seal)

Order written to the chief merchants (*Maliku-t-Tujar*) in charge, of the factories of the *Sarkar-i Khudadad* (Sultan's Government),[7] Ismail Khan, Mir Nasiq Ali, Gulab Khan, Rahat Khan Battani (etc.), nine of you are hereby appointed to the post of Chief merchants. They are required (a) to take care of the business of the ships and factories[8] and the victorious army of the *Sarkar-i Khudadad* in the territories of other countries; (b) to buy, sell and obtain coin and bullion, i.e. gold, silver, etc.[9] and different kinds of cloth,[10] sandal-wood, round pepper, small and big cardamoms, betel-nut, coconut, copra, rice,[11] red sulphur (*kibrit-i ahmar*),[12] and elephants and other commercial goods; (c) to issue firm and true convenants (*qaul*) to get invited and invite merchants from foreign countries;[13] (d) to select trustworthy accountants (*mutasaddi-i kifayatsha'ar*) and alert, experienced, unselfish and honest agents (*gumashta*), who are skilled in accountancy and business, and appoint them over the factories; (e) to look after the management of commercial business without any loss; (f) to maintain accurate records and accounts, while at sea and in port; (g) not to allow any theft[14] or embezzlement; and (h) not to show negligence in managing the entire affairs of the factories (*kothis*) and ships within the kingdom and outside. Considering God and his Prophet (Peace be on him) to be present as witness it is their duty of work for carrying out these duties in accordance with the *Hukmnama* within their own jurisdiction and other factories to the best of their ability. To bring about and get all the above work done is their duty; indeed, deeming themselves responsible they should actively strive towards this end. With the help of Almighty Allah, whenever the four classes (*chahar firqa*)[15] are asked to present themselves at the Court for consultation on some matters, the people of the aforesaid four classes, keeping in mind God and His Prophet as being present and witnessing their conduct and word[16] should submit (for the consideration of the Sultan) whatever they deem in the interest of *Sarkar-i Khudadad* and the welfare of the people and likely to enhance (our) good name and repute. They should do their best to devote their life to the execution of the great task and consider it as their bounded responsibility as has been stated in the Noble Tradition (*Hadith Sharif*) 'Effort is for me and to fulfil is for God'.

Rescript I

The above Chief merchant along with the office secretaries and office accountants that, considering God and His Prophet as present and Witnesses should take oath according to their religion and have reliance upon God, and should count themselves subject to the four kinds of loyalty.[17] They should unite with one heart and one mind in conducting and effecting the business of the *Sarkar-i Khudadad*. If by chance, which God forbid, any one acts contrary to his pledge and joins in violating the loyalty of four kinds, it is necessary that all should join to accuse and shame him, and bring the matter to the knowledge of this Court and punish the culprit harshly so that others may take a lesson from this measure. From the officers-in-charge of the territories (*'ilaqa-daran)* of the various factories under them, they should exact the said oaths according to their faiths and they should put them to work in the business of the *Sarkar-i Khudadad.* Whenever anyone does anything contrary to the four kinds of loyalty, it is the duty of all to see that the culprit is punished according to the above order and the decrees of God and His Prophet. The four kinds of loyalty are: (1) By the eye; (2) By the ear; (3) By the hand; (4) By the tongue. It is with these four things that God gives capability and guidance to His servants. In the execution of business all officials should sit together and consult among themselves and without informing the *mutasaddi,* etc. they should record the statements of each person in their register, and obtain their signatures and put them in a box, setting a seal on the cover. They should follow the [decision taken] in consultation. If the opinion of six or seven persons is the same and in favour of one course of action, and the opinion of three or four is not in favour of that course, the opinion of the majority should be accepted and acted upon accordingly. Relying on God, the majority opinion should be followed. If any inquiry takes place later, the signed documents could be submitted in defence and the [false] reports of interested parties will be rendered futile. Whatever the questions needing answers within their jurisdictions are, should be written out in detail and submitted to the Court so that upon its presentation, whatever orders are issued in response may be carried out without any sign of defiance. In case the matter concerns a large amount of money and the query and reply are of a serious and secret nature, the application and other papers should be written in their own hands and personally brought and submitted at the Court so that His Majesty may record his reply in his own august hand so that it should reach them in confidence. Written in His Majesty's own order: 'Our orders and documents with our seal and writing should be kept in a box closed with a seal on it, in the treasury at the capital through Mir Miran, and copies thereof be left with the [respective] officer'. Order issued in the third month of Ahmadi of the Rasikh (48th) year, 1222 (or 1220) of the Birth of Muhammad (Peace be on him).

151

Five lines in his Majesty's hand: 'Appointments to posts of service and writers in office, candidates should be proposed from amongst Quraishis, Saiyids, Sunnis, and prayerful Hanafis,[18] so that nothing is done contrary to our inclination'.

Rescript II
Ships up to the number of one hundred ships[19] of the Khizri and Ilyasi class[20] are to be constructed, of which immediately 10 ships of Khizri and Ilyasi are to be built from resources of *Sarkar-i Khudadad*, together with men [and] equipment for war, [the work] having been entrusted to you. You are also expected to provide persons who are trustworthy and experienced in war, etc., as well as men of business, so as to engage in commerce wholeheartedly and with dedication. Necessary material like wood, iron, ropes, etc., required for the construction of the vessels *Khizri* and *Ilyasi* is to be purchased and the ships made ready. If for purchase of war equipment, money is not found sufficient, a report should be made to the Court and the required amount obtained. Labourers of all kinds should be paid their wages and the ships built.

Rescript III
The Muscat and Kutch factories, with their order and the seal[21] for the areas of jurisdiction of the factories, have been placed in your charge. You are expected to send reliable and alert people to the above mentioned factories. The charge of the materials should be received by your agents, for which acknowledgements should be given to the older [i.e. the relieved] officials. Whatever qualities of pepper, sandalwood, cinnamon, coconut, betel-nut and rice are needed for trade, you should inform the Court thereof, and get the written order of the *Asif-i Huzur*.[22] The goods should be sold by them through the factories that you have at various places. They should not allow the said goods to be dealt with by anyone except your agents.[23] Every year 600 *rati* of crude sulphur, namely, sulphur of the first quality, should be obtained by purchase from the Muscat factory.[24] The Court should be kept informed, and whenever you are ordered to, you should send it and obtain a receipt for it. Their *Sar-naib* (principal Deputy) who should be attached to each *Asif* should in the jurisdiction of his respective *Kachehri* deal through the agents, in all coined and uncoined precious metal, namely gold and silver and sandalwood, i.e. three items

except the above-mentioned forest produce. The *Asif* should not interfere, but rather help these deputies of theirs. No one else should be
allowed to deal in the above items.

Rescript IV

A sum of four lakhs of *Rahatis*[25] has been placed in your
custody for commerce and buying and selling of gold and silver, coined
and uncoined, cloth, elephants,[26] etc. The articles of commerce should
be made ready so that with God's grace there may be immense profit.
The sandal, cinnamon, pepper, rice, betel-nut and coconut, dry and
wet, *darchini*[27] and elephants, whatever they have asked for trade from
the Court, could be obtained from the *Asifs* at fixed prices after getting
a royal order; they should pay the price thereof to the *Asif* of the
Kachehri and get a receipt. The profits occurring from the sale of the
aforementioned commodities should be credited to the account of
factories under you. Whatever of the coined and uncoined gold and
silver and merchandise is purchased at the Court or by the *Asif* of the
Kachehri or the heads of the *Kachehri*, they should take money in cash.
And, of the aforementioned goods, whatever of them they buy from
the *Asif* of the Kachehri and head of Kachehri and districts (*ta'alluqas*)
they should pay for them in cash. If in these transactions three or four
months pass, there is no harm. They should pay the taxes of the
kingdom, etc. to the officers concerned (*ta'alluqdars*) according to the
norm in the same way as the subjects (*ri'aya*) pay as per rules. Be it
known to each of the four categories appointed in the *Sarkar-i
Khudadad* whatever is received by them, within their jurisdictions, in
cash and kind as acknowledgement thereof entered in the books of the
ledger, with the signature and seal and signature of the officer on the
margins, and below that the sign of the ledger at the end and the
binding (*shiraza*), the seal and signature of his jurisdiction. If it consists
of one sheet, he should put it at the end of it. He should bring it to the
Royal Court, and obtain His Majesty's stamp, special seal and signature
and seal on the front of it, and [thereafter] submit it. The duplicates of
the receipts should be kept in the office and acknowledgements of
receipt should be obtained from each *ta'alluqa* and given according to
the procedure prescribed above. On account of the administration of
the state, four classes have been distinguished according to the requirements and in accordance with their jurisdictions. Every arrangement
(*saranjam*),[28] which is needed for those of each class, should be

brought to the notice of the Court six months before the arrangement (*saranjam*) is due [to be affected], and an order from the Court being obtained in that matter, the required materials should be acquired from the above-mentioned holders of jurisdictions, and among which-ever places these are to be given; these should be distributed. The original of the order [to] you and your officials, which is issued from the Court with the [Sultan's] seal and writing [and] the copy of the order [to] you and [your] factories, together with acknowledgement, promissory note and receipts, [should be kept] in your own presence with a seal stamped on it. The original order with certificates, such as receipts and promissory notes, should be kept in a sealed box in the treasury of the capital, Pattan [Srirangapatnam]. Whenever the clerks of the Court are summoned to the presence, the *Arz Begi* would inform them of this, and one person from amongst you and one *mi'sai* of office and one Hindu writer of the office should attend the Court and remain till the Court is adjourned. Whatever questions and answers take place, you should properly understand them, and whatever relates to your own jurisdiction, you should make submission therefore. Whatever is then pronounced in response thereto [by the Sultan], you should carry out. They should get written the instructions for implementation assigned to them [upon] the representations of one [whole] year; and these should be put in a box, closed with their seal and securely kept. All the four set classes should be present and attend at the aforesaid time. The advantage of this is that all the four classes would be infor-med of each other's affairs and there will remain no obstruction to the management of affairs.

Rescript V

In the entire dominion of the *Sarkar-i Khudadad* agents are to be appointed to serve at 30 places as recorded [below].[29] In propor-tion to the volume of commerce at those places, money should be supplied so that trade may be carried on in coined and uncoined metal, as well as in [several] kinds of cloth, etc. In whatever [goods] profit may be obtained, commerce is to be conducted. In the remaining *ta'alluqas*, the *Sarkar-i Khudadad* should be supplied with 1,000 to 2,000 *Rahatis* every year at [the expected] profit of 5 *fanams* a *Rahati*, excluding expenses. Care should be taken that no commercial transaction may be executed except in coined and uncoined gold and silver. Commerce in other stock, e.g. cloth, should not be undertaken.

The next year (in territories outside the 30 listed factories), another person should be appointed to the post and [the amount of capital] be given to him, raising something over and above the [expected] profit of 5 *fanams* [a *Rahati*]. In the said *ta'alluqas* no individual should be allowed to deal in coined and uncoined gold and silver. It should be impressed upon agents that they should not let anyone's money be used for the grant of a loan and with regard to the *hawala* (bill of exchange), except for a person who makes a deposit of Rs 1,000 as security in return for gold and silver, gems, cloth, etc. If he so wishes, he can take a bill of Rs 1,200 and enter [the trade]. In the other *ta'alluqas* that the thirty agents have been left to serve, the returns are found to exceed [the principal]. In other *ta'alluqas* too servants shall be appointed and profits obtained. Elephants should be purchased from the government at a price, they should be despatched to places where they are required and then sold. If orders are issued for the purchase [of elephants] on behalf of the *Sarkar-i Khudadad*, the elephants should be purchased and obtained at Mahmud Bandar, etc., and sent to the Court.

Rescript VI

In the *ta'alluqas* of the *Sarkar-i Khudadad* wherever textiles of better and fine quality are produced, it is ordered that agents should be posted there and the fine and better sort should be produced economically and purchased and sent to places for sale where it is in demand. Similarly, in other countries where better and fine cloth of the above sort is manufactured, deputies (*na'ibs*) may be sent so that they may buy and bring them and sell them to advantage. Sandal, black pepper, betel-nut, cardamoms, coconut, cinnamon, etc., all such products of the dominions of the *Sarkar-i Khudadad* [should] be sent to [parts of] the dominions of the *Sarkar-i Khudadad* and other countries for sale under deputies. From the place the products in demand [here may be obtained and sold and profit realized].

Rescript VII

The posting of deputies: In accordance with the above, the necessary order should be got written and cardamoms, sandal, black pepper, betel-nut be obtained from the *Asif* of the *Kachehri* and sent to the [several] factories under your jurisdiction and sold there. Should other merchants purchase the aforesaid items from the government and sell them, there is no harm. In the dominions of the *Sarkar-i Khudadad* according to the names listed below, 30 factories (*kothis*) may be installed and deputies be appointed to serve there. There, the abovementioned articles and gold and silver, coined and uncoined, and cloth of every region should be purchased and sold off. Saleable articles (i.e. saleable at advantage) may be sold. Whatever uncoined gold and silver is obtained should be brought from the various factories, and a fourth of it given to the mint, to be collected after getting it coined and giving the expenses to the mint according to the regulations.

The list of the factories is as under:

1. Patan, the Capital
2. Salamabad (Sattimunglum)
3. Vefiemungal (Arivacoochy)
4. Bangalore
5. Bangloor
6. Kolar
7. Murwagal
8. Madan Pillai
9. Zafarabad (Guramkundah)
10. Punganoor
11. Raichouty
12. Faiz-hisar (Gooty)
13. Dharmwar (Dharmawaram)
14. Farrukhyat Hisar (Chittledoorg)
15. Be-nazeer
16. Hurrial
17. Nagpur (Bidnore)
18. Shikarpur
19. Sonda
20. Kurail (Mangalore)
21. Khushalpur
22. Barkur
23. Karwar
24. Jamalabad
25. Bhalkal
26. Fathabad
27. Karoor (Guroar)
28. Kurap (Gurap)
29. Banwasi
30. Gardun Shukoh (Nandydoorg)

Rescript VIII

You should write petitions to rulers of other countries on your own behalf and send them along with robes of honour with manly persons and invite promises (*qaul*) [of good reception] and establish factories in foreign countries. Suitable to need, deputies should be appointed to those factories supplied with money. Various kinds of rarities of those countries should be brought here and sold, and rarities and other commodities of this country and [other] products should be sent to those factories and sold there. The list of 17 factories to be established in other countries is undernoted. For the establish-ment of the factories whatever expenditure is required should be incurred.

1. Kurnool
2. Cheena-Patan (Madras)
3. Pahalcheri (Pondichery)
4. Poonah
5. Kurpah
6. Nagore (in Tanjore)
7. Werage (belonging to Poona)
8. Maligaon (belonging to Hyderabad)
9. Pagar Kotch (belonging to the Rasta)
10. Utnee (belonging to Rasta)
11. Nandair (belonging to Hyderabad)
12. Humnadad (belonging to Hyderabad)
13. Raichore (belonging to Adoni)
14. Muscat
15. Kutch
16. The country of Nasir Khan, i.e. Sind; Karachi Bandar
17. Mahi-Bandar (belonging to the French)

Notes and References

[1] W. Kirkpatrick, *Select Letters of Tippoo Sultan* (London, 1811).

[2] Ibid., Appendix E as contained in the *Hukmnamaha-i Tipu Sultan*.

[3] Nikhiles Guha, *Pre-British State System in South India: Mysore 1761–1789*, (Calcutta, 1985), also uses only Kirkpatrick.

[4] Kirkpatrick, *Select Letters*, p. 234

[5] See M.H. Gopal, *History of Tipu Sultan's Mysore*, p. 20.

[6] Kirkpatrick, *Select Letters*, p. 234.

[7] Tipu was of the view that he was a trustee, a chosen individual of a ruling class and was made accessible to riches, rank and power by the Creator. He was born to serve the people and look after their welfare. The government that he had established was a gift of God. Kabir Kausar (trs.), *Secret Correspondence of Tipu Sultan* (Delhi, 198), p. 307.

[8] Initially the aim was to establish 30 factories in Mysore and 17 in other regions of India and abroad but in fact, a few factories were successfully established; the ones with the most potential of them outside India were at Muscat in Oman (1785) and Jedda. The official-in-charge of the factory was called *darogha*. He was assisted by a *mutasaddi* and *gumashta*. See Mohibbul Hasan, *History of Tipu Sultan* (Calcutta, 1971), p. 345.

[9] The last quarter of the eighteenth century is significant for the import of large amounts of bullion by Indian merchants into India from both the Red Sea as well as the Persian Gulf. The value of precious metal as a country's major source of economy was well known to all economists of the time and Tipu was not unaware of this situation. There were five mints

at Seringapatam. The supply of metal was made by an official called the *darogha* and after the minting was over he received the coins and put them into the treasury, ibid., p. 335.

10 Cloth constituted one of the chief items of export of Mysore. The cloth-weaving industry was mainly concentrated at Bangalore, Waluru, etc. See Francis Buchanan, *Journey From Madras through Mysore, Canara and Malabar* (1807, reprint Delhi, 1988), pp. 40, 326.

11 This constituted one of the 'gruff goods' in Mysore's regular consignments to Muscat. Merchants of the Portuguese and English ports were not allowed to purchase rice in Tipu's dominion. There was no restriction on the purchase of rice from Mysore's inhabitants by the Muscat merchants (Kirkpatrick, *Select Letters,* pp. 238–39).

12 This was one of the major items of import and the main ingredient of gunpowder. It was imported mainly from Muscat (Kirkpatrick, *Select Letters,* p. 209).

13 Earlier as well, the Sultan had invited merchants from foreign countries. On at least one occasion he personally wrote to two of the Armenian merchants, namely Khwaja Seth and Khwaja Heratoon and promised them his full support and cooperation during their stay in his dominion (Kirkpatrick, *Select Letters*, pp. xi-xii.

14 Tipu may be referring to the nature of theft and punishment according to different schools of jurisprudence but I have not been able to trace evidence of such punishment ever being awarded to anyone (*Hukmnamaha-i Tipu Sultan,* Rescript-IX, folios 20b–21a).

15 The four classes were Quraishis, Saiyids, Sunnis and *prayerful* Hanafis and identified by their presence and sitting arrangements in the Court (*Hukmnamaha-i Tipu Sultan,* fo. 23b). See also the subsequent lines of Rescript I.

16 Such invocations are not uncommon in Tipu's orders.

17 See the ensuing lines of the same Rescript.

18 Perhaps these four classes were very firm in their loyalty to Tipu.

19 During the period when Tipu issued a series of commercial orders, he had simultanously also embarked on creating a naval force. Kirkpatrick thinks this was too fantastic a plan to materialize, perhaps on the grounds that it was not possible for Tipu to afford the expenses of the project. We have some estimate of Tipu's income: Macleod would have us believe that Tipu's income was 83,67,549 pagodas and an additional ten lakhs that he had made in 1795. This can be corroborated by Read. Mohibbul Hasan regards it as a highly exaggerated figure since in 1792 Macleod's figure of Tipu's receipts was between 25 and 35 lakh pagodas. To quote Mohibbul Hasan, 'But there could not have been so much difference between demands and receipts considering the structure and efficiency of Tipu's administration' (Mohibbul Hasan, *Tipu Sultan,* p. 344). Yet there are two more instances of Tipu's wealth. Just one or two years before his plan to create a powerful naval force, Tipu, after his defeat in the Third Anglo–Mysore War, was led to sign a treaty (19 February 1792) with the East India Company and its

allies. One of the terms of the treaty was that Tipu had to pay in cash three crores and thirty lakhs as indemnity (*Authentic Memoirs of Tippoo Sultan,* p. 17). Another instance of Tipu's wealth was found after the fall of Seringapatam on 4 May 1799. Tipu's treasure as found in the palace amounted to three millions (currency not mentioned) (*Authentic Memoirs of Tippoo Sultan,* p. 119).

[20] Ships of two different builds, but the distinction between them not made. The only distinction that one can find is in the number of cannons mounted on them. These ships were to be equipped on the modern pattern and named after the prophets, *Khizr* and *Iliyas,* and both were men-of-war. Tipu also desired ships of good quality to be constructed. One such variety was a *dhow* for whose construction the services of shipwrights were hired from Muscat. One kind of *dhow* was the *ghurab,* a three-masted vessel with a sharp bow. The swifter kinds of vessel during Tipu's period were of European model known as the frigate. See Patricia Risso, *Oman and Muscat— An Early Modern History* (London, 1986), pp. 216–17.

[21] A description of the seal made for each factory and identified by the inscription engraved on it, such as *Zarf-i Zahb* (the golden vase or vessel) for the Kutch factory, or *Kan-i Zar* (mine of gold) for the Muscat factory, is given in Kirkpatrick, *Select Letters,* Appendix-e, pp. XXXVIII–IXn.

[22] The term 'Asoph' (as Kirkpatrick has used it) is the corruption of the Persian word *Asif* used for the Chief Governor of a large district under Tipu Sultan (Buchanan, vol. 3, Index). Mohibbul Hasan designates *Asif* as a Civil Governor having jurisdiction over a province (*Tipu Sultan,* p. 337). The *Asif* also imparted justice in the town; see ibid., p. 338. Mohibbul Hasan seems to nearly concur with Kirkpatrick who identifies an 'asoph' as an official-in-charge of a district (see Kirkpatrick, *Select Letters,* Appendix-E, p. XXXVII). But '*Air Asif,* according to Kirkpatrick is the Revenue Department of Tipu's time whereas '*mir Asif* has been interpreted as the Head of the Department of Revenue by Mohibbul Hasan (*Tipu Sultan,* p. 331). It may therefore be inferred that *Asif-i Huzur* was the administrative official directly responsible to the Sultan.

[23] These agents (*gumashtaha*) were Maoji Seth, who had his own agents as well, and Abdullah, the Jew, both of them attached to Tipu's factory at Muscat, Mohibbul Hasan, *Tipu Sultan,* p. 131. For Maoji Seth's agents, Prem and Sewa, see *Waqa-i Manazil-i Rum* (ed.) Mohibbul Hasan, p. 41.

[24] Prudence in purchasing commodities had always been a matter of special consideration for Tipu. In a letter to Mir Kazim (12 January) he asked him to buy sulphur when its price had come down to a moderate level; Mir Kazim had however, to see that the regular supply of sulphur was maintained (Kirkpatrick, *Select Letters,* pp. 231, 282–83.

[25] It was equal to £1,28,000 sterling of Kirkpatrick's period (Appendix, XL).

[26] Mysore's territory extended to the Western Ghats, which were notorious for elephants who always devastated the cultivation and created fear in the adjoining settlements. Hejuru, the high hills of the southern region of Humpa pura Betta, Chica Deva Betta etc. were the main abodes of

159

elephants. Hunting the animal had to be conducted with due religious ceremonies. However, the animal was used as beast of burden for tasks such as carrying timber to rivers, *river* to nearby dockyards and ports, and was also exported to other countries. See Buchanan, *Journey from Madras*, vol. II, pp. 13, 122–23. Elephants were also sent as gifts to the rulers of foreign countries during Tipu's period. References to such gifts are numerous. See *Hukmnama* (*Mutafarriqa*), Asiatic Society of Bengal (xerox copy at the CAS, AMU), f. 14A; also Abdul Qadir, *Waqa'i Manazil-i Rum* (ed.) M. Hasan (Bombay, 1968), pp. 2, 3 & *passim*.

[27] Identified as *Cassia Cinnamon* in George Watt, *Dictionary of the Economic Products of India*, vol. II, p. 319; for other details, see Irfan Habib, *Atlas of the Mughal Empire* (Delhi, 1982), p. 66 (Sheet 16B).

[28] The most appropriate interpretation of this word seems to be 'material', 'ingredient', 'provision' and 'supply' in order of sequence. In other documents of Tipu's period the word *saranjam* is a matter of common occurrence. See Abdul Qadir, *Waqa'i Manazil-i Rum* (original, copy at the CAS, AMU), folios 25a; *Hukmnama* (*Mutafarriqa*), f. 25b (*saranjam i zoruri*) f. 5a (*mazduran waghaira saranjam ta'yyari-i 'am, nawisanida*), etc.

[29] See Rescript VII, folios 17a–18a.

20
Developing Agriculture: Land Tenure under Tipu Sultan

B. Sheik Ali

The system of land tenure existing in Karnataka under Vijayanagar resembled the European fiefs, subject to a certain assessment of revenue under regular measurement or estimate of production. When the Southern provinces fell to the Bijapuris under the command of Randaula Khan in 1644 who established a new government at Sira, no great alterations were made in the existing land tenure. In fact he committed the province to the charge of the Maratha chief, Shahji, and thus kept his new conquests free from the admixture of Turkish traits in land revenue prevailing in Bijapur, namely the Timaryet system or the grant of extensive *jagirs* to their commanders. When Mughal suzerainty was established over the South under Aurangzeb, he introduced the practice of assigning considerable tracts of the best lands to the *mansabdars*. During Haidar's regime also, the abuses of land magnates were not been prevented. He annually collected more than his assessment or rents. Consequently the task of completely developing the management of revenue fell to Tipu, who had acquired great knowledge and experience by his administration of the *jagirs* in Dharmpuri for fifteen years where he had introduced a number of reforms.

On his accession, Tipu modified the land tenure and restored it to what had existed in the lower Carnatic where Mughal influence had not penetrated deeply. Chiefly, he laid down certain rules for the distribution on arable land between the old and the new *rayats*. There were four kinds of land, wet, dry, *hissa* and *ijra*. *Hissa* lands were those where the produce was equally distributed between the state and the peasant and he was not expected to pay any fixed tax—like the *bhagra*

161

lands in Bengal. *Ijra* land was that which was leased to the *rayat* at a fixed rent, like *theka* land in Bengal. Out of these four categories of land every peasant would have an equal share. The grain seeds sown in *ijra* land were greater in quantity than in Hissa land.

Tipu encouraged chiefly two varieties of land tenures, the institution of hereditary property and the fixed rent. The first may be described in technical language as *meeras*, signifying inheritance. According to this the peasant secured the hereditary right of cultivation or the right of a tenant and his heirs to occupy a certain ground, so long as they continued to pay the customary rent of the district. The rent was paid only when the land was cultivated. But the state insisted on the cultivation of the land and that it should not be left fallow on any account. Those who defied this order ran the risk of forfeiting the land which was then bestowed on another. The rent varied under this tenure according to the produce. In the other tenure, system ownership of the land was vested with a landlord who collected the rent from his tenants and paid a fixed rent to the state. On his death the land was passed on to his son, thus respecting the right of succession. Such a system existed in Bednore, Ballam, Mysore and Tayoor provinces. In Canara, all the lands which the landlords did not immediately manage themselves, paid a fixed rent in money or kind. In Baramahal, the farmers held the land directly from the government and there were no landlords in that province.

Tipu introduced the system of collecting the rent in cash. Where the rents were fixed according to the grain, the lands were measured every year. If coins in metals like gold and silver, copper or brass were offered, they were accepted at their current prices in the bazar. These metals were not disposed of but deposited. Farming out the land was abolished and the state undertook the task of collecting the tax directly from the peasants. State officers were strictly instructed not to harass the ryots. They were not to interfere in their daily affairs except at the time of collecting taxes when they should adopt peaceful methods of collection. The rents fixed by the state were fair and moderate.

Those who cultivated dry land were assessed at about one-third of the crop. For the wet or rice lands, the payment was more, nearly half the crop and the tax was received in kind. The mode of estimating the quantity of land was not by actual measurement but by the quantity of seed grains required to sow the arable land. The term used was 'candy' which differed from district to district and from grain to grain. A candy of land meant the extent of land in which a candy of seed grain was sown. A candy consisted of twenty *kudus* and each *kudu* was of ten *seers*. There were varying types of *kudus*. But to assure an equal share the produce was distributed half and half between the state and the farmer. The candy of dry land was almost four times larger than the candy of wet land which was considered much superior to, and hence charged at a higher rate than dry land. The actual differences in rent between wet and dry lands was not 2–3 but 1–6 because the extent of one candy of paddy land was 24 measures, the state's share was 12. For dry land it should have been 8 but actually the state took only 2 measures from dry land for the same area as that of wet land, as the gross yield was only 6 measures. Brahmin cultivators paid only half the usual rent as their womenfolk did not work in the field. The state dues were not very high compared to the rentals in the same period in England, where the peasant paid one-third to the landlord, one-third going as husbandry charges, with only one-third left to him. In Mysore, the state took one-third from the peasant leaving two-thirds to him.

Lands were graded into three categories according to the fertility of the soil and the assessment depended on the productivity of the soil. A farmer cultivated both dry and wet lands and on an average he paid 40 per cent of his income to the state. The cultivation of a dry crop was most extensive and most certain. It was sown in the beginning of June and reaped in January. Nearly 25 varieties of crops were harvested, the principal dry grains being ragi, jari, bajra, dhal, horsegram, Bengal gram and green gram. Rice and sugarcane were the chief wet crops grown near the reservoirs or with Kaveri water. There was even scope for second crop in the lands fed by this river but Tipu discouraged more than one crop as it would reduce the fertility of the soil. Besides these foodgrains, other commercial crops like areca-nut, pepper, cardamom, tobacco and sandalwood brought good revenue, which was collected on the basis of a fixed money rent. Repairs to the tanks were attended to with special care and urgency. These tanks stood in constant need of repairs owing to the heavy rainfall which brought down good quantities of earth, and washed away the embankments in the rainy season. Cultivation of wasteland was encouraged by making it tax-free in the first year, charging one quarter in the second year, and the full thereafter. Tipu made it impossible by his reforms for tax collectors to rob the ryots and the government as in his father's days. That was why even his inveterate foes were compelled to declare, 'that his country was the best cultivated and its population the most flourishing in India'.

Notes and References

[1] Crisp, *The Mysorean Revenue Regulations.*

[2] Wilks, *Report on the Interior Administration of Mysore.*

[3] Zainal-Abidin Shustri, *Fatuhatu-l Mujahidin.*

[4] Buchanan, *A Journey from Madras through the Countries of Mysore, Canara, Malabar.*

[5] Munro, *A Narrative of the Military Operations on the Coromandel Coast— 1780–84.*

[6] Edmonstone, *Official Documents and Papers of Tipu's Government.*

[7] Kirkpatrick, *Official Correspondence and Other Papers.*

[8] Kirkpatrick, *Select Letters of Tipu Sultan.*

21
Tipu Sultan as Modernizer: A Contemporary British Critic

Francis Buchanan

Francis Buchanan, whose later surveys of eastern India are so well known, showed his talents when in 1800–01, at the instructions of the Governor-General Marquis Wellesley, he travelled extensively in the dominions that had belonged to Haidar Ali and Tipu Sultan, to collect all the information he could on 'the state of agriculture, arts and commerce, the religion, manners and customs, the history, natural and civil, and antiquities' of these territories. The resulting detailed account in the form of daily reports was published under the authority of the Court of Directors of the East India Company in 1807, in three volumes, under the title *A Journey from Madras through the Countries of Mysore, Canara and Malabar*.

Composing an official document, Buchanan was obviously biased against the two past Mysore rulers, especially Tipu Sultan. The following two passages from his narrative, one about Haidar Ali, as an agrarian administrator, and Tipu Sultan, as a modernizer, are not without interest.—Ed.

Haidar Ali's Agrarian Administration
Account of arrangements for division of harvest at Kolar

The heap is then [after harvest and the taking away of some petty shares] measured, and divided equally between the government, or renter, and the farmer; but a certain portion is left, which is divided as follows:

From this portion twelve *Seers* for every *Candaca* in the heap are measured, of which the accomptant takes one third, and the remainder goes to the renter. This formerly belonged to the *Daishmucs*, or *Zemeendars*; but these having been abolished by *Haidar*, and officers paid by regular salaries having been established in their stead, it was but fair that government should receive this perquisite. Indeed, most of *Haidar's* operations in finance seem to have been highly judicious and reasonable; and on account of his justice, wisdom, and moderation, his memory is greatly respected by the natives of all descriptions.—*Journey from Madras*, I, p. 300.

Tipu Sultan as Modernizer
Account of Srirangapatnam

The apartment most commonly used by *Tippoo* was a large lofty hall, open in front after the Mussulman fashion, and on the other three sides, entirely shut up from ventilation. In this he was wont to sit, and write much; for he was a wonderful projector, and was constantly forming new systems for the management of his dominions which, however, he wanted perseverance to carry into execution. That he convinced himself to be acting for the good of his subjects, I have no doubt; and he certainly believed himself endowed with great qualities for the management of civil affairs; as he was at the pains of writing a book on the subject, for the instruction of all succeeding princes: his talents in this line, however, were certainly very deficient. He paid no attention to the religious prejudices of the greater part of his subjects; but everywhere wantonly destroyed their temples, and gloried in having forced many thousands of them to adopt the Mussulman faith. He never continued long on the same plan; so that his government was a constant succession of new arrangements. Although his aversion to Europeans did not prevent him from imitating many of their arts; yet this does not appear to have proceeded from his being sensible of their value, or from a desire to improve his country; it seems merely to have been done with a view of showing his subjects, that, if he chose, he was capable of doing whatever Europeans could perform; for although he made broad-cloth, paper formed on wires like the European kind, watches, and cutlery, yet the processes for making the whole were kept secret. A French artist had prepared an engine, driven by water for boring cannon; but so little sensible was the Sultan of its value, that he ordered the water wheel to be removed, and employed bullocks to work the machinery. One of his favourite maxims of policy was, to overthrow everything that had been done in the *Raja's* government; and in carrying this into practice, he frequently destroyed works of great public utility, such as reservoirs, and canals for watering the ground. Although an active prince, he in a great measure secluded

166

himself from his subjects (one of the greatest evils that can happen in an absolute monarchy); and his chief confidant, *Meer Saduc*, was a monster of avarice and cruelty. The people universally accuse *Tippoo* of bigotry, and vain-glory; but they attribute most of their miseries to the influence of his minister. The *Brahmans*, who managed the whole of the revenue department, were so avaricious, so corrupt, and had shown such ingratitude to *Haidar*, that *Tippoo* would have entirely displaced them, if he could have done without their services; but that was impossible; for no other persons in the country had any knowledge of business. Instead of checking them by a constant inspection into their conduct, by exemplary punishment when detected in peculation, and by allowing them handsome salaries to raise them above temptation, he appointed Mussulman *Asophs*, or Lord Lieutenants, to superintend large divisions of the country; and this greatly increased the evil; for these men, entirely sunk in indolence, voluptuousness, and ignorance, confident of favour from the bigotry of their sovereign, and destitute of principle, universally took bribes to supply their wants; and the delinquencies of the *Brahmans* were doubled, to make good the new demands of the *Asophs*, over and above their former profits. Owing to this system, although the Sultan had laid on many new taxes, the actual receipts of the treasury never equalled those in the time of his father. The *Amildars*, under various pretexts of unavoidable emergency, reported prodigious outstanding balances; while they received, as bribes from the cultivators, a part of the deductions so made. Although the taxes actually paid by the people to government were thus much lighter than they had been in the administration of *Haidar*, the industrious cultivator was by no means in so good a condition as formerly. The most frivolous pretexts were received, as sufficient cause for commencing a criminal prosecution against any person supposed to be rich; and nothing but a bribe could prevent an accused individual from ruin. *Tippoo* certainly had considerable talents for war; but his fondness for it, and his engaging with an enemy so much his superior in the art, brought on his destruction; while his early habits, of contending with the *Marattah* plunderers, had given him a ferocity and barbarity, that must prevent every considerate person from pitying his overthrow. The policy in which he succeeded best, was in attaching to him the lower Mussulmans. He possessed in the highest degree all the cant, bigotry, and zeal, so well fitted for the purpose, and which some few men of abilities have succeeded in assuming; but with him, I believe, they were natural. None of his Mussulmans have entered into our service, although many of them are in great want; and they all retain a high respect for his memory, considering him as a martyr, who died in the defence of their religion.

Though *Tippoo* had thus secured the affections of many of his subjects, and though he was perhaps conscious of good intentions, and fondly imagined that his government was fit to be a pattern to all others; yet whoever sees his private apartments, will be sensible, that the mind of the despotic monarch was torn with apprehension. Such is, perhaps, the universal state of men of this description; and although a knowledge of the circumstance may not be sufficient to prevent the ambitious from grasping at this power, nor to induce the person who has once possessed it to return to the calm of private life; yet it may be some consolation to the persons exposed to its baneful influence, to know, that their ruler enjoys less security and tranquillity of mind than themselves.

From the principal front of the palace, which served as a revenue office, and as a place from whence the Sultan occasionally showed himself to the populace, the chief entry into the private square was through a strong narrow passage, wherein were chained four tigers; which, although somewhat tame, would in case of any disturbance become unruly. Within these was the hall in which *Tippoo* wrote, and into which very few persons, except *Meer Saduc*, were ever admitted. Immediately behind this, was the bed-chamber, which communicated with the hall by a door and two windows, and was shut up on every other side. The door was strongly secured on the inside, and a close iron grating defended the windows. The Sultan, lest any person should fire upon him while in bed, slept in a hammock, which was suspended from the roof by chains, in such a situation as to be invisible through the windows. In the hammock were found a sword and a pair of loaded pistols.—*A Journey from Madras*, I, pp. 70–73.

Building a Navy

22

The Mysore Navy under Haidar Ali and Tipu Sultan

Raj Kumar

Recent Indian historical works on British rule in India suffer from a neglect of the naval perspective. We understand from the available sources that Haidar and Tipu possessed naval forces but no systematic research has been conducted on this subject so far in spite of stray references.[1]

The decision of Haidar and Tipu Sultan to fight British colonialism and their recognition that the secret of the success of the East India Company lay in their sea-power led them to contemplate the establishment of a strong navy.[2] In doing so their strategy was to seek the help of the European rivals of the British—the French, the Dutch and the Portuguese. They also succeeded in attracting some British subjects who helped them to build and also command some of their ships.[3]

Haidar created a naval fleet, some good ports and ship building yards.[4] Tipu possessed a number of men of war and had about 10,000 men manning a variety of ships. He issued marine regulation in 1796[5] and ordered the immediate building of forty warships.

Contemporary British records state clearly that Haidar Ali and later Tipu Sultan were most formidable enemies of the British.[6] They maintained a steadfast alliance with the French against their common adversary.[7] Evidence also exists of their efforts to maintain good relations with the Portuguese.[8] The Mysore rulers had also tried to enter into alliances with Afghanistan, Muscat, and Turkey,[9] which necessitated the building of a strong fleet. Moreover their English enemies were strong on the sea, their Portuguese neighbours relied on their navy in their struggle with Indian states, and the Peshwa possessed a

171

fleet of his own. And the conquest of the Malabar coast put Haidar Ali and Tipu in possession of the famous ports and the ship-building yards of that region.

We have evidence that Haidar Ali built vessels in the East India Company's marine yards at Honavar in 1763.[10] He is reported to have had a large fleet which the East India Company claimed to have destroyed in the year 1768.[11] We also understand from the same report that Haidar Ali was going to re-establish the fleet.[12] The Portuguese evidence proves that by 1765 the Mysore navy possessed 30 vessels of war and a large number of transport ships which were commanded by an Englishman with some European officers.[13] The Portuguese records further explain how Haidar Ali planned to build the most powerful fleet in Asia by building a stockade above the waterline in the Gulf of Batical in 1778.[14] Unfortunately, in 1780 Admiral Edward Hughes dealt a fatal blow to this maritime power.[15]

But we know that Tipu's fleet had practical existence as early as 1787.[16] Tipu's interest in the navy is evident from his letter to Ghulam Hussain dated 27 September 1786.[17] The Mysore sovereign turned his thoughts seriously to building a navy after the defeat of 1792. A separate Board of Admiralty was established in September 1786[18] and express orders were issued for the building of 40 warships and a number of transport ships at the Jamalabad, Wajidabad and Majidabad dockyards and other places on the west coast. The details available in the *Hukmnamas* leaves us in no doubt that the Mysore navy would have been the most powerful fleet in Asia and would have compared favourably with the best fleet in existence anywhere in the world but for the sudden death of Tipu in 1799.

Notes and References

[1] Mohibbul Hasan, *History of Tipu Sultan,* Calcutta, 1951; M.H. Gopal, *Tipu Sultan's Mysore* (Bombay, 1971).

[2] Raj Kumar, 'Naval Adventures of Tipu Sultan', Paper presented at the National Seminar on Tipu Sultan, Bangalore, Jan. 1992.

[3] Surendra Nath Sen, *Indian Historical Quarterly,* June 1930.

[4] Ibid.

[5] W. Kirkpatrick, *Select Letters of Tippoo Sultan* (London, 1811).

[6] Mark Wilks, *History of Mysore,* Vol. II (1810, rpt New Delhi, 1989).

[7] Ibid.

[8] Mohibbul Hasan, *Tipu Sultan.*

[9] Kirkpatrick, *Select Letters,* Appendix L.

[10] Public Dept. Diary Nos 40 and 41 (C.B.S. No. 90). Also see the diary of 1766, Nos. 46 and 47.

[11] British Museum, Additional MSS., folio 88. Also see Gopal, *Tipu Sultan's Mysore.*

[12] Ibid.

[13] Officios dos Governadores, Maco 3, No. 44.

[14] Officios dos Governadores, Maco 5, No. 70.

[15] C. R. Low, *History of the Indian Navy,* Vol. I, p. 178.

[16] Officios dos Governadores, Maco 20, No. 95.

[17] Kirkpatrick, *Select Letters,* pp. 414–15.

[18] Ibid., Appendix 'K'.

[19] Ibid.

23
Regulations of
Tipu Sultan's Navy

Mahmud Husain

In the establishment of British rule in South Asia naval supremacy, no doubt, played a vital role. Those who resisted British aggression either did not fully appreciate the value of naval power or lacked the determination and resources to build up a navy which could offer effective resistance to the British naval might.

Of the indigenous rulers, Tipu Sultan was one of the few who recognized the importance of naval power. Indeed his father himself had attempted to build up a navy, but his attempts had proved abortive. In 1768 the desertion of his naval commander, Stannet, caused the loss of many ships. This loss, however, did not deter him from undertaking the task once more. But misfortune persisted and the navy he built for the second time was almost completely destroyed through British action at Mangalore in 1780.

Tipu Sultan, on succeeding his father, first turned his attention to the building up of his army; but even so, he possessed from the beginning a number of war vessels. The chief function of these ships was to protect merchant ships from piracy. Administratively they were placed under the *Malik-al-Tujar* or the Board of Trade. These vessels were obviously no match for the British navy. The Third Mysore War convinced Tipu Sultan of the necessity of a strong navy, and during the last few years of his life he showed great keenness in this connection. By 1794 the Sultan had decided upon the construction of 40 war vessels.

In 1796 Tipu Sultan issued a *hukmnamah* or ordinance which laid down the regulations for the naval building programme which he had undertaken.[1] It is addressed to the *mirs yam* or lords of the

Admiralty who were eleven in number. These *mirs* constituted the Board of Admiralty with their headquarters at Seringapatam. The Board was established in the Jafari month of the *Mauludi* year 1224, reckoned from the birth of the Holy Prophet, corresponding to September 1796.[2]

Next in rank to the *mirs yam* were the *mirs bahr* who were officers of the highest rank to serve on the seas. Two of these were assigned to each squadron of four ships; in modern terminology they may be termed admirals or commodores.[3]

The programme contained in the *hukmnamah* visualized a naval force of forty ships which was to be placed under the care and superintendence of the *mirs yam* as soon as they were ready. They were, moreover, to be built with all possible dispatch. The names given to them all ended with the word 'Bakhsh', e.g., Muhammad Bakhsh, Ali Bakhsh, Sultan Bakhsh, etc. signifying 'bestowed by' or 'gift of' Muhammad, Ali and the Sultan respectively.[4]

The ships were divided into three *kachehris* or divisions, namely, the *kachehri* of Jamalabad or Mangalore, the *kachehri* of Wajidabad or Bascoraje and the *kachehri* of Majidabad or Sadasheogarh. The first of these *kachehris* was to consist of 12 ships and the last two of 14 ships each. With a view to expediting the completion of the project two *mirs yam* assisted by a *mirza-i-daftar* (office superintendent) and a *mutasaddi* (accountant) were appointed at Mangalore from whence they were to superintend the construction of the vessels intended for the Jamalabad division. Two other *mirs yam*, together with a *mirza-i-daftar* and a *mutasaddi* each, were stationed at or near Mir Jan Creek for the purpose of directing the construction of vessels for the Wajidabad and Majidabad divisions.[5]

The Admiralty Board was supplied with a model ship with a tiger figure head according to which all the vessels were to be built. The timber for the ships was to be procured from the state forests and then floated down various rivers to the respective dockyards. Of the ships to be built, 20 were to be line-of-battle, and 20 frigates divided among the three stations, as follows: for Jamalabad were intended 6 line-of-battle ships and 6 frigates. Of these line-of-battle ships, three were to be of 72 guns and the rest of 62 guns each. Of the 72 guns, 30 were to be 24-pounders, 30 were 18-pounders, 6 were 12-pounders and 6 were 9-pounders. Of the 62 guns, 4 were to be 24-pounders, 24 were 18-pounders, 24 were 12-pounders and 10 were 6-pounders. To

Wajidabad 14 ships were assigned, 7 line-of-battle ships and 7 frigates. Majidabad was to have 14 ships.[6]

The number of officers for the fleet fixed in the *hukmnamah* was as follows: there were to be in all 11 *mirs yam*, all stationed at the capital and 30 *mirs bahr*, of whom twenty were stationed on ships, two assigned to each squadron; and ten were to remain at the capital for instruction. The salary of the *mirs yam* and such *mirs bahr* as attended the court was to be fixed according to their qualifications. The twenty *mirs bahr* serving on the ships were to receive a monthly salary of 150 *imamis* or rupees.

The land establishment of each *kachehri* was to consist of three office superintendents, three writers, twelve clerks (*gumashtas*), one judge (*qazi*), two proclaimers, (*naqib*), eleven attendants (*hazirbashi*), eleven literate scouts (*sharbasharan*), and one chamberlain (*farrash*) who had charge of camp equipment and carpets, one torch-bearer or link-boy (*mash'alchi*) and one camel-driver (*sarban*). Their salaries ranged from twenty *rahatis* or pagodas in the case of the office superintendents to two *rahatis* or pagodas in the case of the torch-bearer.

Each ship of the line was to have the following establishment of officers: four *sardars* (officers) denominated First, Second, Third and Fourth, two *tipdars* and six *yuzdars*, along with a number of subordinate officers. The First *Sardar* was to have overall command. The Second *Sardar*, with one *tipdar* and two *yuzdars* under him, was placed in charge of the guns and gunners, the powder magazine and everything else appertaining to the guns as well as of the provisions. The Third *sardar*, with one *tipdar* and two *yuzdars* under him, was in charge of the marines and small arms. He was also to look after spare tools, implements and stores. The Fourth *Sardar* was to have particular charge of the *khalasis* or sailors, and of the artificers belonging to the ship such as blacksmiths, carpenters, etc. He was expected to superintend the cooking of the food and its distribution among the crew. The navigation of the ship was also entrusted to him. Orders for the hoisting and trimming of the sails were to come from him. He was to look after the tools and implements in immediate use which had to be kept in a proper condition. Any damage caused to the ship during war was to receive his immediate attention.

All the above officers were to be carefully selected and only

176

persons of good parentage and some amount of education were to be employed.

The complement of each line-of-battle ship was fixed at 346 men. Thus all the twenty line-of-battle ships together were to have an establishment of 6,920. The establishment was divided into five main categories: the musketeers, the gunners, the seamen, the artificers and the officers; and each category was divided into several sub-categories. Among the musketeers were included *tipdars, sharbasharans, nafir-nawazes* (fifers), *shahnainawazes* (trumpeters), *yuzdars* (lieutenants), *sarkhils* (second lieutenants), *jamadars* (sergeants), and privates. The gunners similarly were categorized as *tipdars, yuzdars, sarkhils, jamadars* and privates. The seamen included *jaqdars, dafadars* and privates. The artificers consisted of smiths and carpenters with a head-smith and head-carpenter. Officers included not only the First, Second, Third and Fourth *Sardars* but also the pilots, *darughas,* physicians and superintendents of offices. Details were given in the *hukmnamah* of the emoluments to be paid to the different classes of men, and these ranged from 24 pagodas in the case of Third and Fourth *Sardars* to 3 pagodas and 6 *fanams* for blacksmiths, fifers and trumpeters, and 3 pagodas to privates. In between these were the salaries of *tipdars* who got seven pagodas and six *fanams* and *sarkhils* who received four pagodas and eight *fanams*. Apart from the regular salary there was also the institution of a subsistence allowance. It is interesting to note that the difference between the salary of the *sarkhil* (lieutenant) and that of the *jamadar* (sergeant) was only four *fanams,* and the *jamadars* received only eight *fanams* more than the privates. There was not the kind of disparity between the salaries of officers and men to which we have become accustomed since British rule. The total monthly expenses of a line-of-battle ship, while in port, came to 1,471 pagodas and 5½ *fanams*. For the twenty such ships, the sum comes to 29,431 pagodas.[7]

Similar details regarding the establishment of the twenty frigates are given in the *hukmnamah,* the total expenditure on the frigates amounting to 16,171 pagodas. Thus the total monthly expenditure on a fleet of forty warships, exclusive of wear and tear, ammunition and stores, came to 45,602 pagodas or approximately 182,400 pounds sterling.

These emoluments were to be received by officers and men

while on shore. At sea they were also to receive rations which were fixed in the *hukmnamah*. As a *mir yam* might occasionally be employed with the fleet—normally he was stationed at the capital—he was in such cases to be provided with decent meals at the expense of the State. Officers, including *mirs yam, mirs bahr, sardars, mirzas-i-daftar,* pilots, *daroghas* and physicians and surgeons were to eat together. Daily rations were to be served out to them on the following basis; rice ¾ *seer, dal* ½ *seer,* ghee 8 *jauz* or *tolas,* meat ½ *chota seer,* salt 3 *jauz,* tamarind 2 *jauz,* turmeric ½ *jauz,* dry garlic ½ *jauz,* coriander seed ¾ *jauz* and black pepper 1 *jauz.*

Musketeers and gunners, both officers and men, were to get the following daily rations: rice 1 *seer, dal* 6 jauz, ghee 4 *jauz,* salt 2 *jauz,* dry garlic ½ *jauz,* onions 1½ *jauz,* coriander seed 1¼ *jauz* and black pepper 1 *jauz,* with kababs or roasted meat once in fifteen days at the rate of a quarter of a *chota seer* per head.

Seamen were to be allowed daily ¾ *seer* of rice, ¼ *seer* of dal, 2 *jauz* of ghee and 2 *jauz* of salt.

Among the other regulations laid down in the *hukmnamah* one related to prayers which were to be said every day, at the five appointed hours of the day. The First Officer or commander was to lead the prayers and deliver the Friday sermon, and the *daroghas* were to recite the five daily calls to prayers.

During the rainy season, it was ordained the ships were to be laid up in the creek, probably Mir Jan Creek, in specially constructed sheds. The duty of supplying materials for the sheds was placed on the civil officials of the district and the labour was to come from seamen.

The *hukmnamah* also refers to the previous orders as regards the erection of fortifications at *Hafiz-hisar* or Batkul and directs the *mirs yam* to examine carefully the ground in the vicinity of *Hafiz-hisar,* to make a thorough survey of it and select sites, and to forward the complete plans and drawings to the Sultan. They were particularly asked to make use of the two hills which perhaps formed the entrance to the harbour. The survey was to ascertain the exact distance between the two hills and the width of the channel or strait formed by them. The depth of water and the number of ships which might lie at anchor between these hills was similarly to be ascertained and reported. Two old ships which were beyond repair, namely the *Fakhru-ul-marakib* and *Fath-i-mubarak,* lying in Mir Jam and Onore respectively were to be dismantled and the steel and other material obtained from them used in the construction of new ships.

Twelve small ships were on the occasion delivered to the *mirs yam*. Of these ten were cargo-boats, five of them at Mangalore and five at Onore. The other two were called *Asadullahis*. All these smaller vessels were to be used for training the naval crew for the ships which were being built. With the same object it was directed that a kind of buoy should be anchored in some suitable place and a flag erected thereon, to serve as a mark for practising with cannon. Instruction was to be imparted to the gunners with the greatest care.

The *hukmnamah* insisted that the timber used in the construction of ships should be seasoned and for this purpose the wood, after being felled and barked should be kept lying from one to two years, and only when, judged by the highest standards, it was perfectly seasoned, was it to be used.

The men recruited for service with the navy were to be sworn in at Seringapatam in the presence of Tipu Sultan himself, and then sent to their respective destinations.

For the accounts of the navy the *mirs yam* and the *Asifs* (collectors) of the districts concerned were made jointly responsible. The movements and warlike operations of ships were similarly placed under the directions of the *mirs yam* and *Asifs*. If, however, the Sultan wished to employ the ships against an enemy he would issue orders in a full council of ministers.

Four *kothis* or business houses, called 'factories' in those times, two at Muscat and two at Kutch, which had already been in existence when the *hukmnamah* was issued, were placed under the *mirs yam* for the purpose of protection. At each of these factories two *yazaks* (platoons of 12 men) of the regular troops were to be stationed. These guards were to be paid by the superintendents of the factories and the *mirs yam* were to make the necessary remittances to them for the purpose. The guards in question were to be relieved annually.

The *mirs yam, mirs bahr* and *sarishtadars* (keepers of records) attached to the three naval stations were to appear personally before the Sultan ten days before each *Id-al-Adha*. They were on this occasion to deliver an account of receipts and disbursements and to report on the progress of the work on construction of the ships. Officers of certain other categories such as *tipdars, mirza-i-daftars* and *daroghas* were in like manner to appear before the Sultan 10 days before each *Id-al-Fitr* for the purpose of giving their respective accounts and reporting generally on the state of affairs in their departments.

The Sultan abhorred the elaborate modes of salutation and greeting that had become all too common among the Muslims of India such as *adab, kurnishat,* etc., which he considered undesirable and degrading in the extreme. In this *hukmnamah*, therefore, he prohibited the practice of rising for the purpose of receiving or greeting anyone, shaking and kissing hands, and embracing each other upon meeting, all of which were declared to be odious customs and contrary to Islam. He directed that all Muslims were brethren and equal and as such they should desist from all these undesirable practices and confine their mutual salutations to *Asalam-u-'alaikum*, 'Peace be with you' with the response *wa 'alaikumus-salam*, 'And with you be peace'.

The project which was put forward for execution in this memorable *hukmnamah* was supplemented by an ordinance dated the 24th *Taqi*, year *Saz* or year 1225 of the Prophet's birth (corresponding to June 1797) which contained some more details of the establishment of artificers attached to the three naval stations.

It is a pity that the naval programme could not be completed before Tipu Sultan met with his glorious end in 1799. What would have happened if he had had the opportunity of building his navy before the final war with the British, is one of the Ifs of history on which it is not worth speculating. But one may here refer to Kirkpatrick's remark on the subject: 'It may be contended, that in proportion as the Sultan might have been able to realize his alarming plan of a marine establishment, we should, as a measure of necessary precaution, have been compelled to augment at a heavy expense, our naval force in India, for the purpose of duly watching his armaments, and keeping them in constant check. This evil ... was averted by the issue of the war of 1799.'

It may well be that the naval building programme of Tipu Sultan was one of the important reasons why the British precipitated a war with him so that his plan might be nipped in the bud.

Notes and References

[1] William Kirkpatrick has translated this *hukmnamah* in his *Select Letters of Tippoo Sultan*, appendix L, pp. ixxviii ff.

[2] Ibid., p. ixxviii. For the reform of the calendar by Tipu Sultan and the new

names given by him to months and years see Kirmani, *Nishan-i-Haidari*, pp. 399–400. See also *Islamic Culture*, Vol. XIV, No. 2. pp. 161–64.

[3] Kirkpatrick, op. cit.

[4] Ibid.

[5] Ibid., p. ixxix.

[6] Ibid., pp. ixxix–ixxx.

[7] For an understanding of the monetary terms of the time of Tipu Sultan see Henderson, *The Coins of Haidar Ali and Tipu Sultan* and Taylor, *The Coins of Tipu Sultan*. The pagoda was a gold coin usually weighing 52½ grams and the *fanam* was the smallest gold coin weighing 5½ grams.

Building
Military
Strength

24
Encampment Charts
of Tipu Sultan's Army

Mahmud Husain

I n the India Office Library there is a small but interesting manuscript containing the regulations for the encampment of Tipu
Sultan's army.[1] It consists of seven tables preceded by a brief introduction. There seems to be no doubt that it was drawn up not only for
Tipu Sultan's army, but under his guidance.[2]

The introduction lays special stress on the proper selection of
that site for encampment of the *lashkar-i-khudadad* (Tipu Sultan's
army). It stipulates that advantage should be taken, wherever possible,
of rivers, streams, shrubs, rice-fields, hills, and thickets, which should
be kept on one side, and, after leaving an open space in the centre,
soldiers should be encamped on the other side. In between the soldiers
and the central court should be located the camp followers, goods and
chattel. The tents were to be pitched in such a manner as to avoid the
wind so that the army might not be troubled with wind and dust. One
should also, so says the introduction, take into consideration the
direction of the wind in the course of fighting, the best plan being to
fight in the direction of the wind and not to oppose it.

After these general remarks the tables that follow give seven
patterns of encampment. The first table (Plate 1) contains a rectang-
ular plan of encampment with an entrance in front only. Guns are
located at all four corners and at the entrance. Two tents in front and
one on each of the three sides seem to be meant for officers. The central
position is occupied by the *bargah-i-mu'alla*, elsewhere mentioned as
bargah-i-khass (Plates 2 and 3) or Tipu Sultan's own tent which is
surrounded on three sides by two rows of tents, one of the inner guard
and the other of the outer guard. In front of the *bargah-i-mu'alla* is the

secretarial office and a little further are two rows of tents for the advance guard at the foot of which are the stables. Still further and exactly opposite the *bargah-i-mu'alla* is the *naqqar-khanah* or the place where the drums were beaten at stated intervals, and there are two rows of shops. To the right of the *naqqar-khanah* is the place for the chief standard. Finally all these are surrounded by the tents of the soldiery.

The second table (Plate 4) has a river bend as the base on one side and the soldiers' tents are pitched in a single row forming the diameter for the semi-circular bend.

The third table (Plate 5) has many features in common with the first table, with the difference that there are four entrances instead of one, and guns are placed close to one another and not only on corners. Moreover, there are shops not only in front but at the back of the *bargah-i-mu'alla*. Stables for camels and elephants are located at the back of the *bargah-i-mu'alla*.

In the fourth table (Plate 2) the *bargah-i-mu'alla* is protected by only one row of guards which is located at a distance of forty yards. The tents of the soldiery are in four groups, two in front and two at the back of the *bargah-i-mu'alla*, the two sides on the right and left of it are not utilized for the purpose.

The fifth table (Plate 6) follows the pattern of the fourth, except that the tents both in front and at the back are arranged in perpendicular rows and not horizontally.

The sixth table (Plate 7) visualizes encampment by the side of a river and the camp is arranged parallel to it, there being a single row of tents in front and another at the back of the *bargah-i-mu'alla*.

The main feature of the seventh and the last table (Plate 3) is that the tents are arranged mainly in two rows on the right and left of the *bargah-i-khass*.

The seven tables together with the introduction throw interesting light on an important aspect of the organization of Tipu Sultan's army.

Notes and References

[1] Ethe, *Catalogue of Persian Manuscripts*, Vol. I, MS No. 2760. A microfilm copy along with an enlargement has been obtained by the Karachi University Library from which the accompanying blocks have been prepared.

[2] Ibid.

Encampment Charts of Tipu Sultan's Army
Drawn up under Tipu's guidance

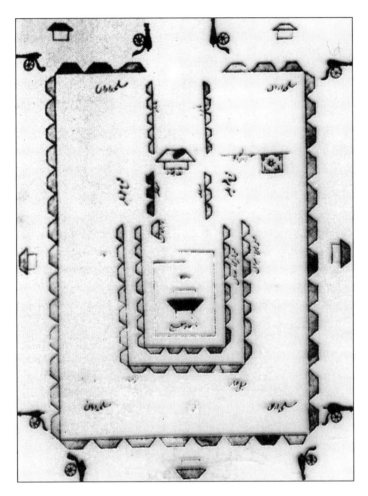

Plate 1

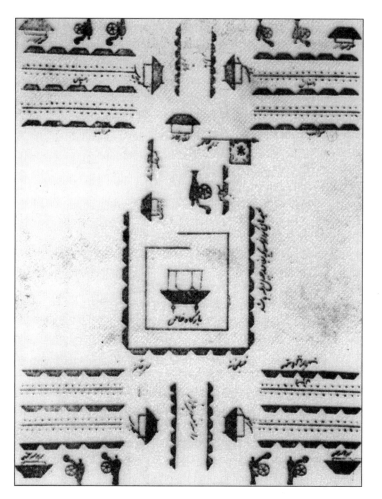

Plate 2

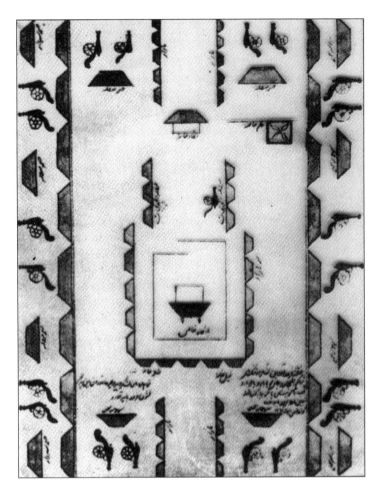

Plate 3

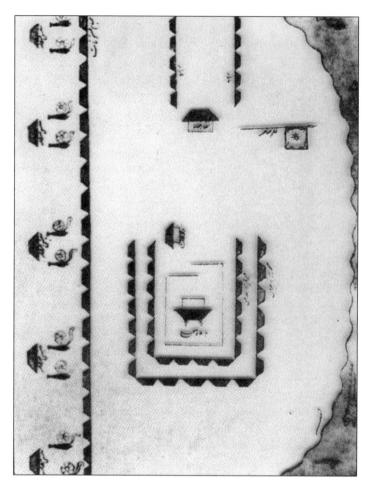

Plate 4

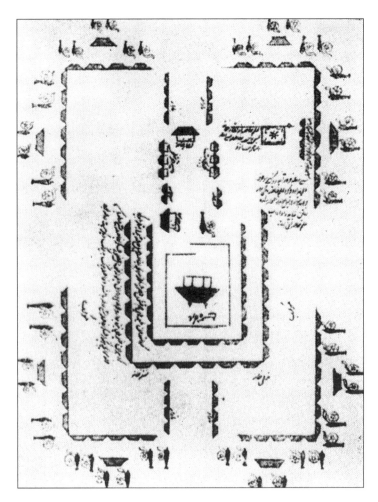

Plate 5

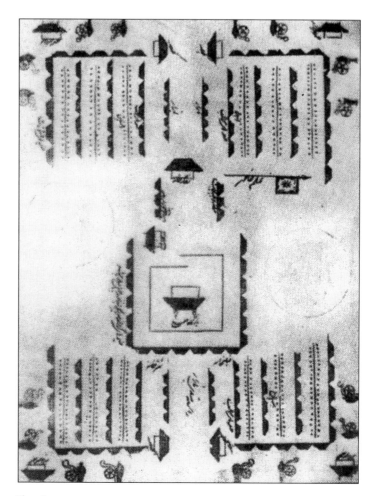

Plate 6

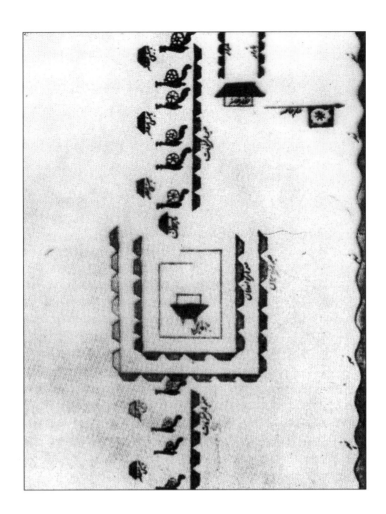

Plate 7

.

25

The Forts of Tipu Sultan: Views by the Daniells

Som Prakash Verma

The presentation of some rare contemporary sketches of the strongholds of Tipu Sultan may legitimately be offered by way of tribute to that extraordinary man. Two British artists, Thomas Daniell (1749–1840) and his nephew William Daniell (1769–1837), who reached Calcutta in the early part of 1786, took extensive tours into the interior parts of India and portrayed buildings and scenes of historical importance. The Daniells visited southern India in 1792–93, and on their route from Bangalore to Srirangam they visited Hosur, Rayakottai, Jagadevipalaiyam, Virbhadradurg and Sankaridurg.[1] By this time, i.e., 1792, these military bases once occupied by Tipu Sultan had passed into the control of the British. Further, the Daniells never aimed to portray all, or only the important monuments. Most likely, they were attracted to the places that lay on the route taken by them. We present here five of the aquatints (watercolour originals reproduced effect of a wash drawing), executed jointly by Thomas and William Daniell. These form part of 44 original aquatints executed by them at present preserved in the India Office Library, London.[2] Thematically, these aquatints encompass India's artistic and architectural heritage from ancient times, especially the development of rock-cut architecture.

The aquatints depict an earthen fort of Tipu Sultan at Hosur, the Rayakottai fort, the Jagadevipalaiyam fort, the Virbhadradurg fort, and the Sankaridurg fort. The latter three crown hills, and are built of dressed stone with masonry work.

The Daniells were most accomplished artists and their depiction of objects, especially in terms of detail and the rendering of solidity and depth is remarkable. In these paintings, the treatment of the monuments is both spacious and lively. The light and shade effect and the distinctive and characteristic tints employed bear affinity with the Neoclassic tradition of landscape painting—a movement which originated in Rome in the middle of the eighteenth century and spread rapidly throughout Europe during the nineteenth century.

In neoclassic style, artists for the first time consciously imitated antique art (sculpture and architecture), and knew they were imitating both in style and subject-matter. In the scenes portrayed by the Daniells the natural surroundings dominate the whole picture. In them, objects shown at a distance, or on a height are shown in diminishing perspectives and appear diminutive. In the aquatints shown here, in the artists' attempt at capturing a full view of a fort in its natural surroundings, only a little space is left in the composition for the central object. However, to make the scene lively and to place it in its cultural setting, men and women (identifiable as Indian) are shown in the foreground, engaged in work like driving bullocks, or sitting at leisure in groups, or wandering in the open. Their tiny figures are in sharp contrast to the size of the other objects shown in the scene.

Since the Daniells craved for accuracy and invariably maintained correctness of proportion and exactness in the rendering of details, their paintings can be taken as very good historical evidence. They made careful sketches and drawings made on the spot in pencil, sepia and water colour. These served as the basis for both aquatints and oil paintings, which latter were obviously artistically more accomplished. The Daniells often used *camera obscura* (a box with a lens which reflected the landscape image on to a sheet of paper) for tracing architectural details, and also the views and angles of the subject-matter. All this lent their work an art historical quality. The historical worth of their oriental paintings is immense, since with the passage of time vital changes have occurred in the landscape. Some of the buildings have totally perished, or been partly destroyed, altered or renovated. Their depiction of monuments is full of dramatic and emotional content.

The Daniells seem fully conscious of Indian topography and their images of India are in general faithful; their artistic imagination is severely veined in. The aquatints under consideration exhibit a spectacular view of nature, and are of great topographical interest.

Although other British artists, such as Samuel Scott, George Lambert, George Chinnery, James Wales, Francis Sawin Ward, Thomas Cussans, James Broff Byers and John Johnson extensively executed oriental scenery and pictures of monuments in India, they did not take up the subject of the aquatints under study.

The Hosur Earthen Fort and Rayakottai Fort

The Hosur and Rayakottai forts (Plates I, II) were of considerable strategic importance being built on the route always taken by the Mysore armies to invade the Carnatic. On this specific route from Bangalore to Carnatic there were numerous forts, and Lord Cornwallis considered the conquest of these places very important during the Third Mysore War.

To conquer Tipu Sultan's earthen fort at Hosur, situated about 28 miles south-east of Bangalore, Cornwallis sent Major Gowdie who got it evacuated by Tipu's troops on 15 July 1791. The garrison tried to blow up the fort but failed in their attempt due to Gowdie's sudden advance.

Major Dirom writes:

> The enemy were preparing to abandon the place, but, dilatory on all occasions, the unexpected approach of this brigade forced them to a precipitate retreat. They spiked the guns, burnt the carriages, and as they went off, fired a mine, which blew up one of the bastions; but a train they had laid to the magazine, luckily did not take effect, so that the damage done to the place was not great, and both a quantity of powder and other ammunition, and a considerable store of grain, which the garrison had not time to remove, were found in the fort.[3]

The Daniells, who portrayed this military post, were at Hosur in 1792, i.e., barely a year after the British seizure of this place. In their aquatint, Tipu's fort is visible in the distance on a diminished scale. The fort has now totally disappeared, and the glory of this fortified place can be experienced by us only through Daniells' work. However, the two shrines depicted here on either side (in the foreground), i.e., Sudeshvara (on the right) and Ganesha (on the left) still survive. These offer definite clues to the location of Tipu's earthen fort. The description of Hosur fort as given by Dirom confirms the details depicted in the aquatint:

189

Tippoo, sensible of the importance of Oussoor, had lately made great exertions to improve its defences. The works of the old fort were enclosed within a new rampart, flanked with good bastions, and surrounded by a wide ditch, excavated from the solid rock, which, already filled on three sides, would soon have been completed also on the fourth, to such depth as to be filled with water from a large tank which covers the south side of the fort. Protected by another tank on the north, and on the east by an extensive tract of low rice fields, which are watered by those tanks, it can only be attacked with advantage on the west side, where its defences would be such, when the present plan should be completed, as would enable it to stand a regular siege.[4]

The rampart with bastions and a vast tract of low fields and water-logged areas may be seen in the aquatint.

Rayakottai fort was another important outpost used by Tipu Sultan's forces on their military campaigns. The fort was built on a granite rock and consisted of two forts connected by a rampart: one at the foot of the rock, and the other on top of the rock. Immediately after Hosur, Gowdie's next move was to capture Rayakottai, and after an assault he succeeded in seizing the lower fort on 20 July 1791. Husain Ali Khan Kirmani thus describes the event:

> Colonel Gowdie, with his division of troops after the capture of Nundi Gurh, marching, by the route of Bangalore and Hussoor, first subdued the hearts of the Killadars of Rai Kote with but little trouble, and by shewing them a sum of money and firing a few shots at the foot, it was surrendered; and having left a garrison in it, he returned.[5]

Dirom's detailed account provides additional details on this fortified place:

> The killedar refusing to surrender, the major next morning attacked the lower fort, which encloses the pettah. He soon carried it by assault, and, pursuing the fugitives, got possession of the two first walls, which form a sort of middle fort, between the lower fort, and that which defends the summit of this stupendous rock. The place was known to be too strong by nature to be reduced, if the garrison were resolute in its defence. Major Gowdie was therefore directed to return to the army, if it was not given up on the first attack; but having made a lodgement on the hill, where the troops were covered

190

from the fire of the upper fort, and having reason to think the garrison were intimidated, he requested leave to continue the attack. A battalion, with two other iron twelve-pounders, was sent on the 22nd July to join this brigade, and enable him to breach another of the walls, which was within his reach. The major's spirited measures were also enforced by a movement of the army at the same time, towards Rayacotta, when the killedar proposed a parley, which soon ended in his giving up the place, on condition of security to private property, and his being permitted to go with his family to Carnatic.[6]

The British flag shown flying on the gateway of the fortified wall on the extreme left in the aquatint testifies to British control on the Rayakottai fort.

The vast landscape shown encompassing this fort hints at its massive structure. It is important to note that the rampart with strong bastions encircling the granite rock, clearly shown in the Daniells' work is now hardly traceable.

Jagadevipalaiyam

The fort of Jagadevipalaiyam (Plate III) is built on top of a hill, and is portrayed by the Daniells in diminished scale in the distant background. In this aquatint the painters' emphasis is on the scenic beauty of the surroundings, and the fort itself has little significance. Nevertheless, it is important to note that the rampart with bastions encircling the fort, depicted here with precision as seen by the Daniells in 1792, has now totally disappeared. Once again, we realize the historical value of the Daniells' work as providing a visual record of our architectural heritage much of it now entirely lost.

Virbhadradurg Fort

The depicturi of Virbhadradurg fort (Plate IV) is also on similar lines. Here we find the ascending rugged passage, paved with stone blocks, approaching the fort is the immediate focus of the painters' view, and the fort above is depicted in greatly diminished perspective, and thus once again, the scenery becomes prominent. One feels that perhaps the distance between the fort and the rugged passage is probably exaggerated. Here too, the outer walls encircling the citadel shown by the Daniells, have now disappeared. Nevertheless, the main fort is still intact.

191

Virbhadradurg fort (Verbudderdroog) is listed by Dirom in the list of districts ceded to the English East India Company under the terms and conditions of the Definitive Treaty, Article III, of 18 March 1792 at Seringapatam.[7]

Sankaridurg Fort

The aquatint, of Sankaridurg fort (Plate V) is shown on a flat-topped hill. It is now in a ruined condition, and the rampart encircling the hill top and its summit has totally disappeared.

Notes and References

[1] Antonio Martinelli and George Michell, *Oriental Scenery, Aquatints by Thomas and William Daniell* (New Delhi, 1998), pp. 16–17.

[2] Ibid., p. 9, (colour plates 91–95).

[3] Major Dirom, *A Narrative of the Campaign in India which Terminated the War with Tippoo Sultan in 1792* (London; reprint, 1974), pp. 31–32.

[4] Ibid., p. 32.

[5] Miles, *The Reign of Tipu Sultan*, p. 142.

[6] Dirom, *Narrative*, pp. 34–35.

[7] Ibid., pp. 277–78.

The Forts of Tipu Sultan
Aquatints by Thomas Daniell and William Daniell

Plate I: Hosur fort

Plate II: Rayakottai fort

Plate III: Jagadevipalaiyam fort

Plate IV: Virbhadradrug fort

Plate V: Sankaridurg fort

Select Bibliography

Records and Documents of Tipu Sultan

Tipu Sultan, *Dreams of Tipu Sultan*, original (autograph) in India Office Library, translated by Mahmud Husain, Karachi, n.d.

Tipu Sultan, *Hukmnamas*, comprising six letters of instructions issued to envoys proceeding to Constantinople and Paris, all dated 17 November 1785. Asiatic Society, Calcutta, Persian MS No. 1677.

Tipu Sultan, *Hukmnamaha-i (Tipu Sultan)*. India Office Library, London, Persian MSS, I.O. 4685. All orders and regulations in this belong to the period 1792–96.

Tipu Sultan, *Select Letters of Tippoo Sultan, etc.*, arranged and translated by W. Kirkpatrick, London, 1811. These are translations or abstracts of Persian material, largely contained in the preceding two volumes.

Tipu Sultan, 'Original Documents of Tipu Sultan and his officials, 1783–99' [in Persian], India Office Library, London, MS I.O. 4683.

Tipu Sultan, *The Mysorean Revenue Regulations*, Persian MS 'under the seal of Tippoo Sultaun', translated by B. Crisp, Calcutta, 1792; reprinted in Nikhiles Guha, *Pre-British State System in South India: Mysore*, Calcutta, 1985, pp. 175–219. It has not yet been investigated if the original text of these Regulations is identical with the text of any of the Regulations contained in the preceding manuscript in the India Office Library.

Waqai-i Manazil-i Rum [official diary of Tipu's embassy to

Constantinople] (incomplete), 1786, edited by Mohibbul Hasan, Bombay, 1968.

Zainul Abidin Shustari, *Fathu'l Mujahidin*, prepared under the supervision of Tipu Sultan, 1783, Maulana Azad Library, Aligarh Muslim University, 56/2. Several manuscript copies are in Asiatic Society Library, Calcutta, and India Office Library, London.

Other Contemporary Works and Records

Aitchison, C.U., *A Collection of Treaties, Engagements and Sanads*, Vols. VI, IX, Calcutta, 1909.

Beatson, Alexander, *A View of the Origin and Conduct of the War with Tippoo Sultan, c.*, London, 1800.

Buchanan, Francis, *A Journey from Madras, through the Countries of Mysore, Canara and Malabar, etc.* (1800–01), 3 vols., London, 1807.

Cornwallis, Marquis, *Correspondence of Charles, First Marquis Cornwallis*, edited by C. Ross, 3 vols., London, 1859.

Dirom, Major, *A Narrative of the Campaign in India, Which Terminated the War with Tippoo Sultan in 1792*, 2nd edn., London, 1794.

Forrest, W.G. (ed.), *Selections from the State Papers Preserved in the Bombay Secretariat*, Maratha Series, Vol. I, Bombay, 1885.

———, *Selections from the State Papers Preserved in the Bombay Secretariat*, Home Series, Vol. II, Bombay, 1887.

———, *Selections from the State Papers Preserved in the Foreign Department of the Government of India*, 1782–85, 3 vols., Calcutta, 1890.

Kirmani, Husain Ali Khan, *Nishan-i Haidari* [completed, 1802], lithographed, Bombay, 1890, translated by Colonel W. Miles, published in two separate vols. *History of Hyder Naik*, London, 1842; and *The History of the Reign of Tipu Sultan*, London, 1844.

Love, H.D. (ed.), *Vestiges of Old Madras*, 3 vols., London, 1913.

Mautort, L.F., *Memoirs (1752–1802)*, Paris, 1895.

Munro, I., *A Narrative of the Military Operations on the Coromandel Coast, 1780–84*, London, 1789.

Oakes, Captain Henry, *An Authentic Narrative of the Treatment of the*

English Who were taken Prisoners . . . by Tippoo Saib, with an
Appendix containing an Account by Lt. John Charles Shean,
London, 1785.

*Official Documents Relating to the Negotiations carried on by Tippoo
Sultan with the French Nation and Other Foreign States for
Purposes Hostile to the British Nation, to Which is added
Proceedings of a Jacobin Club formed at Seringapatam, etc.*,
published by Order of the Governor-General-in-Council,
Calcutta, 1799. A large part of this collection is reprinted in
Kabir Kausar (ed.), *Secret Correspondence of Tipu Sultan*, New
Delhi, 1980, pp. 47-263.

Pissurlencar, P.S. (ed.), *Antigualhas, Estudos e Documentos sobre a
Historia dos Portuguese na India*, Vol. I.

Scurry, J.,*The Captivity, Sufferings and Escape of James Scurry, written
by Himself*, London, 1824.

Venkatesh, Suman (trs.), *The Correspondence of the French During the
Reign of Haidar Ali and Tipu Sultan*, Vols. II and III,
Bangalore, 1998.

Wilks, Mark, *Report on the Interior Administration, Resources and
Expenses of the Government of Mysore under the System
prescribed by the Order of the Governor-General in Council
dated 4th September 1799*, Bangalore, 1864.

Secondary Works

Ali, B. Sheik, *English Relations with Haidar Ali*, Mysore, 1963.

———, *Tipu Sultan*, New Delhi, 1971.

Anonymous, *Authentic Memoirs of Tippoo Sultan, with a Preliminary
Sketch of the Life and Character of Hyder Aly Cawn, by an
Officer of the East India Company*, London, 1799.

Briggs, H.G., *The Nizam: His History and Relations with the British
Government*, 2 vols., London, 1861.

Brittlebank, Kate, *Tipu Sultan's Search for Legitimacy: Islam and
Kingship in a Hindu Domain*, Delhi, 1997.

Cunat, C.H., *Histoire du Bailli de Suffren*, Rennes, 1852.

Forrest, Denys, *Tiger of Mysore: The Life and Death of Tipu Sultan*,
Bombay, 1970.

Guha, Nikhiles, *Pre-British State System in South India: Mysore 1761–
1799*, Calcutta, 1981.

Hasan, Mohibbul, *History of Tipu Sultan*, 2nd edn., Calcutta, 1971.

Henderson, J.R., *The Coins of Haidar Ali and Tipu Sultan*, Madras, 1921.

Hosain, Hidayat, 'The Library of Tipu Sultan', *Islamic Culture*, Hyderabad (Dn.), XIV (1940), pp. 139–67.

Kareem, C.K., *Kerala under Haidar Ali and Tipu Sultan*, Ernakulam, 1973.

Khan, Mahmud ('Mahmud' Bangalori), *Tarikh-i Saltanat-i Khudadad* (Urdu), Bangalore, 1939.

Kincaid, C.A., and O.B. Parasnis, *A History of the Maratha People*, Oxford, 1925.

Martineau, A., *Bussy et l'Inde Francaise*, Paris, 1935.

Michaud, Joseph, *History of Mysore under Hyder Ali and Tipu Sultan*, (French), Paris, 1801; English translation, 1926 (rpt., New Delhi, 1985).

Mill, James, *History of British India*, edited by H.H. Wilson, Vols. 3–6, London, 1848.

Panikkar, K.M., *Malabar and the Dutch*, Bombay, 1931.

Parsons, Constance E., *Seringapatam*, London, 1931.

Sen, Ashok, 'A Pre-British Economic Formation in India of the Late Eighteenth Century: Tipu Sultan's Mysore', in *Perspectives in Social Sciences-1*, edited by Barun De, Calcutta, 1977.

Sen, Surendranath, *Studies in Indian History*, Calcuta, 1930. The essays include, 'Hyder Ali's Fleet', pp. 146–50, and 'The Shringeri Letters of Tipu Sultan', pp. 155–69.

Sinha, N.K., *Haidar Ali*, 3rd edn., Calcutta, 1959.

Smith, V.A., *Oxford History of India*, 2nd edn., London, 1922.

Taylor, Rev. Geo. P., *The Coins of Tipu Sultan*, Calcutta, 1914 (rpt., New Delhi, 1989).

Thompson, Edward, *The Making of the Indian Princes*, London, 1943.

Wilks, Mark, *Historical Sketches of the South of India, etc.*, [original edn., London, 2 vols., 1810 and 1817], edited by Murray Hammick, 2 vols., Mysore, 1930.

————, *Notes on Mysore*, Bangalore, 1864.

Wilson, W.J., *History of the Madras Army*, 2 vols., Madras, 1882.

Contributors

B. Sheik Ali. Eminent historian of Karnataka. Formerly Professor of History, Mysore University; and Vice-Chancellor, Goa University. Author of *The Hoysala Dynasty, Tipu Sultan, Tipu Sultan: A Study in Diplomacy and Confrontation,* and *English Relations with Haidar Ali.*

Irshad Husain Baqai. We have not been able to trace much information about Mr Baqai. His paper, reprinted here, was published in 1943. He also contributed to the *Proceedings of the Indian Records Commission* in the 1940s.

Francis Buchanan. A surgeon, he travelled widely in Burma in 1794, and was asked by Wellesley, after the fall of Tipu, to tour Mysore, Malabar and Canara. Buchanan compiled a very careful report of the areas he travelled through in 1800–01; it was officially published as *Journey from Madras* in 3 volumes by the English East India Company. He was called upon to conduct a still more ambitious survey of the Company's territories in Bengal and Bihar, in 1807–12. These district-wise surveys were published in abridged form by Montgomery Martin in 1838; his surveys of Bihar districts have been separately printed. He died in 1829.

A. Subbaraya Chetty. He was Teacher, R.B.C.C.C.'s High School, Perambur, Madras, in 1944, when he read his paper at the Indian History Congress session. No further information is available.

197

BARUN DE. Formerly Professor and Director, Centre for Studies in Social Sciences, Calcutta; and Director, Maulana Abul Kalam Azad Institute, Calcutta. Has written extensively on eighteenth and nineteenth-century India. Author, jointly with A. Tripathi and B. Chandra, of *Freedom Struggle*; and editor of *Perspectives in Social Sciences, I: Historical Dimensions.*

MOHIBBUL HASAN. Author of the standard biography of Tipu Sultan, originally published in 1951, and then in a revised and enlarged edition in 1971. He also wrote *A History of Kashmir under the Sultan* and a biography of Babur. He was Professor of History in Jamia Millia, New Delhi, and in University of Kashmir, Srinagar. He died in 1999.

MAHMUD HUSAIN. Professor, Dacca University, and, then, Vice-Chancellor, Karachi University (Pakistan). He published a translation of the *Dreams of Tipu Sultan.*

N. KASTURI. Lecturer in the Department of History, Mysore University, in 1935, when he wrote the paper published in this volume. Author of the book, *History of British Occupation of India.*

IFTIKHAR A. KHAN. Lecturer in History, Centre for Advanced Study in History, Aligarh Muslim University. Has written papers on Indian maritime history.

A.P. IBRAHIM KUNJU. Professor of History, Farook College, Kozhikode, Kerala, in 1960, when he presented his paper.

K. SAJAN LAL. Was Professor and Head of Department of History, Osmania University, at the time (1957) he contributed the paper to this volume.

GEORGE M. MORAES. Professor of History, Bombay University; author of *Kadamba Kula—A History of Ancient and Medieval Karnataka, Mangalore, A Historical Sketch,* and *A History of Christianity in India (AD 52–1542).*

ISHTIAQ HUSAIN QURESHI. Was Professor in History at Delhi University in 1945 when he wrote the paper published here. He had already published his *Administration of the Sultanate of Delhi.* Subsequently, the doyen of Pakistani historians, he published books on Akbar and Mughal administration. He also edited a multi-volume history of Muslim political movement in India.

D.S. ACHUTA RAU. Was teaching at Maharaja's College, Mysore, when he published the paper reprinted in this volume (1952). He also published other papers on Haidar Ali.

B.A. SALETORE. Author of *Maratha Dominion in Karnataka* and *Social and Political Life in the Vijayanagar Empire,* and editor of *Fort William—India House Correspondence,* Vol. IX (1782–85), besides other works.

JADUNATH SARKAR. A great master of the history of the seventeenth and eighteenth centuries. Major works are *A History of Aurangzeb* (5 vols.), *Shivaji and His Times,* and *Fall of the Mughal Empire* (1939–1803) (4 vols.). His industry was indefatigable. He published voluminously, but everything from his pen bears the mark of care and his command of sources in many languages. He died in 1958.

M.P. SRIDHARAN. Professor (retd.), Calicut. Has worked on French records relating to Mysore.

C.S. SRINIVASACHARI. One of the founders and early General Presidents of the Indian History Congress. Retired as Professor of History, Annamalai University. His studies of the historical material in the Private Diaries of Ananda Ranga Pillai (1736–61) are an important contribution to the history of the Carnatic during that period. He authored *History of Madras, The Inwardness of British Annexation in India* and *Vignettes of the Walajahi Dynasty,* and edited *Selections from the Orme Manuscripts.* He was editor of the *Journal of Indian History* from 1931 till his death in 1951.

SOM PRAKASH VERMA. Professor of History at Aligarh Muslim University. Has published the monumental biographical dictionary and catalogue, *Mughal Painters and Their Work,* and a book on *Material Life as Depicted in Mughal Painting,* besides a number of monographs and papers on art history.

Index

Index

Index